Music for More
than
One Piano

Music for More than One Piano

AN ANNOTATED GUIDE

Maurice Hinson

INDIANA UNIVERSITY PRESS
Bloomington

George Crumb's description of his *Music for a Summer Evening* is
quoted from the backliner of Nonesuch Record H 71311 and is
used by permission.
The editorial note on *Fantasy* in a by Alexander Scriabin appeared
in the Bartlett and Robertson edition (1940) of this work and is
reprinted by permission of Oxford University Press.

Manufactured in the United States of America

Library of Congress Cataloging in Publication Data

Hinson, Maurice.
Music for more than one piano.

Includes indexes.
1. Piano music (Pianos (2))—Bibliography.
2. Chamber music—Bibliography. I. Title.
ML128.P3H52   1983   016.7864'95   82-49245
ISBN 0-253-33952-9
1 2 3 4 5 87 86 85 84 83

To My Parents

Contents

Preface

Music for more than one keyboard instrument dates back at least to the piece "For Two Virginals" by Giles Farnaby (ca.1560–ca.1620), found in the *Fitzwilliam Virginal Book*. The line of development continued with Bernardo Pasquini, J. S. Bach and three of his sons (Carl Philipp Emanuel, Wilhelm Friedemann, and Johann Christian), Clementi, Mozart, Liszt, Brahms, and Busoni, and into the twentieth century. The two-piano medium continues strong today, but contemporary composers, in their desire for new timbres, have tended to favor more diverse and previously untried groupings. Hence much recent music is written for two pianos plus other instruments (or voice or tape) or for more than two pianos. Many two-piano works composed since the 1940s have been written for specific two-piano teams and usually on commission.

The first multi-piano concert was held in Rio de Janeiro on October 5, 1869. Thirty-one pianists at sixteen pianos were assembled on one platform for the first of Louis Moreau Gottschalk's "monster concerts." It appears that such ensembles are again coming into vogue. Composers, performers, and audiences all seem to favor music for more than one piano. Most of the great composers of the last 250 years have written for the medium, and a sizeable repertoire now exists. The sense of synergism that comes to a player in a multi-piano team is a special feeling. It is similar to what orchestral musicians may experience when they hear the instrumental drama taking place around them. (Webster defines *synergism* as "cooperative action of discrete agencies such that the total effect is greater than the sum of the two effects taken independently." In other words, the whole is greater than the sum of the parts.)

Almost all music can be performed by twenty fingers. In fact, the natural tendencies of multi-piano playing make it a symphonic medium. As the contemporary composer Gilman Collier says, "I firmly believe all piano four-hand music should be played on two pianos when available" (note in the score of *Prelude and Fugue* g). Some two-piano teams, notably Gold and Fizdale, play piano duets on two pianos.

As in my earlier books—*Guide to the Pianist's Repertoire*, 1973, and its *Supplement*, 1980, which describe solo piano literature; *The Piano in Chamber Ensemble*, 1978; and *Music for Piano and Orchestra*, 1981 (all published by Indiana University Press)—my aim here is to answer the key questions: What is there? What is it like? Where can I get it?

Selection. The following criteria were followed to make this volume manageable: 1. All compositions listed are written for two or more keyboard instruments, alone or with other parts. 2. The time span covered is mainly from 1700 to the present, but a few works written before 1700 are included because of their special musical interest. The listing contains some music composed before the invention of the piano, but these works have been tried on two pianos and found to be effective on modern instruments. 3. In selecting composers an attempt was made to cover all standard composers and to introduce contemporary composers of merit. 4. Works originally written for piano and other media (piano and orchestra, piano quartet, etc.) are included if they were arranged for two pianos by the composer and if the distribution of material is approximately equal. 5. Outstanding transcriptions by such composers as J. S. Bach, Busoni, Debussy, Prokofiev, Ravel, and Webern and by such two-piano teams as Gold and Fizdale, and Bartlett and Robertson, are included. 6. Information on works listed but not described has been obtained from publishers' catalogues. Special effort has been made to examine as many contemporary works as possible, both published and unpublished.

The sonic capabilities of the piano have been so stretched during this century that the word *pianistic* has become much more encompassing. New sound sources are exploited from above, below, and within the piano, as well as from the keyboard, assisted by numerous distorting gadgets or with the fingers, fists, palms, and arms. The use of these techniques by two or more pianists creates an even more heightened and frequently exciting experience. Some avant-garde music requires a new, multi-dimensional technique of multi-piano playing—a dexterity of hand and finger movement that is not based primarily on scales and arpeggios. I sometimes think there is no avant-garde any more because there seems to be no "main garde." It is difficult to see who is ahead of the times because we cannot even agree on what the times are. Even so, I have used *avant-garde* to indicate a work or style that in the early 1980s was considered experimental and/or advanced in technique.

For many of the contemporary works discussed in this volume, an understanding of the compositional processes that go into their writing would aid memorization and help produce a more nearly correct performance. Elliott Carter supports this idea:

> The special demands of modern scores can only be solved by repeated efforts to play and listen to them, for their minute performance indications have to be understood in the context of the music itself and are often to be taken more as underlying qualities of the score than as literal demands. . . . Matters of dynamic inflection, balance, and rapidity of change of these, especially when they are treated as independent items of discourse . . . pose serious acoustical problems in halls as well as many live-performance problems with instruments and the reactions of players.[1]

Another writer emphasizes that

At some point it is necessary for players to study the compositional process to realize a more correct performance: indeed, as some have pointed out, in many avant-garde works, this is not the sort of composition in which analysis precedes composition—the analysis *is* the composition.[2]

And to continue with the idea, "analysis is a direction for a performance."[3]

Because of constant change in the publishing world it is impossible to list only music currently in print. Some important works known to be out of print are listed here because of their merit, and many of them can be located at second-hand music stores, in the larger university or municipal libraries, or more especially in the Library of Congress and the British Museum Library. Many excellent recent works are available in manuscript form from the composers. A certain amount of subjectivity is unavoidable in a book of this nature, but I have attempted to be as fair and objective as possible. Composers who wish to submit works for possible inclusion in future editions are encouraged to do so.

Acknowledgments. Many people in many places have generously given me their help. I gratefully acknowledge the assistance of Martha Powell, Music Librarian of the Southern Baptist Theological Seminary; Elmer Booze and Rodney Mill of the Library of Congress; David Fenske, Music Librarian at Indiana University; Marion Korda, Music Librarian at the University of Louisville; Fernando Laires of the Peabody Conservatory of Music; Norma and Leonard Mastrogiacomo of Florida State University; my graduate assistant Dan Landes; my students who played through much of this music with me; and the Southern Baptist Theological Seminary for making possible the typing of the manuscript and the aid of graduate assistants through the years. The American Composers Alliance Library, the Danish and Finnish Music Information centers, and the Canadian Music Centre have been most helpful, as have the many composers who have graciously supplied me with scores and tapes.

Without the generous assistance of numerous publishers this volume would not be possible. Special appreciation goes to John Pope of Boosey & Hawkes, Inc.; Gerald Siani of Belwin-Mills Publishing Corp.; Donald Gillespie of C. F. Peters Corp.; Susan Brailove of Oxford University Press; Ernst Herttrich of G. Henle Verlag; Barry O'Neal of Associated Music Publishers; Mike Warren of Alphonse Leduc; Terry Rothermich of Magnamusic-Baton, Inc.; and George Hotton of Theodore Presser Co.

Investigating the repertoire for this book has been exciting, sometimes mind-boggling, educational, and fun. The English pedagogue Edith Crawshaw hit at the heart of the matter: "What fun it is to play together." I fully endorse her view. The words of Francis Bacon are appropriate as I conclude this volume: "Read not to contradict and confute, nor to believe and take for granted, nor to find talk and discourse, but to weigh and consider." I hope the reader will carefully weigh and consider the music presented here and realize the magnificent scope of the repertoire for more than one piano.

Louisville, Kentucky   Maurice Hinson
January 1983

Notes

1. Elliott Carter, "To Think of Milton Babbitt," PNM 14:2/15:1 (1975): 30–31.
2. Edward T. Cone, "Analysis Today," in *Problems of Modern Music,* edited by Paul Henry Lang (New York: W. W. Norton & Co., 1960), p.36.
3. Eric Salzman, *Twentieth-Century Music: An Introduction* (Englewood Cliffs, NJ: Prentice-Hall, Inc., 1967), p.160.

Using the Guide

Arrangement of entries. All composers are listed alphabetically. Sometimes biographical or stylistic comments follow the composer's name and dates. Under each composer's name, individual works are listed by year of composition, opus number, or title, or by a combination of the three. If nothing is indicated after the title, e.g., *Suite, Sonata, Duo, Structures, Kentuckiana,* etc., the reader may assume that the work is for two pianos. The terms "arranged," "transcribed," and "reduction" are all used to mean the same thing for this book. I have used the term found on the particular score.

Descriptions. Descriptions have been limited to general style characteristics, form, particular and unusual qualities, interpretative suggestions, and pianistic problems inherent in the music as well as unusual ensemble problems. Editorial procedures found in a particular edition are mentioned. The term "large span" is used when spans larger than an octave are required. "Expanded tonality" refers to techniques commonly found in contemporary writing up to ca. 1950. "Octotonic" refers to lines moving in the same direction one or more octaves apart. "Shifting" or "flexible meters" indicates that varied time signatures are used with the space mentioned (a few bars, a movement, the entire work). "Proportional rhythmic relationships" indicates five notes are to be played in the space for four. The designation "3 with 2" means three notes in one voice are played with (against) two notes in another. "Chance music" (aleatory) is described or mentioned, not analyzed, since it has no definitely ordered sequence of events. "Graphic notation" means that only approximate pitch and relative motion are indicated. "Spatial" notation is used for music in which a plan for the physical location of sound sources is an integral part of the structure, either explicit or implied.

Grading. An effort has been made to grade the piano parts in representative works of each composer. Five categories of grading are used: Intermediate (Int.), for the above-average high school pianist; Intermediate to Moderately Difficult (Int. to M-D); Moderately Difficult (M-D), for the above-average college pianist; Moderately Difficult to Difficult (M-D to D); and Difficult (D), for advanced pianists. To provide a better understanding of this grading, the following standard works will serve as guides for the basic levels:

Int.: F. Poulenc, *L'Embarquement pour Cythère*
M-D.: D. Milhaud, *Scaramouche*
D.: I. Stravinsky, *Concerto for Two Solo Pianos*

These categories must not be taken too strictly but are only listed for general indications of technical and interpretative difficulties.

Details of entries. When known, the date of composition is given after the title of the work. Then, in parentheses, are as many of the following as apply to the particular work: the editor, the publisher, the publisher's number, and the copyright date. When more than one edition is available, the editions are listed in order of preference, the most desirable first. The number of pages and the performance time are frequently listed. Timings in all cases are approximate. The spellings of the composers' names and of the titles of the compositions appear as they do on the music being described. Specifically related books, dissertations or theses, and journal articles are listed following individual compositions or at the conclusion of the discussion of a composer's work, and a more extended bibliography appears at the end of the book.

Sample Entries and Explanations

Johannes Brahms. *Sonata* f Op.34b 1854 (Br&H; CFP; IMC) 41 min. The piece is in the key of f minor; the opus number is 34b; the date of composition is 1854; the publishers are Breitkopf and Härtel, C. F. Peters, and the International Music Co; and the work takes approximately 41 minutes to perform.

György Ligeti. *Drei Stücke für zwei Klaviere* 1976 (Schott 6687) facsimile edition, 20pp., 16 min. The work was composed in 1976; Schott is the publisher; 6687 is the publisher's number; the work is available only in a facsimile edition of the composer's MS; the score is 20 pages long; and the work takes approximately 16 minutes to perform.

Other assistance. See "Abbreviations" (pp. xv–xviii) for terms, publishers, books, and periodicals referred to in the text, and the directories, "American or Parent Companies of Music Publishers" and "Addresses of Music Publishers" (pp. xix–xxvii), to locate publishers. Six special indexes direct the user to entries in the text for music in special categories.

Abbreviations

AA	Authors Agency of the Polish Music Publishers	CMC	Canadian Music Centre
ACA	American Composers Alliance	CMP	Consolidated Music Publishing
AMC	American Music Center	CPE	Composer/Performer Edition
AME	American Music Editions	CSMP	Crystal Spring Music Publishers
AMP	Associated Music Publishers	D	Difficult
AMT	*American Music Teacher*	DCM	*Dictionary of Contemporary Music,* ed. John Vinton (New York: E. P. Dutton, 1974)
APNM	Association for the Promotion of New Music		
		Dob	Doblinger
		DSS	Drustva Slovenskih Skladateljev
ARG	*American Record Guide*	DVFM	Deutscher Verlag für Musik
B&VP	Broekmans & Van Poppel	EAM	Editorial Argentina de Música
BB	Broude Brothers		
BMC	Boston Music Co.	EBM	Edward B. Marks
BMI	Broadcast Music, Inc., Canada	EC	Edizioni Curci
		ECS	E. C. Schirmer
Bo&Bo	Bote & Bock	EFM	Editions Françaises de Musique/ Technisonor
Bo&H	Boosey & Hawkes		
Br	Bärenreiter		
Br&H	Breitkopf & Härtel	EMB	Editio Musica Budapest
BrM	British Museum	EMM	Ediciones Mexicanas de Música
ca.	circa		
CAP	Composers' Autograph Publications	EMT	Editions Musicales Transatlantiques
		ESC	Max Eschig
CeBeDeM	CeBeDeM Foundation	EV	Elkan-Vogel
		FSF	Fast, Slow, Fast
CF	Carl Fischer	FSV	Feedback Studio Verlag
CFP	C. F. Peters		
CHF	Cheský Hudebni Fond	Gen	General Music Publishing Co.

GS	G. Schirmer	MIC	See Danish Music
GTPR	*Guide to the Pianist's*		Information Service
	Repertoire, by	MJ	*Music Journal*
	Maurice Hinson	MM	*Modern Music*
	(Bloomington:	M&M	*Music and Musicians*
	Indiana University	MQ	*Musical Quarterly*
	Press, 1973).	MR	*Music Review*
GWM	General Words and	MS, MSS	manuscript(s)
	Music Co.	MT	*Musical Times*
Hin	Hinrichsen	Nag	Nagel's Musik-
IMC	International Music		Archive
	Co.	NK	Norsk
IMI	Israel Music Institute		Komponistfoerning
IMP	Israel Music	NME	New Music Edition
	Publications (see IMI)	NMO	Norsk Musikförlag
Int.	Intermediate	NMS	Norska Musikförlaget
IU	Indiana University	Nov	Novello
	School of Music	NYPL	New York Public
	Library		Library
JALS	*Journal of The*	OBV	Oesterreichischer
	American Liszt		Bundersverlag
	Society	OD	Oliver Ditson
JF	J. Fischer	OdB	OdB Editions
JWC	J. W. Chester	OMB	See Conselho Federal
K	Kalmus		da Ordem dos
K&S	Kistner and Siegel		Músicos do Brazil
LAP	Los Angeles Public	OUP	Oxford University
	Library		Press
LC	Library of Congress	PIC	Peer International
L'OL	L'Oiseau-Lyre		Corporation
MA	*Musical America*	PNM	*Perspectives of New*
MC	Mildly contemporary		*Music*
MCA	M.C.A. Music (Music	PQ	*Piano Quarterly*
	Corporation of	PWM	Polskie Wydawnictwo
	America)		Muzyczne
M-D	Moderately difficult	R&E	Ries & Erler
Mer	Mercury Music Corp.	Ric	Ricordi
MFPO	*Music for Piano and*	Ric Amer	Ricordi Americana
	Orchestra, by		S.A.
	Maurice Hinson	Ric BA	Ricordi Argentina
	(Bloomington:	Ric BR	Ricordi Brazil
	Indiana University	SA	Sonata-Allegro
	Press, 1981).	Sal	Salabert

SB	Summy-Birchard	UCLA	University of California, Los Angeles
SBTS	Southern Baptist Theological Seminary Music Library	UE	Universal Edition
SDM	Servico de Documentacão Musical da Ordem dos Músicos do Brazil Av, Almte. Barroso, 72–7° Andar 20000 Rio de Janeiro (RJ), Brazil	UME	Uníon Musical Española
		UMP	United Music Publishers
		USSR	Mezhdunarodnaya Kniga (Music Publishers of the USSR)
SP	Shawnee Press	VU	Vienna Urtext Edition (UE)
SZ	Suvini Zerboni		
TP	Theodore Presser Co.	WH	Wilhelm Hansen

American Agents or
Parent Companies of Music Publishers

1. Associated Music Publishers, Inc., 866 Third Avenue, New York, NY 10022.
2. Belwin-Mills Publishing Corp., 25 Deshon Drive, Melville, NY 11746.
3. Boosey & Hawkes, Inc., 200 Smith Street, Farmingdale, NY 11735.
4. Brodt Music Co., P. O. Box 9345, Charlotte, NC 28299.
5. Alexander Broude, Inc., 225 West 57th Street, New York, NY 10019.
6. Broude Bros., Ltd., 170 Varick Street, New York, NY 10013.
7. Henri Elkan Music Publisher, 1316 Walnut Street, Philadelphia, PA 19107.
8. Elkan-Vogel Inc. (see Theodore Presser), Presser Place, Bryn Mawr, PA 19010.
9. European American Music Corp., 195 Allwood Road, Clifton, NJ 07012.
10. Carl Fischer, Inc., 56–62 Cooper Square, New York, NY 10003.
11. M C A Music, 25 Deshon Drive, Melville, NY 11746.
12. Magnamusic-Baton, 10370 Page Industrial Boulevard, St. Louis, MO 63132.
13. Edward B. Marks Music Corp., 1790 Broadway, New York, NY 10019.
14. Oxford University Press, Inc., 200 Madison Avenue, New York, NY 10016.
15. C. F. Peters Corp., 373 Park Avenue South, New York, NY 10016.
16. Theodore Presser Co., Presser Place, Bryn Mawr, PA 19010.
17. E. C. Schirmer Music Co., 112 South Street, Boston, MA 02111.
18. G. Schirmer, Inc., 866 Third Avenue, New York, NY 10022.
19. Shawnee Press, Inc., Delaware Water Gap, PA 18327.
20. Southern Music Publishing Co., 1740 Broadway, New York, NY 10019.
21. Summy-Birchard Co., 1834 Ridge Avenue, Evanston, IL 60204.
22. Location or American agent unverified.

Addresses of Music Publishers, Library Locations, and National Information Centers

A number following the name of a publisher corresponds to that of its American agent or parent company (see previous directory).

Ahn & Simrock
  Meinekestrasse 10
  1 Berlin 15, West Germany
J. Albert
  139 King Street
  Sydney, Australia
Editorial Alpuerto
  Madrid, Spain
Alsbach   15
Alpeg   15
American Composers
  Alliance—Composers
  Facsimile Editions
  170 West 74th Street
  New York, NY 10023
American Music Center
  145 West 58th Street
  New York, NY 10019
American Music Editions
  263 East 7th Street
  New York, NY 10009
Johann André
  Frankfurterstrasse 28
  D-605 Offenbach
  West Germany
Arcadia Music Publishing Co.
  10 Sherlock Mews
  Baker Street
  London W1M 3RH England
Ariadne
  Vienna, Austria
Arno Press
  3 Park Avenue
  New York, NY 10016

Arizona State University
  Music Library
  Tempe, AZ 85281
Ars Viva Verlag   2, 9
  Mainz, Germany
Artia   3
  Smeckach 30
  Prague I, Czechoslovakia
Edwin Ashdown, Ltd.   3, 4
Association for the
  Promotion of New Music
  2002 Central Avenue
  Ship Bottom, NJ 08008
Association of Irish Composers
  15 Herbert Street
  Dublin 2, Ireland
Augener   17
Authors Agency of the Polish
  Music Publishers
  ul. Hipoteczna 2, 00–950
  Warsaw, Poland
Axelrod (see Shawnee Press)
Bärenreiter Verlag   9, 12
  Heinrich Schütz Allee 35
  35 Kassel-Wilhelmshöhe
  Germany
Barger & Barclay
  P. O. Box 22673
  Ft. Lauderdale, FL
M. P. Belaieff   15
Berandol Music Ltd.
  (Canada)   1
Bèrben   16
Gerald Billaudot, Editeur   16

14, rue de l'Echiquier
Paris 10, France
Ernst Bisping
Cologne, Germany
Boelke-Bomart Music Publications
through Jerona Music Corp.
81 Trinity Place
Hackensack, NJ 07601
F. Bongiovanni
Bologna, Italy
Boston Music Co.
116 Boylston Street
Boston, MA 02116
Bosworth & Co. Ltd.
14/18 Heddon Street
London W1 England
Bote & Bock   1
Breitkopf & Härtel   1
Postschliessfach 74
Walkmühlstrasse 52
6200 Wiesbaden 1
West Germany
Breitkopf & Härtel
Postschliessfach 107
Karlstrasse 10
701 Leipzig C1, East Germany
British Museum
Great Russell Street
London, England WC1
Broadcast Music Canada   1
Max Brockhaus
Leipzig, West Germany
Broekmans & Van Poppel   15
Canadian Music Centre
1263 Bay Street
Toronto, Ontario M5R 2C1
Canada
Carisch, S. P. A.   3
Via General Fara 39
20134 Milan, Italy
Casa Amarilla
San Diego 128
Santiago, Chile

CeBeDeM (Centre Belge de
Documentation Musicale)   7
4, boulevard de l'Empereur
B-1000 Brussels, Belgium
C. A. Challier   22
Chappell & Co.   16
Cheský Hudebni Fond (rental
library)
Parizska 13
110 00 Prague, Czechoslovakia
J. W. Chester   5
Choudens   15
Cleveland Public Library
Cleveland, OH
Franco Colombo, Inc.   2
Composer-Performer Edition
330 University Avenue
Davis, CA 95616
Composers' Autograph
Publications
P. O. Box 671
Hamilton, OH 45012
Composers Press (see Seesaw
Music Corp.)
Conselho Federal da Ordem dos
Músicos do Brasil
Av. Almte, Barroso, 72–7°
Andar
20000 Rio de Janeiro (RJ)
Brazil
Cornell University Library
Ithaca, NY 14853
Costallat   16
Cranz   20
Crystal Spring Music
Publishers
P. O. Box 7422
Roanoke, VA 24019
J. Curwen & Son (England)   20
Danish Music Information
Center
Skoubogade 2, 2
1158 Copenhagen K Denmark

Glen Rock, NJ 07452
H. T. FitzSimons, Co. Inc.
  615 North LaSalle Street
  Chicago, IL 60610
Flammer (see Shawnee Press)
Foetisch   17
C. Foley   10
Forberg   15
A. Forlivesi & Co.   2
  Via Roma 4
  Florence, Italy
Frank Music Corp.
  1350 Avenue of the Americas
  New York, NY 10019
Fredonia Press
  3947 Fredonia Drive
  Hollywood, CA 90068
Galaxy Music Corp.   17
Galliard, Ltd.   17
Gebauer, W.   22
  Leipzig, Germany
General Music Publishing Co.,
  Inc.
  P. O. Box 267
  Hastings-on-Hudson, NY 10706
Musikverlag Hans Gerig   2, 12
  Cologne, Germany
A. Goll
  Vienna, Austria
Goodwin & Tabb
  London, England
Grunert, Emil
  Leipzig, Germany
Hain Verlag
  Heidelberg, Germany
Hamelle & Co. (France)   8
Wilhelm Hansen   12
Harcourt Brace Jovanovich
  757 Third Avenue
  New York, NY 10017
Otto Harrassowitz
  P. O. Box 2929
  6200 Wiesbaden, Germany
Frederick Harris Music Co., Ltd.

P. O. Box 670
  Ontario, Canada
  L6J SC2
Harvard University Library
  Cambridge, MA 02138
F. K. Heckel
  Mannheim, Germany
Heinrichshofen's Verlag
  (Germany)   15
G. Henle Verlag   4, 12
Henn Editions
  8 rue de Hesse
  Geneva, Switzerland
Heugel & Cie.   16
Hinrichsen Edition
  (England)   15
Ludwig Hoffarth
  Dresden, Germany
Friedrich Hofmeister (Germany) 15
Hug (Switzerland)   15
Impero Verlag
  Wilhelmshaven, Germany
Indiana University Music Library
  Bloomington, IN 47405
International Music Corp.
  511 Fifth Avenue
  New York, NY 10017
Israel Music Institute   3
Israeli Music Publications   5
Izdanje Udruzenja
    Kompozitora Makedonije
  Zagreb, Yugoslavia
Japan Federation of Composers
  Shinanomachi-Bldg.,
  · 602 33-Shinanomachi
  Shinjuku-ku, Tokyo, Japan
Jean Jobert   8
P. Jürgenson
  Moscow 200, USSR
C. F. Kahnt   15
Edwin F. Kalmus   2
Kenyon Publications
  17 W. 60th St.
  New York, NY 10023

Kistner & Siegel
  c/o Concordia
  Publishing House
  3558 S. Jefferson Avenue
  St. Louis, MO 63118
Kronos Press
  25 Ansdell Street
  London W8 5BN England
Alphonse Leduc   4, 8
Leeds Music Ltd. (Canada)   14
Leeds Music Corp. (see MCA
  Music)   11
Henry Lemoine & Cie.   8
Alfred Lengnick & Co., Ltd (see
  Frederick Harris Music Co.)
  421a Brighton Road
  South Croydon, Surrey
  England
Library of Congress
  Music Division
  Washington, D.C. 20540
Lienau   15
Collection Litolff   15
L'Oiseaux-Lyre, Editions de   19
  Les Ramparts, Monaco
Lopes Edition   25
Los Angeles Public Library
  630 West Fifth Street
  Los Angeles, CA 90071
Lottermoser, Carlos S.
  Rivadavia 851
  Buenos Aires, Argentina
Margun Music Inc.
  167 Dudley Road
  Newton Center, MA 02159
Media Press
  2617 Gwynndale Avenue
  Baltimore, MD 21207
Mercury Music Corp.   16
Merion Music Co.   16
Béla Mery
  Budapest, Hungary
Mezhdunarodnaya Kniga (Music
  Publishers to the USSR)   21

Midbar Music Press
  639 West End Avenue, Apt. 7A
  New York, NY 10025
Price Milburn
  Wellington, New Zealand
Millikin University Library
  Decatur, Il 62522
Mobart (see Boelke-Bomart
  Music Publications)
Hermann Moeck Verlag   2, 12
Möseler Verlag   12
Willy Müller (see Süddeutscher
  Musikverlag)   15
Murdoch   22
Musikverlag Hans Gerig   2, 12
Myklas Press
  P. O. Box 929
  Boulder, CO 80306
Nagel's Musik-Archive   1
New Music Edition   16
New York Public Library
  Library of the Performing Arts
  Lincoln Center
  New York, NY 10023
A. Nöel   22
Pierre Noel   16
Nordiska Musikförlaget   12
Norsk Komponistforening   5
  (Society of Norwegian
  Composers)
  Klingenberggaten
  Oslo 1, Norway
Norsk Musikförlag   12
Norton Critical Scores
  W. W. Norton
  500 Fifth Avenue
  New York, NY 10036
Northwestern University
  Music Library
  Evanston, IL 60201
Novello & Co., Ltd.
  145 Palisade Street
  Dobbs Ferry, NY 10522
Nymphenburg

Munich, Germany
Oberlin Conservatory Library
  Oberlin, OH 44074
OdB Editions
  37 Camden Park Road
  London NW1 9AX England
Oesterreichischer
  Bundesverlag   1
Ongaku No Toma Sha (Japan)   16
Paragon Music Publishers
  57 Third Avenue
  New York, NY 10003
Paxton & Co., Ltd.   2
Peer International Corp.   20
Pembroke Music, Inc.   10
Plymouth Music Co., Inc.
  170 N. E. 33rd Street
  Ft. Lauderdale, FL 33334
Polskie Wydawnictwo
  Muzyczne   13
  (Polish Music Publications)
Rahter   1
Ramsey, B.   5
Redcliffe Edition
  Arlington Park House
  London W4 4HD England
Reuter & Reuter Forlags AB
  Regeringsgatan 45
  Stockholm, Sweden
G. Ricordi & Co. (International)   18
Ricordi Americana (see
  G. Ricordi & Co.)   18
Ricordi BA (Argentina)   18
Ricordi BR Brazil   18
Ries & Erler (Germany)   15
J. M. Rieter-Biedermann
  Leipzig, Germany
Robitschek   22
Rongwen Music, Inc.   6
C. M. F. Rothe
  Leipzig, Germany
R. D. Row   11
Editions Salabert   18
Sassetti & Cia.

R. Nova do Almada, 60
  Lisbon 2, Portugal
Schauer   1
Schlesinger,
  Schemusikhandlung   17
Arthur P. Schmidt Co.   21
Schott   9
Schott Frères   15
  Brussels, Belgium
Schroeder & Gunther   1
J. Schuberth & Co.
  Zietopring 3
  Wiesbaden, Germany
Seesaw Music Corp.
  1966 Broadway
  New York, NY 10023
Maurice Senart (see Salabert)
Shawnee Press, Inc.
  Delaware Water Gap, PA 18327
Hans Sikorski   2
Carl Simon (see Breitkopf &
  Härtel)
N. Simrock   1
Societé d'Editions Musicales
  Internationales   22
Soundings Press
  984 Canyon Road
  Sante Fe, NM 87501
The Southern Baptist Theological
  Seminary
  Music Library
  2825 Lexington Road
  Louisville, KY 40280
Southern Illinois University
  Music Library
  Carbondale, IL 62901
Soviet Composer (Sovetskii
  Kompozitor)
  (see Otto Harrassowitz)
Jack Spratt
  17 West 60th Street
  New York, NY 10023
Steingräber Verlag
  Auf der Reiswiese 9

Offenbach (M) Germany
Stockhausen-Verlag
  5073 Kuerten, Germany
Süddeutscher Musikverlag
  (Willy Müller)   15
Sundry Music Publishing House
  Silliman University Press
  Silliman University
  Sumaguete City
  Philippines 6501
Supraphon   3
Edizioni Suvini Zerboni   3
Swedish Music Information
  Center
  Birger Jarlsgatan 6B
  Box 5091
  S-102 42 Stockholm, Sweden
Tischler & Jangenberg
  Nibelungenstrasse 48
  D-8000 Munich 19
  West Germany
Toledo Public Library
  Toledo, OH
Tonos Verlag (see Seesaw Music
  Corp.)
United Music Publishers   16
Universal Edition (Vienna,
  London, Zurich)   9
University of California, Los
  Angeles
  Music Library
  405 Hilgard Avenue
  Los Angeles, CA 90024
University of Colorado

Music Library
  Boulder, CO 80309
University of Louisville
  Music Library
  Louisville, KY 40292
University of Toronto
  Music Library
  Toronto, Canada M5S 1A1
University of Virginia
  Music Library
  Charlottesville, VA 22903
University of Wisconsin
  Music Library
  Madison, WI 53706
Editores Vitale
  Rua Franca Pinta 42
  Caixa Postal 380
  Sao Paulo (SP) Brazil
Warner Brothers
  75 Rockefeller Plaza
  New York, NY 10019
Waterloo Music Co.   4
Josef Weinberger, Ltd.   3
Joseph Williams Editions   17
Willis Music Co.
  7380 Industrial Road
  Florence, KY 41042
Wright State University
  Music Library
  Dayton, OH 45435
Editore Gugliemo Zanibon   2, 15
Zen-On Music Co., Ltd.   21
Wilhelm Zimmerman,
  Musikverlag   15

Publishers No Longer in Business

Bessell, W.	Hainauer	Prochazka	Stahl
Church, J.	Haslinger	Reuhle, C.	Wernthal, O.
Cocks	Naderman	Richault	Wood, B. F.
Diabelli	Praeger & Meier	Rogers, W.	Woolhouse, C.
Lafleur			

Music for More
than
One Piano

A

Jean Absil (1893–1974) Belgium
Cinquième Rhapsodie Op.102 1959 (CeBeDeM 1968) 16pp., 6 min. Sur de
vieux noëls français. One movement with contrasting sections of
tempos and dynamics, brilliant toccata style, flexible meters, parallel
chords, expanded tonality, chromatic scales, octave passages. Requires fleet fingers. M-D.
Assymétries Op.136 1968 (CeBeDeM) 23pp. 11 min. Facsimile score. Andante mysterioso et allegro scherzando: 7/4. Andantino: 6 + 4/8. Allegro vivo: 15/8. Octotonic chromatic scales, much use of thirds and
chords, strong dissonance and rhythm, freely tonal, parallel chords,
molto stringendo ending. M-D.

Julian Aguirre (1868–1924) Argentina
Cancion No.3 (Ric BA).
Danza Argentina (Ric BA).
Huella (Ric BA).

Isaac Albeniz (1860–1909) Spain
Spanish Rhapsody Op.70 (IMC) 12 min. Originally composed for two
pianos in 1886. A magnified genre study, concert-popularistic in tone,
Lisztian with hiccoughs of undigested Impressionism. M-D.

Thomas Albert (1948–   ) USA
Devil's Rain 1977 (AMC). 2 folded leaves. A number of musical examples
(patterns) are given, to be repeated at will or according to instructions. Certain sections are to proceed "approximately together."
Aleatory, avant-garde. Requires experience in the style. M-D.

Haim Alexander (1915–   ) Israel, born Germany
Alexander teaches piano, harpsichord, and composition at the Rubin
Academy of Music in Jerusalem.
Six Israeli Dances (IMP 1960; IU) 22pp. Pastorale; Shepherds' Dance;
Spring Dance; Peasants' Dance; Reapers' Dance; Dance of the Sab-
ras. Freely tonal, written in the spirit of folk music but not based on
any existent folk material. "Israeli children are called sabras (sabra =
cactus) as they are said to have as thorny a shell and as sweet an

1

inside as the cactus fruit" (from the score). Modal, generally homophonic with some alteration of melody between hands. M-D, with last piece the most difficult.
Sonata Brevis (MS available from composer).

Humberto Allende (1885–1959) Chile
Pequeña Suite (Universidad de Santiago de Chile, Santiago).

Carlos Almeida (1906–   ) Brazil
Introdução e dança brasileira (Fermata do Brazil 1947; IU) 14 pp., 7 min. Originally for piano and orchestra, reduction by composer. Recitative-like introduction leads to the strongly rhythmic Brazilian dance. Tonal. M-D.

Eyvind Alnaes (1872–1932) Denmark
Marche Symphonique Op.16 (WH 13693; LC) 29pp. Grandiose sweep; many large chords, scales, and octaves; Reger style. M-D.

Ladislav F. Aloiz (–   )
Nine Variations, Finale and Fugue Op.28 (Jurgenson 1894; BrM) 23pp. Written in a Schumannesque style with a certain Slavic flavor. Exceedingly pianistic; academic fugue. M-D.

René Amengual (1911–1954) Chile
Introducción y Allegro 1939 (Casa Amarilla).

Jurriaan Andriessen (1925–   ) The Netherlands
Concerto for Two Pianos without Orchestra 1944 (Donemus) 11 min. Facsimile of MS. Allegro molto; Adagio; Allegro. Written in a neoclassic style oriented toward Stravinsky. Flowing figuration and chordal melodies, fast canonic unisons. M-D.

Louis Andriessen (1939–   ) The Netherlands
Ittrospezione III 1965 (Donemus) 8pp. Fragment for two pianos with tenor saxophone ad libitum. Pointillistic, serial, proportional rhythmic relationships, thin textures, dynamic extremes. M-D to D.
Séries 1958 (Donemus 1964) Facsimile. 9 min. One movement divided into 12 short sections. Twelve-tone, Webernesque, aleatory, expressionistic, complex organization, flexible meters, varied notation. D.

George Anson (1912–   ) USA
Kid Koncerto (Willis 1961). I'm Mad; I'm Sad; I'm Bad; I'm Glad. Diatonic and chromatic scales, clusters, parallel chords, rapid alternation between hands. Int.

Hugo Anson (1894–1958) Great Britain
The Lonely Sailing Ship (OUP 1934) 4pp. Developed in the manner of a

very free dialogue between the instruments. Freely tonal, atmospheric. "The actual ship which suggested the idea of this piece to the composer was a derelict vessel, allowed to ride at anchor. . . . The movement must be rather dragging and the tempo very slow" (from the score). Int. to M-D.

Jorge Antunes (1942–   ) Brazil
Reflex per due pianoforti 1971 (SZ 1973). 2 playing scores, each with 10 loose leaves. 6 min. Explanations in Italian. Certain "preparations" required; instructions included for use of rulers, soft marimba mallets, guitar picks, a water glass, etc. Avant-garde. M-D.

Violet Archer (1913–   ) Canada
Three Sketches 1947 (Waterloo) 7 min. Little Prelude. Impromptu. Gigue Scherzo. M-D.

Anton Arensky (1861–1906) Russia
Arensky possessed an exceptional understanding of the two-piano idiom. All his works display strong melodies, graceful fluidity, and careful workmanship and reflect the cultural climate in which he created. Most movements of the suites are Int. to M-D.
Suite I Op.15 (IMC; Bo&H; GS; Bosworth) 12½ min. Romance. Waltz: the best-known movement and probably the most frequently performed piece in the two-piano literature. Polonaise: highly embellished lyrical themes. Charming, graceful, and effective.
Suite II Op.23 (CFP; Jurgenson). Silhouettes; Le Savant; La Coquette; Polichinello; La Reveur.
Suite III Op.33 (Jurgenson) 18½ min. Variation form. Theme; Dialogue; Valse; March triomphale; Menuet; Gavotte; Scherzo; March funèbre; Nocturne; Polonaise.
Suite IV (GS). Prelude; Romance; Le rêve; Finale.
Suite V Op.65 Children's suite, 8 canons. Originally for piano duet. (Philipp—IMC) Prelude (Canon by Augmentation). Aria (Canon at the Second). Scherzino (Canon at the Third). Gavotte (Canon at the Fourth). Élégie (Canon at the Fifth). Romanze (Canon at the Sixth). Intermezzo (Canon at the Seventh). Alla Polazza (Canon at the Octave); also available separately as *Polonaise* Op.65/8 (GS).

Paul Arma (1905–   ) France, born Hungary
Sept transparences 1967 (Lemoine) 24pp., 14 min. Short contrasting pieces; freely tonal, neo-Classic. Details carefully worked out. Large span required. M-D.

Richard Arnell (1917–   ) Great Britain
Suite D Op.73 (Hin) 15 min. Prelude; Invention; Pas de Deux; Allegro

Transformation; Finale; Epilogue. Spontaneous and unpretentious, nothing unusual in the harmonies. Performers not made to indulge in redundant musical pyrotechnics. M-D.

Maurice Arnold (1865–1937) USA
Valses Élégantes Op.30 (Br&H 1893; LC) 17pp. For two pianos, eight hands. Four waltzes in a concert setting, late Romantic (Max Bruch) style. M-D.

Edward Arteaga (1950–   ) USA
Venturi (Berandol).

Michael von Asantshewsky (1838–1881) Russia
Festival Polonaise Op.12 (K&S; LC) 23pp. Pompous, solemn, marcato, pesante repeated chords, short contrasting lyric sections. M-D.

Joseph Ascher (1829–1869) Germany
Guillaume Tell, Grand Duo Concertante (Schott).

Algernon Ashton (1859–1937) Great Britain
Suite Op.50 (Hin; R&E) 71pp. Praeludium; Pastorale; Scherzo; March triomphate; Finale. Traditional writing, Brahms influence, overly long. M-D to D.
Toccata Brillante Op.144 (Leuckart 1912; BrM; LC) 23pp. Dedicated to Rose and Ottilie Sutro. Square phrases, strong rhythms. M-D.

Jan Astriab (1937–   ) Poland
Phrases (AA). For piano and harpsichord. 10 min.

Louis Aubert (1877–1968) France
Aubert was a pupil of Diemer and Fauré. A remarkably fine pianist, he was at one time world-famous as the composer of *Habanera* for orchestra (1918).
Suite Brève Op.6 1901 (Durand; Willamette University, Salem, Oregon 97301) 23pp. Menuet; Berceuse; Air de Ballet. Impressionistic; strong dance influence, somewhat in the style of Chabrier. M-D.
Fantaisie Op.8 (Durand).

Georges Auric (1899–   ) France
Equally hostile to Wagnerianism and Impressionism, Auric cultivated a witty, sharp-edged style opposed to all Romanticism. His many film scores have brought him outstanding success.
Une Valse pour deux pianos 1949 (ESC 1955) 8pp. A fine encore. Light, graceful, charming, and in good taste. Clever *pp* ending. Int. to M-D.
Partita 1953–55 (ESC 6944   1958) 40pp. Three untitled movements written in an idiosyncratic free-serial style. Constantly changing meters, many metronome marks, more serious than the earlier *Valse*. M-D.

Double-Jeux I 1970 (Sal) 13pp. Light, transparent, freely tonal, flexible meters. M-D.

Double-Jeux II 1971 (Sal) 6pp. Expressionistic. M-D.

Double-Jeux III 1971 (Sal) 28pp. More venturesome tonally, rhythmically, and melodically than the first two *Double-Jeux,* and more involved than the earlier pieces. Auric's style continues to evolve, but all three *Double-Jeux* follow the basic style of the *Partita*. M-D.

Thomas Austen (1913–   ) Great Britain

The Keel Row (Galaxy 1939) 4 min. Based on an eighteenth-century Northumbrian folk tune. Strongly syncopated rhythms contrast with gliding and flowing melodies; chromatic harmonic treatment; "very fast" mid-section; broad conclusion with a final glissando. M-D.

B

Milton Babbitt (1916–) USA
A Solo Requiem (CFP 66877) 25 min. For two pianos and soprano solo.
  Text from Shakespeare, G. M. Hopkins, G. Meredith, A. Stramm,
  and J. Dryden.

Victor Babin (1908–1972) USA, born Russia
Three March Rhythms 1941 (Bo&H 1953). Military: strong rhythms, witty
  conclusion. Funereal: somber. Processional: four-voice fugue, effective introduction, colorful ending. M-D.
Fantasia on Themes by Georg Phillip Telemann (EV 1950; Bo&H 1965)
  16pp. Babin imitates a style of composition suitable to the thematic
  material; the work is commendably free of harmonic anachronisms.
  M-D.
Three Fantasies on Old Themes 1948 (Augener). The Piper of Polmood:
  clever dance tunes, flamboyant mid-section. Hebrew Slumber Song:
  quiet and sad. Russian Village: festive and exuberant, vivid. Amiable
  light music. M-D.
Six Etudes (Bo&H; UE). Available separately. Tempo giusto con fuoco.
  Adagietto cantabile. Veloce. Vivace (based on "The Flight of the
  Bumble Bee"). Quasi una Siciliana. Allegro molto, dramatico. Concert studies exploiting various problems encountered in the two-
  piano medium. M-D.

Carl Philipp Emanuel Bach (1714–1788) Germany
Four Little Duets W.115 (Gold and Fizdale—GS; Br 499 1942) 11 min.
  Allegro; Poco adagio; Poco adagio; Allegro. All four works are filled
  with a felicitous delicacy. "The melodic lines unfold above the bass
  as if etched with a fine silver stylus—a conversation turned into
  music, and the image of an age in which spirited taste and profound
  sensibility could still be so happily united." (Hannsdieter Wohlfarth,
  from record jacket of Nonesuch H-71357). The GS edition includes
  realized ornaments. M-D.

Johann Christian Bach (1735–1782) Germany
Sonata G Op.15/5 (Schott 2445; Phillip—IMC 1252; Nag; Ric; Stein-

graber) 13 min. Allegro. Tempo di Menuetto: trills present some ensemble difficulty. This pleasant, light-textured, flowing work was written by J. S. Bach's youngest and possibly least-appreciated son. It displays a natural, relaxed, jovialness that clearly distinguishes the early Classical style from that of the Baroque. Requires clarity, precision, and vitality. M-D.

Johann Sebastian Bach (1685–1750) Germany.

Two Fugues from the Art of Fugue (CFP). Two mirror fugues; Bach added counterpoint to the original version. The second fugue is the inversion and mirror of the first in all parts. Requires two experienced pianists. M-D to D.

Concerto c S.1060 1729–36 (CFP; Br&H; IMC; GS; CF; Eulenberg). Allegro; Adagio; Allegro. S.1060 and S.1061 were arranged by Bach for two keyboard instruments and orchestra. Both were originally composed for two violins, or violin and oboe, and contain movements in concertante style. M-D.

Concerto C S.1061 1727–30 (CFP; Br&H; IMC; GS; CF; Augener) 20 min. For two keyboard instruments and orchestra, but may be performed without orchestral instruments. First movement: no tempo indication. Adagio ovvero largo: brooding siciliano, scored without orchestra. Fuga: an exhilirating and glorious finale. M-D.

Fourteen Canons S.1087 1742–46 (C. Wolff—Br 1977). These canons were discovered in 1974 on a MS sheet forming the last page of the composer's own copy of the *Goldberg Variations*. Bach's title is *Various Canons upon the First Eight Bass Notes of the Preceding Aria*. All the canons are of value as pieces of construction, and some are as interesting—musically—as some sections of the *Goldberg Variations*. But none come up to the level of the best variations of the famous set. M-D.

Wilhelm Friedemann Bach (1710–1784) Germany

Friedemann spent his entire life in a constant and restless search for a satisfactory mode of expression. He was torn between the powerful heritage of his father and the stylistic demands of a new age.

Sonata F F.10 (CFP; IMC; OUP; Durand; *Bach Gesellschaft*, vol.43, pp.47–68) 20pp., 20 min. Allegro moderato; Andante; Presto. Canonic and imitative writing permeate all three movements; the last one is especially imaginative and lively. Baroque in outward appearance, emotionally colored and subtle in its individual motives, this work stands as both a rare document of its time and an eloquent portrait of its creator. M-D.

Ernst Bachrich (–)

Variations on a Theme of Beethoven Op.8 (A. Goll).

Svend-Erik Bäck (1919–   ) Sweden

Tollo (Swedish Music Information Center). For two pianos and electronic alterations. Has plenty of shape, thrust, and guts; free, nontonal style. Electronic effects are subtle and aimed at causing changes in sound color. M-D.

Ernst Bacon (1898–   ) USA

"The mood and temper of Mr. Bacon's works are chiefly a meditation on nineteenth-century rural America. He is full of our Scotch-Irish folklore, knows it from the inside, speaks and writes it as his own musical language. Mr. Bacon's work is remarkably pure in its expressive intent" (Virgil Thomson, *The Art of Judging Music*, pp.153–54).

The Battle of Jericho (AME 1962). For two pianos or piano duet. 8pp. Clever, strong rhythms.

Burr Frolic 1944 (AMP) 19pp. Based on American folklore. Plain harmony, never note-heavy, ingeniously evocative of our back-country musical style. "Moderately fast, and with puckering precision" (from score). Int. to M-D.

The Coal-Scuttle Blues (AMP 1944; SBTS; AMC) 20pp. A sedate and professional mingling of boogie, blues, and jazz idioms. Composed with Otto Luening. M-D.

Kankakee River 1935 (AMC).

River Queen (AME 1962; AMC) 6pp. Depicts President Lincoln's stern-wheel yacht; charming and picturesque in every way. Pretty in sound; derives its interest from melodic, rhythmic, and prosodic design rather than from oratory or from any kind of punch. M-D.

Henk Badings (1907–   ) The Netherlands

Badings follows the Brahms-Reger-Hindemith tradition.

Balletto Grottesco 1939 (UE) 10 min. Intrada; Marcia Funebre; Ballo; Intermezzo; Rondo Popolare. A suite of dances ranging from a funeral march to a rousing rumba conclusion. Int. to M-D.

Balletto Notturno 1975 (Donemus) 12 min. Giuoco delle Campane Lontane; Giuoco degli Arabeschi Sinuosi. Freely tonal, dramatic gestures. Large span required. M-D.

Balletto Serioso 1955 (Donemus) 25 min. Lento introduction; theme, four variations; Tempo di Valsa; Largo. This large work is tonally oriented and uses bi- and polytonalities. Requires advanced pianism throughout. D.

Foxtrot 1953 (Donemus) 2½ min. Jazz and blues influence, thin textures. Int. to M-D.

Raymond Baervoets (1930–   ) Belgium

Scherzo 1957 (CeBeDeM 1972) 25pp., 4 min. Facsimile of MS. One movement. Freely serial, octotonic, trills, full chordal skips, flexible meters, fast scales, repeated notes and octaves. M-D to D.

Riverberi 1980 (CeBeDeM) 44pp., 13½ min. One movement. Complex and highly organized with strong serial implications, pointillistic, clusters, harmonics, extreme dynamic range, rhythmic proportional relationships. Requires advanced musicianship and seasoned ensemble performers. D.

Zbigniew Baginski (1949–   ) Poland
Baginski teaches at the Warsaw State School of Music.

Refrain for Two Pianos 1975 (AA 1979) 31pp., 12 min. Performance directions in Polish and English. Mixture of traditional and experimental notation; uses key signatures; clusters; harmonics. Special sounds produced by pressing finger hard on string and sliding finger over string, striking strings with timpani sticks, and striking piano frame with hard object while depressing damper pedal. Much overlapping of lines between instruments, pointillistic, avant-garde. Improvisation required. M-D.

Shad Bailey (1946–   ) USA
Joyieux 1973 (Myklas 1975) 6pp. Octotonic, material equally shared, MC. M-D.

Sonata 1974 (Myklas 1978) 10 min. Allegro moderato; Lento, secco with precision; Moderato; Allegro, with exuberance. Carefully fingered, reflects a firm grasp of contrapuntal technique, material well dispersed between the two instruments, MC. Large span required. M-D.

Edward Bairstow (1874–1946) Great Britain
Variations on an Original Theme (OUP 1932).

Michael Baker (1941–   ) Canada, born USA
Baker writes in an essentially conservative idiom that is both an expression of temperament and the outgrowth of a desire to produce works that will afford pleasure to both performers and audiences.

Capriccio 1964 (F. Harris 1975) 22pp., 8 min. Flowing, melancholy, percussive and flamboyant, brilliant and showy writing, contrasting sections, strong Romantic flavor, MC. Parts are of equal difficulty. M-D.

Mili Balakirew (1837–1910) Russia
Symphony II d 1908 (Zimmermann; LC). Arranged for two pianos by the composer. A gargantuan work. The third movement, Romanza, could be extracted and used separately. Requires much endurance. M-D.

Edward Ballantine (1886–1971) USA
Three Variations on Mary Had a Little Lamb (A. P. Schmidt 1952; LC)

18pp. In the styles of Brahms, Johann Strauss, and John P. Sousa. Much fun. M-D.

Esther Ballou (1915–1973) USA
Beguine (ACA).
Sonata 1958 (Mercury; AMC) 30pp., 14 min. Allegro rhythmico: propulsive octotonic ideas, freely tonal, flexible meters, thin textures, low trills, Presto coda. Teneremente: flowing chromatic lines contrasted with pedalled sustained sections, ethereal chordal conclusion. Allegro: alla breve, based on a long–short rhythmic pattern, boisterous passages contrasted with legato cantando sections, fast repeated notes, bitonal implications, fugato section leading to coda. M-D.

M. Balutet (–   ) France
Suite Caracteristique Op.26 (A. Nöel 1899; LC). Montagnards; Marins; Moissonneurs. Dated but contains some effective use of the instruments. M-D.

Jacques Bank (1943–   ) The Netherlands
Two for Four (Donemus 1979). For four pianists playing two pianos. 13 min. First; Second; Third. Serial influence, dynamic extremes, changing meters, strong staccato accents, tremolo with both hands, ostinato-like figures, glissandi, cluster harmonics, long trills, atonal. D.

Samuel Barber (1910–1981) USA
Barber was a full-blooded Romantic and large-scale thinker even in his smaller works.
Souvenirs Op.28 1952 (Gold, Fizdale—GS) 20 min. A highly successful arrangement of the original four-hand work. These six pieces are a satirical evocation of once-popular social dances—Schottisch, One-Step, Galop, etc. Lightweight, basically diatonic, long harmonic sentences, sustained pedal-points and harmonic ostinato patterns, clever, wide audience appeal. Displays expert craft, fine melodic invention, imaginative scoring, much rhythmic charm. M-D.

Neil Barkla (–   ) Great Britain
Miniature Suite 1940 (OUP 1947; BrM) 16pp. Allegro; Andante; Presto. Pleasant, MC, attractive melodies. Int. to M-D.

Klarenz Barlow (1945–   ) Germany, born India
Textmusic 1971 (Feedback FB 7305K) 4pp., 89 bars, 15 min. Version 10 for two pianos. "Take a text consisting of a number of words, phrases, or sentences. Prepare the keys of the piano in the following way: A key somewhere in the middle of the keyboard is marked with the first letter of the chosen text. The next keys of the same color,

alternating to left and right (or vice versa) are treated with the succeeding letters in the text; if a certain letter occurs a second time, it should be dropped, and instead the next letter which has not yet occurred taken, until every letter of the text is represented on the keyboard. This procedure is then repeated with the keys of the other color, and then a third time, without taking the color of the keys into consideration" (from the score). Avant-garde, clever, some surprising sonorities. M-D.

Béla Bartók (1881–1945) Hungary

Rhapsody Op.1 1904 (Bo&H) 17pp. This brilliant work was originally for solo piano. Bartók rewrote it for piano and orchestra, and from that version, made an arrangement for two pianos. Structurally it is related to the Rhapsodies of Liszt with an opening slow lassú followed by the fast friss. Themes are based on gypsy modifications of Hungarian tunes. M-D.

Suite Op.4B 1905–7, 1941 (Bo&H). Originally written for orchestra (*Suite* Op.4) in 1905–7; rewritten for two pianos in 1941. Displays a variety of late nineteenth- and early twentieth-century styles, especially those of Liszt, Strauss, Debussy, and Ravel. Opens and concludes around B♭. Serenata: lyrical theme undergoes various transformations; development section displays a wide variety of pianistic sonorities. Allegro diabolico: SA, devilish and ferocious, strong climaxes in the fugal development and in the recapitulation. Scene of the Puszta [lowland plains of Hungary]: Impressionistic; opens with a lonely, unaccompanied rubato melody. Per finire: opening hornlike theme contrasts with a vigorous and active triplet rhythm. Impetuous and exciting writing. D.

Sonata for Two Pianos and Percussion 1937 (Bo&H) 25 min. Two (or three) players required for the percussion ensemble: 3 timpani, xylophone, 2 side drums, bass drum, cymbals, suspended cymbal, triangle, tam tam. Assai lento—Allegro molto: contains the most complexities. Lento ma non troppo: great color in this "night music" movement. Allegro non troppo: a lively dance movement that disappears in a C tonality. Traditional designs are used in the three movements (SA, ABA, and rondo) but they are given new dimensions and perspectives by the varied and colorful instrumentation. Percussive qualities of all instruments emphasized. The timpani and the xylophone have important thematic parts while the other percussion provide colorful and somewhat heavy sonorities and rhythmic emphasis. Thematic unification is not an aim of this work, which moves beyond the range of the pianistic and approaches a tonal landscape just shy of orchestral. All the percussion help create that landscape.

Recorded by Bartók and his wife on *Turnabout* TV 4159. One of the three or four greatest works in the two-piano literature. Great ensemble difficulties. D.

Seven Pieces from the Mikrokosmos (Bo&H 1947) 34pp. Arranged by the composer from *Mikrokosmos* 69, 113, 123, 127, 135, 145, and 146. Bulgarian. Chord and Trill Study. Perpetuum Mobile. Short Canon and Its Inversion. New Hungarian Folk Song. Chromatic Invention. Ostinato. In addition to these pieces, nos. 43a, 44, 145a, and 145b of the original *Mikrokosmos* are written for two pianos. See: Ivan Waldbauer, "Bartók's Four Pieces for Two Pianos," *Tempo,* 53/54 (1960): 17–22.

Stanley Bate (1911–1959) Great Britain
Three Pieces 1943 (AMP; LC). Prelude, 16pp. Pastorale, 11pp.: siciliano rhythms. Rondo, 28pp.: driving. Conceived as a suite but the movements are not related. M-D.

Sophie Gräfin Wolf Baudissin (1821–1894) Germany
Variations on an Original Theme Op.8 (C. A. Challier).

Hans Bauernfeind (1908–   ) Austria
Festliches Spiel (Oesterreichischer Bundesverlag 1954) 10pp. This "Festive Piece" is the overture to the musical play *A Comedy in the Palace* (words by Ewald Seifert). As the production is intended for school children, the style is natural and the musical lines flow easily. Octotonic, MC. Int. to M-D.

Waldemar von Baussnern (1866–1931) Germany
Duo (Steingräber 2594; LC) 37pp. Kraftvolle, nicht rasche Viertel; Ernst und ruhig; Lebhaft. Reger style, mainly thick and turgid writing throughout, concluding dancelike section. M-D.

Arnold Bax (1883–1953) Great Britain
The Devil that Tempted St. Anthony 1928 (Chappell) 15pp. Atmospheric Lento section contrasted with an agitated and nervous Allegro. M-D.
Hardanger 1927 (Chappell) 3½ min. Short contrasting sections, dancelike, with acknowledgments to Grieg. M-D.
Moy Mell 1917 (or *The Happy Plain*) (JWC) 9 min. A one-movement Irish tone-poem, nineteenth-century oriented, dramatic and expressive. Careful balance of dynamics and tone is necessary. M-D.
The Poisoned Fountain 1928 (Chappell) 4 min. Impressionistic and atmospheric, short. Color and flexibility required. M-D.
Red Autumn (Chappell 1943) 12pp. Rhapsodic, freely tonal, parallel chords in one piano against octotonic passages in the other, surprise ending, colorful. M-D.
Sonata E 1930 (Chappell; University of Virginia) 47pp., 18½ min. The

first two movements (Molto moderato; Lento espressivo) are rhapsodic. Finale (Vivace e feroce) is energetic, demanding, and vigorous. M-D.

Paul Bazelaire (1886–1958) France
Chasse, Scherzo (Leduc).

Amy Beach (1867–1944) USA
Suite Founded Upon Old Irish Melodies (J. Church 1924; UCLA; Toledo
    Public Library). Prelude, 28pp., 6½ min. Old-Time Peasant Dance,
    23pp. The Ancient Cabin, 25pp. Finale, 35pp. Well-contrasted pictur-
    esque movements based on nineteenth-century harmonic and pian-
    istic practice. M-D.
Variations on Balkan Themes Op.60 (A. P. Schmidt 1906). Twelve varia-
    tions in two books. Lyric; traditional handling of materials. M-D.

Conrad Arthur Beck (1901–   ) Switzerland
Sonatine (Schott 4909 1956) 24pp. Allegro; Andante sostenuto; Rondo.
    Thin textures, dissonant, octotonic, excellent development proce-
    dure, thoroughly realized neoclassic writing, freely tonal. Rondo (in
    6/8) has the most charm. Large span required. M-D.

Burton Beerman (1943–   ) USA
Beerman teaches at Bowling Green State University, Bowling Green,
Ohio.
Sounds and Wails of the Past (ACA 1981) 12pp. Aleatory; repeat given
    fragments; performers have to sing the given part (falsetto if neces-
    sary) while playing; harmonics; pedal depressed for long sections. A
    quick random sequence of nonsense syllables has to be improvised.
    Avant-garde. D.

Vincenzo Bellini (1801–1835) Italy
Grandes Variations de Concert sur un theme des "Puritains." Hexameron
    Variations. Searle 654 (Schuberth 1870) Written by Liszt, Herz, and
    Thalberg. Shorter than the solo piano version. One of the grandest of
    the Romantic extravaganzas. See also entry under Liszt. M-D.

Paul Ben-Haim (1897–   ) Israel, born Germany
Ben-Haim is one of the most representative composers of Israel. His
works reflect the oriental flavor of his environment within the framework
of Western musical tradition.
Capriccio 1960 (IMP) 12 min. Originally for piano and orchestra, arranged
    for two pianos by the composer. The main mood of the work is
    indicated by a quotation from a Sephardic love song, which heads the
    score. The slow opening, given to the first piano, contains the main
    thematic material expressed in a free, rhapsodic manner. The theme
    is given to the second piano, and eventually both performers have it

before a set of variations begins. The final variation is a rondo, in which the theme receives a toccata-like working out. New episodes are introduced, the pace slows, and the opening mood returns before the short, fast coda. M-D.

Arthur Benjamin (1893–1960) Great Britain, born Australia

Caribbean Dance on Two Jamaican Folk-Songs, Linstead Market and *Hold'im Joe* (Bo&H) 3 min. These keyboard settings of folk songs are not as effective as *Jamaica Rhumba*. There is much repetition of the rhumba rhythm but little interweaving of the two folk songs. M-D.

From San Domingo (Bo&H 1946) 3 min. Similar to *Caribbean Dance*. Light-textured, stylized dances; uses knuckle-raps on the piano lid. Great fun and a charming piece of foolery. M-D.

Jamaicalypso (Bo&H 1957) 8pp. Based on a Jamaican folk song. Rhythmic, fetching, vivacious. M-D.

Jamaica Rhumba (Bo&H) 1½ min. Syncopated 3-3-2 beat throughout, tosses two tunes back and forth, una corda throughout. M-D.

Two Jamaican Street Songs (Bo&H 1944) 11pp. Mattie Rag; Cookie. Contrasting. Requires well-developed ensemble, especially in "Cookie." M-D.

Niels Viggo Bentzon (1919–   ) Denmark

Sonata Op.51 (WH 3993 1956) 60pp., 18 min. Fluente, ma non troppo presto; Tempo quasi passacaglia; Rondo—Allegro. Three contrasted movements filled with effective and well-defined material. Full textures demand considerable virtuosity, many octave-doublings give body to a harmonic scheme based on thirds and hammered into traditional formal shapes by the relentless energy of ostinato motor rhythms. Exploits full resources of both instruments. D.

Bones and Flesh Op.334 1973–74 "Concerto for Two Pianos" (WH 1974) 70pp., 18 min. Facsimile. Alman: freely tonal, melodic ideas clearly designed, flexible meters, full chords, much contrary motion, ostinato-like figures, rather subdued dynamic plan. Atavistic Parenthesis: recurring opening syncopated chordal figure, polytonal implications, pointillistic, extended arpeggiation, patterns tossed between instruments, fades away to calm closing. Dry Book: many chromatic arpeggios and scalar passages, strong rhythms in a driving tempo, wide dynamic range, repeated notes; a Lento section four pages before the end slows the movement. Presto: frenetic, syncopated dancelike full chords bring the work to a resounding conclusion. This work is highly effective, worth the effort, and exploits both instruments and performers in the finest sense of the word. D.

Nicolai Berezowsky (1900–1953) USA, born Russia
Berezowsky's music is noted for its appealing quality, melodic content, and coloristic harmony.
Fantasy Op.9 1931 (AMP 1944) 12 min. Originally for two pianos and orchestra, arranged for two pianos by the composer. The format is essentially fast–slow–fast, with numerous themes and motives. The concluding section forms a free recapitulation of the many thematic materials introduced and utilized in the early passages. These materials are reduced to capsule size, and the work concludes with virtuoso octaves and three final B octaves in Lento tempo. M-D.

Josef Berg (1927–1971) Czechoslovakia
Sonata for Piano and Harpsichord in Classical Mode 1962 (CHF).

Arthur Berger (1912–   ) USA
Three Pieces for Two Pianos 1961 (Boelke-Bomart 1977) 23pp., 8 min. Includes performance directions and instructions for preparing one note on each piano. Pieces have no titles, only tempo indications. Appealing, involved, serial, pointillistic, harmonics, changing meters, plucked strings, clusters, expressionistic. These pieces "were composed with no predetermined plan whatsoever. I was relying on a certain immediacy in the application of techniques I had been exploiting in other works of the years immediately preceding" (composer, quoted in Bayan Northcott, "Arthur Berger: An Introduction at 70," MT, 123, No.1671 [May 1982]: 325). Large span required. M-D to D.

Jean Berger (1909–   ) USA, born Germany
Caribbean Cruise (Broude Brothers 1958) 5 min. Based on Latin American dance rhythms. Mainly diatonic with some dissonance, a little Americana mixed in with the opening measures of "O Susanna." Prominent use of thirds in both pianos, large chords. Int. to M-D.

Wilhelm Berger (1861–1911) USA
Variations e Op.61 1895 (Br&H) 34pp. Traditional style, octaves, skips. Contains some brilliant writing. M-D.

Joseph Berggrum (–   ) USA
Chorale and Fugue on a Theme by J. S. Bach (Brodt 1968) 11pp. Andante. Careful and equal treatment of performers with chorale transferred between instruments. M-D.

Adolphe Bergt (1822–1862) Germany
Sonata Op.1 (CFP).

Luciano Berio (1925–   ) Italy
Memory 1970–72 (UE). For electric piano and electric harpsichord. 8 min.

Linea 1973–74 (UE 15991). For two pianos, vibraphone, and marimba. 15 min. Opens slowly, soft with slipping overlaps, decorative. The title refers to the music's concern with lines, not to the struggle game of Linus and Apollo in Xenakis's piece of the same name. M-D to D.

Charles-Wilfrid de Bériot (1833–1914) France
De Bériot studied with Thalberg and taught at the Paris Conservatory.
Sonata Op.61 (Hamelle; University of Colorado). Allegro moderato; Sérénade; Finale. Outer movements are freely tonal around B♭, Sérénade in E♭. Sounds like "fin de siècle" French international; similar to Widor, Franck, and Vierne. Traditional pianistic figuration. Large span required. M-D.

Lennox Berkeley (1903–   ) Great Britain
Capriccio, Nocturne and Polka Op.5 1938 (JWC) 7 min. Contrasted, clear textures, rhythmic ingenuity, makes the most out of slight material. M-D.
Sonatina Op.52 (JWC 1959) 20pp., 12 min. Moderato; Andante; Allegro con brio. Neoclassic, undemonstrative style expressed in a controlled MC harmonic language but distinctly personal. Interpretative problems. M-D.

Isak A. Berkovich (1902–   ) USSR
Piano Concerto Op.44 (AMP 1977) For student and teacher. 26pp. From the series Teaching Literature of the Soviet Piano School. Allegro; Andante con moto; Allegro assai. This work "accords the student the special opportunity of performing with one's teacher, and the teacher and student together in a performance role participate in a learning and musical experience. In this way the student's musical horizon is developed" (from the score). MC. Int.

René Bernier (1905–   ) Belgium
Epitaphe Sonore (d'après l'epitaphe symphonique pour grand orchestre). 1976 (CeBeDeM). Facsimile. 7 min. Frequent tempo changes, freely tonal, dancelike, MC. Quotes Lamartine at beginning: "Un seul être vous manque et tout est dépeuplé." M-D.

Mario Bertoncini (1932–   ) Italy
Cifre 1964–67 (CPE). The pianos are placed with their keyboards forming a right angle. A bow made of hair (from a stringed instrument) is inserted between the piano strings on the outer side of the strings. There are two positions for the bow: between the dampers and the bridge of the instrument, and in the middle of the strings. The pianists' hands, dipped in powdered rosin, slide up and down the bow hairs. Graphic notation; performers free to follow whatever course of

musical events they wish; infinite possibilities exist. Avant-garde. M-D to D.

Bruno Bettinelli (1913–   ) Italy
Sonatina 1955 (Zanibon 1971) 34pp., 9 min. Allegro con semplicità: soaring angular melodies. Andante: legato melodies. Vivace: staccato. Contrapuntal, light and clear textures, freely tonal with strong dissonance. M-D.
Ricercare (Carisch 21986 1976) 21pp., 9 min. Lento opening in low, clusterlike sonorities leads to a linear Più mosso, with clusters and flexible meters; Lento returns; and Più mosso concludes work. Chromatic triplets, fast repeated notes, effective final bar is Lento; expanded tonality, MC. Requires large span. M-D.

Jürgen Beurle (1943–   ) Germany
Kontra (Moeck 5184). For three or more pianos. Facsimile of MS.

J. M. Beyer (–   ) USA
Movement for Two Pianos (AMC). 3/4; many chromatics and tone clusters. Second piano exploits seven eighth-notes per bar. Some 4 and 5 against 7 make for problems. M-D.

A. Biales (–   ) USA
Passacaglia 1963 (UCLA) 8pp. Freely tonal, variations handled carefully and efficiently, some meter changes, neo-Hindemith style. M-D.

Albert Biehl (1835–1899) Germany
Eight Duos Op.128 (Br&H).

Michael von Biel (1937–   ) Germany
Für Zwei Klavier 1, 2, 3 1961 (Feedback 7118 1971) 5pp., 20 min. Three pieces treated in aleatory fashion. One section takes 90 seconds for one piano but only 50 seconds for the other piano. This takes place four different times in four different sections. Pointillistic, clusters, harmonics, wood of piano slapped, strings muted with hand, avant-garde. D.

Adolphe Blanc (1828–1885) France
Sonatine Concertante Op.64 (Lemoine 1885; BrM) 15pp. Allegro non troppo; Andante; Scherzo; Finale. Somewhat in style of the Arensky suites. Int.

Émile R. Blanchet (1877–1943) Switzerland
Ballade Op.57 (ESC 1937; LC) 24pp. One movement in nineteenth-century Romantic style, cadenza for Piano I before closing. M-D.

Allan Blank (1925–   ) USA
Interplay 1963–64 (AMC) 18pp. "The first three metronome indications

approximate the basic tempo" (from the score). One continuous atonal movement. Pointillistic, flexible meters, octotonic, expressionistic, broad dynamic range. Both instruments have almost entirely separate parts that "interplay." Ensemble problems. D.

Pavel Blatný (1931–   ) Czechoslovakia
Ballette 1956 (CHF) 15 min. Five contrasting movements, neoclassic, colorful, strong Stravinsky influence. Well laid out for both instruments. M-D.
Prolog and Scherzo 1966 (CHF) 32pp. Prolog: consists of sections marked Adagio, Allegro, Alla marcia, and Andante and exploits repeated chords, trills, octaves, and syncopation. Scherzo: employs long trills, a marcato theme, octotonic writing, arpeggiated chords; *pp* closing leads directly to a slower Trio, in which Scherzo material is reworked; a Da Capo al Segno repeats part of the Scherzo; ends with a coda. Freely tonal, ideas are cast in neoclassic style. Limited musical material reveals a richness and variety of detail. M-D.

Ernest Bloch (1880–1959) USA, born Switzerland
Evocations 1937 (GS 1938) 41pp. Transcribed by the composer from the *Symphonic Suite*. Contemplation. Houang-Ti, God of War. Renouveau. A tone-poem of lustrous oriental configuration and coloring that takes full advantage of the timbre range of the orchestra. The two-piano version is not as effective, as it cannot fully replicate the orchestral color. M-D.

Friedemann Blüthner (1949–   ) Germany
Opera 14 (Zanibon 1972) 16pp., 10 min.

Konrad Boehmer (1941–   ) Germany
Zeitläufte 1962 (Tonos 7217 1968) 31pp., parts. 15 min. For two pianos, English horn, clarinet, bass clarinet, horn, and trombone. Highly organized, serial, pointillistic, extreme registers exploited, dynamics attached to most notes, flexible meters and tempi. Piano parts are of equal difficulty. Somewhat in the style of the Boulez *Structures* for two pianos. D.

Leon Boellmann (1862–1897) France
Fantaisie dialoguée Op.35 (Durand).

Philippe Boesmans (1936–   ) France
Fanfare I (Jobert 1972). For two pianos, two hands (one player). 4 leaves, and 1 leaf of explanations in French. Conventional and avant-garde notation, much use of aleatory writing. M-D.
Sur Mi (Jobert 1974) 7 leaves, 13 min. For two pianos, electronic organ, and percussion (cymbals and tam tam). Explanations in French. Four copies necessary for performance. Spatial and traditional notation,

complex chords and rhythmic problems, pointillistic, dense textures, dynamic extremes. Contains almost insurmountable ensemble problems; only for the best equipped avant-garde performers. D.

Rob du Bois (1934–   ) The Netherlands

Allegro 1978 (Donemus 52.1750) 12pp., 6½ min, photostat. For four pianos. Much the same material is played by all the pianists, with each instrument following one bar later. Freely tonal, clever, neo-classic. Int. to M-D.

A Combination of Voices 1968 (Donemus) 8 min. Free serial treatment, pointillistic, dynamic extremes, proportional rhythmic relationship, thin textures. Requires large span. D.

René de Boisdeffre (1838–1906) France

Scherzo-Sérénade Op.9 (Heugel; LC) 11pp. Nineteenth-century style with strong Mendelssohn influence. Int. to M-D.

William Bolcom (1938–   ) USA

Frescoes 1971 (EBM 1975) 32pp., 27 min. For two pianos, harmonium, and harpsichord, played by two performers. Each player has a piano; one also has a harmonium, the other a harpsichord. War in Heaven. The Caves of Orcus. "These *Frescoes* are written or painted with a wide brush, and must be played with the same energy and abandon they were written in" (from the score). Improvisation, free and metered time, plucked strings, clusters, flutter pedal. Time bubbles contain elements whose order can be varied at will and expanded as needed. Instruments not synchronized in some sections, in "Tug of War" sections they "pull" at each other. Bolcom draws on the Book of Revelation, *Paradise Lost,* and the *Aeneid* for visions of death, destruction, and apocalyptic war. Reminders of old battle-pieces and rags are interspersed. Wildly bombastic music; amazing handling of the four instruments. D.

Interlude for Two Pianos 1963 (EBM) 11pp., 8 min. Includes performance directions. Serial, expressionistic, proportional rhythmic notation, free-style, "as little pedal as possible to the end," avant-garde. D.

Claude Bolling (1930–   ) France

Sonata for Two Pianos, Percussion and Double Bass (Les Editions Bleu Blanc Rouge 1973) parts. Piano I (classic) 30pp. Piano II (jazz) 34pp. Percussion required: cymbal, hi-hat, snare drums, small tom tom, big tom tom, bass drums. This sonata "has been composed to allow two pianists of different styles to play together. It is not necessary for the classical pianist to be versed in jazz, nor the jazz pianist to have studied his classics. Even, it's heartily recommended that each of the two styles retain their individuality, and thereby accentuate the contrast" (from the score). The work is divided into three contrasting sections. The "classical" pianist's part has elements of Chopin and Rachmaninoff mixed with a Gershwin flavor. The "jazz" pianist's part reflects the influence of Duke Ellington, while the formal structure of the work depends on traditional forms and resources. The work holds together remarkably well in spite of its opposite styles. M-D.

Maarten Bon (1933–   ) The Netherlands
Let's Go Out for a Drive (and Polute the Air) 1970 rev. 1974 (Donemus) 20 min. For three pianists and a trombonist, accompanied by a conductor.
Boréal 1980–81 (Donemus) 5 min.

Johann Heinrich Bonawitz (1839–1917) Germany
In 1872–73 Bonawitz conducted the Popular Symphony Concerts in New York.
Concerto for Two Pianos (GS).

Melanie Bonis (1858–1937) France
Scherzo-Valse (Leduc; LC) 9pp. Similar in style to Chaminade. M-D.
Variations (ESC).

Bernard van den Boogarde (1952–   ) The Netherlands
Military Games 1969–70 (Donemus 1976) 16pp., photostat. For two pianos and tape. Performance directions in Dutch. Pointillistic, dynamic extremes, clusters, harmonics, fast complex figuration, improvisation with clusters. The piano parts are written to bring out characteristic sounds of the electronic tape and create differentiated sound material. Avant-garde. D.

Wim Boogman (1955–   ) The Netherlands
Muziek voor 2 piano's—de vriendschap ("Music for two Pianos—the Friendship") 1981 (Donemus) 9 min.

Enrico Bormioli (1895–1944) Italy
Canzone Sivigliana (SZ 1940) 12pp., 5 min. ABA, rich impressionistic harmonies, fluid melodies, appealing. M-D.
Gitana 1940 (SZ).
Sincopati (SZ). Jazz-inspired. M-D.

Alexander Borodin (1833–1887) Russia
Symphonie II b (W. Bessell; LC) 27pp. Arranged for two pianos by the composer. M-D.

Alexander Uriah Boscovich (1908–   ) Israel, born Hungary
Boscovich teaches at the Israel Academy of Music in Tel Aviv; most of the younger generation of Israeli composers have studied there with him.
Semitic Suite 1960 (IMP 4.144). Allegretto; Andantino—rubato

teneramente; Folk Dance; Andantino; Pastorale; Dance. Short movements, mainly ABA. Leans heavily on Oriental characteristics of Jewish music, although Boscovich does not arrange actual folk music. Pleasant melodies reflect impressions of the landscape. Large leaps and fast changes in register. M-D.

Fritz von Bose (1865–   ) Germany
Duo Op.13 (K&S).

Peter Böttinger (–   ) Germany
Capriccio für Peter Schreiber 1974 (Döring) 11pp., photostat. For piano and harpsichord.

Pierre Boulez (1925–   ) France
Boulez's piano scores contain some of the most arduous celebration in musical history. They also pose awesome digital difficulties even for the virtuoso. His one foray into the two-piano medium is no exception.
Structures (UE) Vol.I, 1956, 21 min. Vol.II, 1961, 23 min. Book I is based on "the first of the three fragments of the mode of 36 pitch levels of Messiaen's etudes." Book II consists of two sections: the first is a thoroughly fixed ten-minute movement, while the second includes two "pieces," six "texts," and four "insets." Boulez has mapped out the overall form of the second section, but it is up to the players to decide—ideally while performing—which choices to make among the pieces, texts, and insets. Rhythm, dynamics, attack, and pitch are serialized, a kind of compendium of possible techniques of total serialization. A major problem for the performers are the durations, which are ordered arithmetically (from one to twelve 32nd notes). "Despite the fact that they are precisely measurable, they change with the tempos and become increasingly difficult to measure in quicker movement" (Leonard Stein, "The Performers Point of View," PNM [Spring 1963]:65). A "mind-wrenching experience." A challenge for only the most mature pianists. D.

Roger Boutry (1932–   ) France
Třásné (Sal 1967) 5 min. Allegro moderato; Allegretto; Vivace. Strong rhythms, many ninth and eleventh chords, octotonic. M-D.

York Bowen (1884–1961) Great Britain
Suite Op.111 (OUP 1946) 16½ min. Prelude: mainly quiet. Rigadoon: ABA, spirited. Intermezzo: a highly ornamented poem, Rachmaninoff influence. Tarantella: most-effective movement, published separately; requires agile fingers. Pleasantly pianistic, MC, good subjects in all movements. M-D.
Arabesque Op.119 (OUP 1947) 10pp. A fanciful one-movement work. Augmented triads, a few ninth chords, roulades, unfolding varia-

tions, varied keys, engaging thematic material adroitly developed. M-D.

Paul Bowles (1910–   ) USA
Sonata C 1946 (GS) 33pp. Strict tempo: staccato octave theme divided between players. Molto tranquillo: broad, flexible melodies. Absolutely strict tempo: played with no pedal, percussive, strong rhythmic chords, dynamic extremes, freely tonal, polymetrical. The first two movements are written in Bowles's most poetic early-Ravel vein, while the finale imitates African drum sounds and rhythms. A strong yet charming musical work. M-D.
Night Waltz 1948 (AME 1958; AMC; Arizona State University Library) 12pp. Opens with flowing lines in Piano I over rhythmic push in Piano II; next section has more rhythmic emphasis and fuller chords; colorful chromatic broken chordal figuration leads to a staccato morendo closing. Charming and attractive, MC. M-D.

George Frederick Boyle (1886–1948) Great Britain
Danse Negre (H. Elkin 1939) 7pp.
Minuet Antique (H. Elkin 1939) 9pp.

Eugene Bozza (1905–   ) France
Sonate pour deux pianos (Leduc 1963) 51pp. Andante maestoso: broad opening moves to Allegro moderato, Tranquillo, Più vivo, and Vivo. Andante molto moderato: melodic and expressive, builds to big climax, subsides into a Lent and misterioso *ppp* closing. Allegro vivo: many sixteenth-note passages, octaves, chord trills, broken chords. Quartal and quintal harmonies and melodies. Requires strong rhythmic drive. D.

Mario Braggiotti (1909–   ) USA
Variations on Yankee Doodle (GS 1950; LC) 36pp. In the manner of Bach, Beethoven, Chopin, Debussy, and Gershwin. Clever; contains some tricky passages. M-D.

Johannes Brahms (1833–1897) Germany
Brahms brought two-piano writing to its highest level. His originality in the medium is unique.
Sonata f Op.34b 1854 (Br&H; CFP; IMC) 41 min. This is perhaps the best version of *Piano Quintet* Op.34a, although the two-piano version was composed before the quintet scoring took place. Allegro non troppo: five strongly contrasted and well-organized themes. Andante: romantic, surging, beautiful. Scherzo: broad-scale, martial, effective contrasting Trio. Finale: quiet opening, presto coda. One of the most comprehensive and serious works of its time. Requires mature pianism in all aspects. D.

Five Waltzes Op.39 (CFP; Hughes—GS L1530). Nos.1, 2, 11, 14, and 15 from the original cycle for piano duet. Brahms arranged them for two pianos for Karl Tausig and his wife. Each waltz is a study in rich harmony, full texture and tone, and rhythmic complexity. Of special note are the consecutive octaves in No.14 and consecutive sixths in No.15. Most are Viennese waltzes but there is a Ländler influence, with the emphasis rhythmically changed. M-D.

Variations on a Theme by Haydn Op.56b (Br&H; CFP 3892; Simrock; GS; K; IMC 2556; Schauer; Norton; Lengnick) 20 min. One of the masterpieces of the repertoire, highly pianistic. The theme, St. Anthony's Chorale, is extracted from a Haydn woodwind divertimento; eight variations follow. Study this work in conjunction with the orchestral version. Masterful treatment of both instruments in an endless inventiveness of polyphonic design never before or since equalled in two-piano writing. Rhythms include siciliano, hemiola, cross, and polyrhythms. Bell motif of chorale returns throughout the composition. Finale is a passacaglia in half notes based on the chorale. Brahms frequently played this work with Clara Schumann. Although better known in its orchestral form, it was originally written for two pianos. D.
See: Allen Forte, "The Structural Origin of Exact Tempi in the Brahms-Haydn Variations," MR, 18 (May 1957):138–49.

Symphony III Op.90 (Simrock). Arranged by Brahms.

Symphony IV Op.98 (Simrock). Arranged by Brahms. Both of these symphony arrangements came into being simultaneously with the orchestral scores, probably as a means of hearing the symphonies immediately.
See: Herbert F. Peyser, "Johannes Brahms—The Master as Teacher," MA, 67 (February 1947):3, 224, 357.

Wim Brandse (1933–   ) The Netherlands
Brandse was born in Utrecht, Holland, attended the Dutch schools of music, and completed his graduate work in Aachen, Germany. He is Professor of Composition, Counterpoint and Harmony at the Conservatory of Music in Zwolle, Holland, and has written several books on solfege. All the pieces below are published by (GS). They are short, well-made, freely tonal, MC, and display graceful invention. Int.

Bagatelle (GS 1980) 3pp.

Burlesca

Carnival

Humoreque

Impromptu

Nocturne

Overture

Rondino

Fritz Brandt (1902–   ) Germany
Sonata c Op.111 (Ernst Bisping).

Henry Brandt (1913–   ) USA, born Canada
Sonata for Two Pianos 1930 (ACA) 21 min.
Four Chorale Preludes 1932 (ACA) 12 min.
Double Crank Hand Organ for Two Pianos 1933 (ACA).

Rudolf Braun (1869–1925) Germany
Divertimento (Dob 189__) 23pp.

Cesar Bresgen (1913–   ) Austria, born Italy
Konzert für zwei Klaviere Op.13 1934–35 (Müller SM 1008A) 35pp. Allegro vivace, energico. Adagio; Molto vivace. Written in the "old" (alten Stil) concerto-grosso style, with the two instruments treated individually. Octotonic, flexible meters, freely tonal, brilliant closing. M-D.
Bilder des Todes (Dob 1973) 44pp., 19 min. For two pianos and two players on kettledrums and percussion. Toccata: fast-moving, chromatic sixteenths in both piano parts; mid-section becomes more lyric and sustained; an agitato section concludes the movement with a strong punch; large span required. Variationen: staccato and marcato figuration contrasted with octotonic melody, syncopation, and triplet figuration in crescendo. Intermezzo I: melody accompanied with secco chords; serious. Ricercare I: linear treatment of ideas. Intermezzo II: grace-note octotonic melody; short. Ricercare II: unraveling eighth-note figuration in one piano while other comments and amplifies line. Epilog: free, long pedals, maestoso ending. Exciting writing in this suite. D.

Dora Estella Bright (1863–1952) Great Britain
Variations for Two Pianofortes on an Original Theme by Sir G. A. Macfarren (Ashdown 1894; BrM).

Frédéric Brisson (–   ) France
Hymne Triomphale, Fantaisie Brillante Op.41/1 (Schott 18?).

Benjamin Britten (1913–1976) Great Britain
Introduction and Rondo alla Burlesca Op.23/1 1940 (Bo&H) 23pp., 10 min. This large-scale work opens with a serious Grave in d and leads to a lively Allegro moderato, brilliant octave conclusion. Achieves some arresting color effects and is expressively articulate. M-D.
Mazurka Elegiaca Op.23/2 1941 (Bo&H) 15pp., 7½ min. Written in memoriam to Paderewski while Britten was in the USA, exploits Polish tunes. Builds to climax in mid-section, concludes *ppp*. Includes a few key changes. There is atmosphere and a haunting if

somewhat elusive beauty about the piece. There are two or three incorrect or missing accidentals in the second piano part. M-D.

Jane E. Brockman (1949-   ) USA
Brockman received three degrees from the University of Michigan. She is presently a member of the music faculty of the University of Connecticut, Storrs, CT 06268.
Two Piano Quartet 1980 (MS available from composer). For two pianos, flute, and cello. 13pp. Adagio. Widely spaced chromatic and non-tonal sonorities unfold naturally to provide an emotional and rhapsodic movement. Multi-layered rhythms and elastic melodic intervals are effectively used to produce the end-result. Serial influence. D.

Vera Brodsky (1909–   ) USA
In 1932 Brodsky and Harold Triggs gave two-piano concerts in an extensive tour of the USA.
Fuller and Warren (Cowboy Tune) (JF 19361 LC) 8pp. Composed jointly with Harold Triggs. Freely set, rhythmic and cheery. Int. to M-D.

Reidar Brøgger (1886–1956) Norway
Etude de Concert Op.20 (NMO 1946) 19pp. Traditional figures, late nineteenth-century style, Brahms influence. M-D.

Earle Brown (1926–   ) USA
Brown has been one of the most consistently innovative composers of his generation. He pioneered the exploration of "open form," in which the sonorities are specified but the sequence of events is not determined in advance. He also uses a type of graphic notation based on the concept of proportional notation, in which time is divided into relative units whose duration is suggested by the spacing of the notational signs. This results in a variable kind of form where the performer plays an active part. The performer's choice and the randomness attendant on it are essential elements of Brown's art.
Folio and Four Systems 1952–54 (AMP 1961). For two or more pianos and/or various instruments. 8 sheets. October 1952: for piano, graphic notation, performance time determined by performer, aleatory. November 1952 ("Synergy"): for piano(s) and/or other instruments or sound-producing media, graphic notation, aleatory. December 1952: for one or more instruments and/or sound producing media; score is a picture of space at one instant, which must always be considered as unreal and/or transitory; performer must set this in motion; aleatory. MM 87; MM 135; March 1953 (2 sheets): for piano or simultaneous performance by two pianos; "performances rather than compositions" (from the score); pointillistic fragments. Music for "Trio for Five Dancers" June 1953: "A transcription of graphics

which relate to physical position and movement in space into a 'literal' and indigenous sound-event in comparable time" (from the score). 1953: for piano; may be played in any sequence. Four Systems. January 1954: for piano(s) and/or other instruments or sound-producing media; may be played in any sequence, either side up, at any tempo(i). "Outer limits": title refers to the range extremities of any instrument, group of instruments, or other sound-producing media. M-D.

Twenty Five Pages 1953 (UE 15587 1975). For one to 25 pianos. Includes performance directions. "The *Twenty Five Pages* may be played in any sequence; each page may be performed either side up; events within each two-line system may be read as either treble or bass clef; the total time duration of the piece is between eight minutes and 25 minutes, based on 5 seconds and 15 seconds per two-line system as probable but not compulsary time extremities. After the 'Folio' experiments of 1952–3, this is the first extended work using what I call 'time notation' (durations extended in space relative to time, rather than expressed in metric symbols as in traditional notation) and which has since been called proportional notation" (from the score). Aleatory, clusters, dynamic extremes, ten different attacks, avant-garde. D.

Corroboree 1964 (UE 50 15308). For three or two pianos. 12 min. 12 lines of music. Includes detailed directions. The title is an Australian word meaning "a nocturnal festivity with songs and symbolic dances by which the Australian aborigines celebrate events of importance." A noisy festivity, a tumult. Five types of piano sonorities are used: single notes, chords, clusters, pizzicato, and muted sounds on the strings. "By means of frequency, tempo and density controls, these five 'colours' are distributed among the pianos to make the continuity a kind of sonic-spatial 'conversation'" (from the score). Aleatory, avant-garde. M-D.

Dave Brubeck (1920–   ) USA

Four by Four 1946 (AMP 1976) 23pp. Allegro. Largo. Moderato. Moderato. Early contrasting pieces written when Brubeck was studying with Darius Milhaud at Mills College. Freely tonal, octotonic, neoclassic, flexible meters. The outside cover reads "for piano 4-hands" but the first page says "for two pianos, four hands." M-D.

They All Sang Yankee Doodle (AMP 1976) 39pp. Dedicated to the memory of Charles Ives. A set of variations on "Yankee Doodle." This tune is interwoven with other folk and national melodies for a musical collage. Brubeck explains his approach to the piece in the "Composer's Notes." Exploits many pianistic devices, MC. M-D.

Howard Brubeck (1916–) USA
Tamale (AMC) 7pp. Some Latin American rhythmic influences, lively
and vigorous, octotonic handling of main theme, a few tempo
changes, glissandi, many seventh chords, clever. Would make a good
opening program number or an effective encore. M-D.

Max Bruch (1838–1920) Germany
Fantasie d Op.11 (Br&H 1861; Hamelle) 12pp. One movement with
varied sections: Allegro molto energico l'istesso tempo; Adagio ma
non troppo; Vivace assai, ma energico. Bruch has a gift for moving
with grace among the passions. M-D.

J. Ludwig Bruhns (–) Austria
Kanonische Suite Op.2 (Simrock).

Ignaz Brüll (1846–1907) Austria
Brüll's late Romantic style reflects his friendship with and admiration of
Johannes Brahms.
Tarantelle Op.6 (AMP).
Sonata d Op.21 (Brockhaus 1876; Robitschek; LC) 22pp. Allegro;
Scherzo; Andante ma non troppo; Finale—Allegro ma non troppo.
Well worked-out; tuneful ideas. M-D.
Duo Op.64 (Dob; LC) 17pp. Theme with Variations; Andantino pastorale;
"In Arabischer Weise." Brahms influence, both instruments musi-
cally exploited. M-D.

Joanna Bruzdowicz (1943–) Poland
An der schonen blauen Donau ("The Beautiful Blue Danube") (Choudens
1974) 19pp. For two pianos and tape.

Valentino Bucchi (1916–) Italy
Racconto Siciliano (Carisch 21789 1968) 52pp. Five untitled movements,
based on a theme from *Cavalleria Rusticana*. Palm clusters at climax
of fourth movement. Well organized. M-D.

Ernest Bullock (1890–) Great Britain
Introduction and Fugue e 1932, rearranged 1951 (J. Williams 1955; BrM)
14pp., 6½ min. Adagio introduction leads to a busy chromatic fugue.
M-D.

Emil F. Burian (1904–1959) Czechoslovakia
American Suite 1926 (Supraphon). Strong jazz influence, M-D.

Cecil Burleigh (1885–) USA
Mountain Pictures Suite Op.42 (CF). Crags and Cascades; Shepherd's
Song; Distant Haze; Avalanche. Impressionistic, chordal melodies in
ninths and thirteenths. M-D.

Francis Burt (1926–   ) Great Britain
Musik für zwei Klaviere Op.4 (Bo&Bo) 30pp. Contrasting sections, atonal. Well-developed pianism required. M-D.

Alan D. Bush (1900–   ) Great Britain
Three Pieces (Murdoch).

Geoffrey Bush (1920–   ) Great Britain
An Oxford Scherzo 1949 (Galliard; BrM) 12pp. An excellent recital piece with contrasting sections and sudden shifts of meter. Lyric section has contrapuntal moments. Int.
Sonata on Themes by Arne (Galliard) 5 min.
Whydah Variations 1961 (Novello) 11 min. Based on a theme by English composer Balfour Gardiner. Harmonic asperity and a certain explosiveness of both rhythm and dynamics. Full keyboard techniques utilized brilliantly. M-D.

Ferruccio Busoni (1866–1924) Italy
Busoni, once praised for his Bach transcriptions, later vilified as a "recomposer," is now beginning to be properly understood. As two-piano repertoire, these works are an asset to players tired of the more hackneyed literature.
Duettino Concertante "After Mozart" (Br&H 5190 1921) 19pp., 7½ min. Based on the third movement of the Mozart *Piano Concerto* F, K.459. This transcription compares favorably in artistic stature with the original. A spontaneous and effective rondo, with transparent textures and rococo fioraturas. M-D.
Fantasia Contrapuntistica 1912 (Br&H 5196 1921) 68pp. Originally for piano solo, arranged for two pianos by the composer. Chorale variations on "Ehre seit Gott in der Höhe" followed by a quadruple fugue on a Bach fragment. Chorale variations; Fuga I; Fuga II; Fuga III; Intermezzo; Variatio I; Variatio II; Variatio III; Cadenza; Fuga IV; Chorale; Stretta. Around three fugues from Bach's *Art of Fugue* and the torso of the triple fugue, left half-completed when Bach died, Busoni builds a grandiose structure of his own, with variations, cadenza, four completions of the triple fugue, and a new quadruple fugue and coda added. Represents a daring version of an unfinished fugue by Bach. The whole work represents the culmination of Busoni's lifelong Bach studies. D.
Fugue G (Br&H 1894). A transcription of the J. S. Bach *Fugue* S.884/2.
Improvisation on the Bach Chorale "Wie wohl ist mir, O Freund der Seelen," S.517 (Br&H 4941 1917) 30pp. Based on a song from the *Anna Magdalene Notebook*. A large-scale transcription. Loud dynamics, octave scales, chordal trills, Andante con moto mid-section, big climax, full but quiet closing. M-D.

Henri Busser (1872–1973) France

Minerve Op.7 1896 (Lemoine 1905; LC) 7pp. Ouverture de Concert. Arranged for two pianos by the composer.

Hercule aux Jardins des Hespérides, Poème Symphonique Op.18 (Lemoine 1907; LC) 21pp. Originally for orchestra, arranged for two pianos by the composer. Numerous sections, Impressionistic. D.

Sylvano Bussotti (1931–   ) Italy

Bussotti considers himself a self-taught composer. His artistic skills also extend to graphics, painting, and drama.

Tableaux vivants, avant la passion selon Sade 1964 (Ric 130962). "His crowning achievement, which makes use of theatrical effects, diagrams, drawings, surrealistic illustrations, etc., with thematic content evolving from a dodecaphonic nucleus, allowing great latitude for free interpolations and set in an open-end form in which fragments of the music are recapitulated at will, until the players are mutually neutralized. The unifying element of the score is the recurrent motive D-E♭(Es)-A-D-E, spelling the name De Sade, interwoven with that of B-A-C-H" (BBD, 1971 Supplement: 38). Clusters, harmonics, pointillistic, fistfull sonorities, avant-garde. D.

C

Roberto Caamaño (1923–) Argentina

Dialogos Op.26 1965 (IU) 24pp., 14½ min. Quarter note = 72; Quarter note = 60; Interludio; Quarter note = 60. Twelve-tone, changing meters, expressionistic, much use of tremolo in second movement, dramatic gestures, careful distribution of material between instruments. Requires large span. M-D to D.

George Cacioppo (1926–) USA

Cacioppo studied at the University of Michigan with Ross Lee Finney and Roberto Gerhard and took further study with Leon Kirchner. His background in mathematics, physics, and acoustics is extensive.

Cassiopeia 1962 (in *Score—An Anthology of New Music—*GS 1981) 2pp. "Lettered symbols with number subscripts represent pitch. White pitch symbols are played as harmonics. Loudness is proportional to size of pitch symbol. Time values: a) may be proportioned to the linear space between pitch symbols; b) may be developed spontaneously and variably during the performance. Four Networks: Fields of intersecting sound paths. Each of the four networks consists of a number of pitch-defined paths of sound" (from the score). Contains more performance directions. The piece is a mass of connected lines with indicated points lettered and numbered. Aleatory, avant-garde. D.

Charles Wakefield Cadman (1881–1946) USA

Dancers of the Mardi Gras (FitzSimons 1934; LC) 22pp. Arranged for two pianos from the orchestral score by the composer. The work takes its name from the Negro side of the Mardi-Gras, although no Negro themes have been used. It reflects the fantastic, the grotesque, and the bizarre spirit of the carnival. This sectionalized fantasy has much color, even in the two-piano arrangement. M-D.

John Cage (1912–) USA

It seems that Cage has reached the point in his work where there is no shape, no beginning, no ending, and, above all, no sense of progress. He has recently said, "I am now involved in *dis*-organization and a state of mind which in Zen is called no-mindedness . . . in making processes, the nature of which I don't forsee." But these statements are as false as they are true! For discussions of Cage's style see GTPR, pp. 131–32 and *Supplement* to GTPR, pp. 60–61.

A Book of Music 1944 (CFP 6702 1960). For two prepared pianos. 67pp., 30 min. Preparation takes about two hours. In two large parts with a series of short solos near the end of the second part. Thin textures, many repeated notes. Cage substitutes for the classical chromatic scale a gamut of pings, plucks, and delicate thuds that is both varied and expressive and that is different in each piece. This work could easily be subtitled "The Well-Tampered Claviers." M-D.

Experiences No. 1 1948 (CFP 6708A 1961) 3pp., 6 min. Written for the dance by Merce Cunningham. Without accent, quietly, 2/2, thin textures, Satie-like, Impressionistic, long lines and long pedals, lyric. M-D.

Music for Amplified Toy Pianos (CFP 6724 1960). Has to be made up by the publisher on special order. Ozalid, many plastic inserts.

Three Dances 1945 (CFP 6760 1960) 61pp., 20 min. For two prepared pianos. Preparation takes two hours. "Mutes of various materials are placed between the strings of the keys used, thus effecting transformations of the piano sounds with respect to all their characteristics" (from the score). Basically thin textures, percussive treatment of instruments, long trills. The two outer dances are strongly rhythmic while the middle dance is more restful and less active. M-D.

Winter Music 1957 (CFP 6775) 20 separate sheets, to be performed, in whole or part by one to 20 pianists. "The notation, in space, five systems left to right on the page, may be freely interpreted as to time. An aggregate must be played as a single ictus" (from the score). Other performance directions. Clusters, harmonics, avant-garde. M-D.

Charles Camilleri (1931–   ) Malta
Camilleri believes strongly in the possibility and value of a synthesis of cultures and philosophies and draws on Oriental, African, European, and American sources for inspiration and material.

Taqsim 1967 (Fairfield 1975) 32pp., 16 min. "Taqsim means 'division' and this work is divided into three movements with a prelude in the form of the improvised 'Taqsim,' or its counterpart the 'Alap.' The former is the name of such preludes found in the music of North Africa, and the latter in the music of the Indian sub-continent. They both have the same function: establishing the character and the mood of the work to follow" (from the score). The first movement is an accompanied melody. The second is "basically monodic and heterophonic in character. The polyphonic nature of the music is a natural extension of heterophony. The 'piacevole' section of this movement acts as a contrast to the micro-tonal inflections of its outer sections and is developed through idiomatic two-piano writing" (from the score). In the final movement color chords support a folklike melody with a mid-section that recalls rhythmic elements and xylophone sounds from Africa. Evenly laid out between the instruments with much contrast. Complex writing that requires mature musicianship. D.

Gustav Campa (1863–   ) Germany
Allegro Appassionato (Br&H).

Phillip Cannon (1929–   ) Great Britain, born France
Galop Parisien Op.4 1951 (Kronos) 18pp., 3½ min. A vivacious tribute to the excitement of Paris. Would make a brilliant program opener or a sparkling encore. Galop and waltz are combined at the climax. M-D.
Sonata per Ballo (Kronos 1979). As its name suggests, this work is strongly related to the spirit of dancing. M-D.

Charles Capro (1954–   ) USA
Capro studied at Montclair State College, Ramapo College, and the Manhattan School of Music. He is active as a composer and performer of live electronic music.
Crabcar Phase for Two Pianos 1975 (in *Score—An Anthology of New Music*—GS 1981) 2pp. "Begin at 1, and proceed playing each line up to and through 10. In line 10 the first A♭ is absent and all the notes have been moved ahead one position, although the rhythm is the same. This phasing process is continued with each note moving ahead one position on each repeat. When the two pianos are again in phase (unison) pick it up at line 9, and regress by playing lines 8 through 1. Piano I has the option of playing this piece in any register provided the contour is unchanged and the choice of register is adhered to for the entire piece" (from the score). Each line becomes progressively more complex. Avant-garde. M-D.

Cornelius Cardew (1936–1981) Great Britain
Two Books of Study for Pianists/Music for Two Pianos (Hin 1966) 3 scores. Totally organized, pointillistic, aleatory, avant-garde. The third score is Cardew's written-out version showing where and when the notes should be played. D.

John Carmichael (–   ) Australia
Bahama Rumba (Augener 1960) 7pp. Bright and attractive, requires a response to inner rhythm that cannot always be notated on paper, as well as subtle dynamic control. Int. to M-D.
Tourbillon, Valse Brillante (Augener 1961) 12pp. Allegro-vivace. Similar in style to Saint-Saëns, Int. to M-D.

John F. Carré (1894–) USA
Concertino 1968 (Schroeder & Gunther; University of Wisconsin) 19pp.
Whitecaps (JF 1956; LC) 9pp. Flowing. Int.

Robert Casadesus (1899–1972) France
Casadesus was a pianist of international repute and had many fine compositions to his credit. He frequently performed two-piano works with his wife and sometimes works for three pianos with his wife and son.
Six Pieces Op.2 1920 (Durand 1938) 51pp. Algérienne (Andantino misterioso). Russe (Pas vite). Sicilienne (Doux et balance). Française (Animé). Espagnole (Viv). Anglaise (Avec beaucoup d'entrain). Flowing melodic lines are full of shapely suppleness. Combines melodies originally heard separately, often leading to ingenious formal modifications through telescoping recapitulations. Contrasting moods, Impressionistic. M-D.
Dances Méditerranéenes Op.36 (CF 1945; UCLA). Published separately. Sardana: vigorous and propulsive. Sarabande: Lento, quiet opening, subtle effects achieved with bimodal and bitonal combinations; builds to large climax. Tarantelle: perpetual motion, brilliant. This set of evocative, atmospheric dances is characterized by a kind of linear writing called "accidental dissonance" and a musical gourmet's appreciation for native rhythms. Large span required. M-D.

Alfredo Casella (1883–1947) Italy
Pupazzetti 1916 (RIC; JWC). Five Marionette Pieces. The composer suggests either one or two pianos. Marcietta (Little March). Berceuse. Serenata. Nocturne. Polka. Polytonal and iridescent harmonies, atmospheric, contrasting touches and dynamics. Requires mature musicianship and large span. M-D.

Paolo Castaldi (1930–) Italy
Anfrage 1963 (Ric 131792 1971). A collage of bits and pieces from other scores, numerous interpretative directions, avant-garde. M-D.

Mario Castelnuova-Tedesco (1895–1968) Italy
Alt Wein (Viennese Rhapsody) 1923 (Forlivesi; Arizona State University Library) 50pp. Originally for solo piano, transcribed by the composer. Alt Wien (Walzer). Nachtmusik (Notturno). "Memento mori" (Fox-trot tragico). Chromatic, nostalgic, effective. Carefully exploits both instruments and requires plenty of "give and take" between the performers. M-D.
Duo-Pianism—Impromptu for Two Pianos on the Names of Hans and Rosaleen Moldenhauer, Greeting Cards Op.170/9 (Forlivesi; LC) 10pp., facsimile. Hans Moldenhauer (author of *Duo-Pianism*) and his wife, Rosaleen, provide the melodic material: 25 letters of the En-

glish language (*x* is left out) are represented by a chromatic two-octave scale; therefore Hans = E, A, B♭, E♭. Accompaniment shows waltz influence, lyric. M-D.

René de Castéra (1873–1955) France
Jour de Fête au Pays Basque Op.9 1907 (Edition Mutuelle; LC) 27pp. Pièce Symphonique. Arranged for two pianos by the composer. M-D.

Jacques Castérède (1926–   ⁻) France
Feux Croisés 1963 (Salabert 1968) 72pp., facsimile. Quasi una Marcia; Vivamente; Lento misterioso; Animato e martellato. Large-scaled, dissonant, virtuosic. D.

Niccolo Castiglioni (1932–   ) Italy
Omaggio a Edvard Grieg (Ric 133212 1981).

Norman Cazden (1914–1980) USA
Stony Hollow Op.47a (Jack Spratt 1962) 15pp. Tonal, spirited, clever. Lengthy for its ideas. M-D.

Emmanuel Chabrier (1841–1894) France
Rhapsody España 1883 (Bo&H [separate parts]; Belwin-Mills [2 complete scores]; Ashdown) 15pp. Effectively transcribed by the composer. Loaded with colorful effects, including glissandi and sensuous rhythms. Racy and distinguished writing. M-D.
Souvenirs de Munich 1887 (IMC; EMT). Fantaisie en forme de quadrille sur les thèmes favoris de *Tristan et Isolde* de Richard Wagner. Pantalon; Ete; Poule; Pastourelle; Galop. A musical parody based on Wagner's *Tristan und Isolde*. Exuberant, witty, colorful, and rhythmic. Wagner made a great impression on Chabrier. M-D.
Tre Valzer Romantici 1883 (IMC; Bèrben; Enoch; Ashdown) 48pp., 13 min. Available separately from IMC; the Bèrben edition contains a number of misprints. Presto impetuoso: a popular concert and encore number. Moderato. Animato. Elegant salon pieces. Suave, facile, brilliant pianistic writing. Polish and grace are prerequisities. M-D.

Joel Chadabe (1938–   ) USA
Diversions (AMC 1967). Performance directions include discussion of nonmetered notation, duration of held notes, notation of speed in terms of attacks per second, "Tempo X" as a tempo slightly slower than as fast as possible, spatial notation (the space between dots always equals one second, and notes are to be played as they appear spatially). Some special effects indicated by dots, slashes, and wedges. Atonal, clusters, much disjunct motion. Avant-garde. M-D.

Francis Chagrin (1905–1972) France, born Rumania
Concert Rumba (Lengnick 1948) 18pp., 7½ min. Neat in form; lies well on

the keyboard. Requires two players of considerable skill, one who addresses the dreamy theme and the other who tends the rumba rhythm. MC. M-D.

Boris Aleksandrovich Chaikovskii (1925–   ) USSR
Sonata (Soviet Composer 1976 MK 2/1976 no.381) 40pp.

Luciano Chailly (1920–   ) Italy
Sonata Tritematica No.11 Op.259 1961 (in un sol tempo) (EC) 34pp. Twelve-tone, Molto adagio is followed by three extended and contrasted themes; quiet conclusion. M-D.

J. Clarence Chambers (–   ) USA
A physician by profession and a musician by avocation, Chambers composed this suite in a direct, uncomplicated, light popular style. José and Amparo Iturbi played and recorded it.
All American. Satirical Suite for Two Pianos (Belwin-Mills 1948; AMC) 22pp. Chicken in the Hay. Lush. Bloozey-Woozey. Parade of the Visiting Firemen. Int. to M-D.

Cécile Chaminade (1857–1944) France
La Sévillane Op.19 (Enoch; Ashdown) 9pp. Fanfare introduction, repeated notes, trills, fast runs, brilliant closing. M-D.
Intermezzo Op.36/1 (Enoch; EBM).
Andante and Scherzettino Op.59/1,2 (Enoch 1894; GS). Charming, unpretentious, tasteful, and sensitive first-class salon writing. The two parts blend in elegant fluency. Uses the lower register of the piano melodically, a device also typical of Brahms. Int. to M-D.
Valse Carnavalesque Op.73 (Enoch; Northwestern University Library) 17pp. Presto, clever scintillating outer sections; flowing, lyric midsection. M-D.
Le Matin Op.79/1; *Le Soir* Op. 79/2 (Enoch 1895; Bo&H; Ashdown; LC). Originally for orchestra, arranged for two pianos by the composer. Contrasting sections, facile and flowing, cool and colorful ending for both pieces. Int. to M-D.
Duo Symphonique Op.117 (Enoch 1905; Wright State University Library; LC) 15pp. Allegro energico, contrasting sections, virtuosic, flowing themes, varied tonalities, dramatic conclusion. M-D.
Cortege Op. 143 (Ashdown).

John Barnes Chance (1932–   ) USA
Introduction and Capriccio (Bo&H 1966) 20pp. Originally for piano and 24 winds, arranged for two pianos by the composer. Neoclassic orientation, freely tonal, octotonic, secco style, tremolo and repeated chords, glissandi, linear textures, *pp* conclusion. M-D.

Theodore Chanler (1902–1961) USA
The Second Joyful Mystery (AMP 1943; AMC). One movement, fugal, chromatic, contrasting moods, after a quotation from Dante's *Purgatory*. Breathes a spirit of mystical inspiration, which reminds one of César Franck. Main subject is an arpeggiated figure that is skillfully and colorfully woven. The conclusion rises to an ecstatic glow. M-D.

Brian Chapple (1945–   ) Great Britain
Scherzos 1970 (JWC). For four pianos, 17 min. Includes quotations from six nineteenth-century piano works. The middle section includes a three-minute passage in which two of the pianists play in any order, any or all of twelve quotations, including some from the work itself; while the third pianist plays a continuous slow-moving solo and the fourth interrupts at regular intervals. M-D.

Abram Chasins (1903–   ) USA
Chasins, an outstanding pianist, treats the two-piano medium brilliantly and effectively.
Artist's Life (JF 1933; LC) 28pp. This virtuoso concert transcription is based on the Johann Strauss waltz. Every nook and cranny of the keyboard is investigated! Glittering. M-D to D.
The Blue Danube Waltzes (Johann Strauss—Schulz-Evler) (JF 1926; LC) 23pp. Four waltzes freely adapted and arranged for two pianos. Virtuoso treatment; naive melodies set with dizzying chromatic harmony. This ingenious arrangement preserves the joyous moods of the original, but instead of imitating the richness of the orchestration, Chasins chooses the clearer, more sparkling sound of the pianos. M-D to D.
Carmen Fantasy (JF 1937). Similar in style and texture to the above; based on themes from Bizet's opera *Carmen*. M-D.
Fledermaus Fantasy (OD 1948) 28pp., 8½ min. Based on themes by Johann Strauss. Fast harmonic rhythm, contrasting sections, glissandi, furioso closing, delightful. Eminently pianistic. M-D.
Parade (JF 6767 1934) 21pp. Transcribed from the orchestral version by the composer. Strong march rhythms, triplet chords alternate between hands, freely chromatic, *ppp* closing. M-D.
Period Suite 1948 (Chappell) 14 min. Prelude; Bourrée; Pavane; Rigaudon; Sarabande; Fugue. Six "classical" movements in nineteenth-century pianistic style. Pavane is Ravel-like; Sarabande has thin textures and is perhaps the finest movement. M-D.
Rush Hour in Hong Kong (Belwin-Mills). Transcribed from solo piano version by the composer. Even more attractive for two pianos. Int. to M-D.

Wilbur Chenoweth (1899–   ) USA
Fiesta (GS 1944) 10 min. Effective writing that sounds much more difficult
than it is. Int. to M-D.

Erik Chisholm (1904–1965) South Africa, born Great Britain
The Forsaken Mermaid 1940 (Dunedin Publications; UCLA Music Library) 155pp., 50 min. A ballet in five scenes, originally written for
two pianos. Contains story of the ballet. Prologue: A garden under
the sea. Scene I: The harbour of a fishing village in Skyre. Scene II:
The same, on the night of Hallowe'en, a few months later. Scene III:
The same, during a storm, several months later. Epilogue: A garden
under the sea. Parts of the work can be performed when it is not
practical to program the entire piece. Romantic-Impressionistic
style, effective and attractive. M-D.

Frédéric Chopin (1810–1849) Poland
Rondo C Op.73 1828 (GS; CFP; OUP) 8½ min. Brilliant and glittering
salon style, ingratiating, lively. Contrasting ideas are linked to the
tuneful rondo theme, which is varied at its entrances; the episodic
material is also greatly varied. A model of two-piano writing from
which Arensky and others learned much. Its originality is most obvious in the luxuriant passage-work, which is such an integral part of
the piece. Requires facile fingers and sensitive rubato. M-D.
Sonata b♭ Op.35 (Durand 1907; LC) 44pp. Transcribed for two pianos by
Camille Saint-Saëns. Some sections (the last movement especially)
are more involved than in the original version. M-D to D.

Larry Christiansen (1941–   ) USA
Contrasts for Two Pianos (CAP).

Henry Leland Clarke (1907–   ) USA
Give and Take 1977 (ACA) 9pp. Poco allegro; two sections. Each instrument goes its own merry way but the two work together nicely. The
"give and take" occurs when the two instruments play together or
alone. Tonal. Int.

Rosemary Clarke (1921–   ) USA
Variation on an Original Theme 1966 (MS available from composer: %
Music Dept., University of Wisconsin, Platteville, WI 53818; LC).
Sixteen-bar theme, announced by Piano I, is followed by four contrasting variations and a finale. Neoclassic, expressive melodies,
logically derived harmonies, varied rhythms, traditional formal
scheme, MC. M-D.

Muzio Clementi (1752–1832) Italy
Clementi enjoyed performing in public with his great pupil John Field and

thus wrote these two sonatas, which are masterpieces of their kind. Clementi's robust, ample treatment of the piano and the occasional hard intensity of some of his ideas appealed to the young Beethoven, who occasionally unconsciously echoed what he had learned from the older master's compositions.

Two Sonatas Op.12, Op.46 (CFP; GS: Bèrben 1594; Bosworth). Both sonatas are in B♭. I: Allegro assai; Larghetto espressivo; Presto. II: Allegro di molto—Allegretto; Tempo di Minuetto. Graceful, fluent, predictable, fun to play, brilliant, poetic in places, well put together. Idiom and style recall early works of Beethoven. Concise, charming; music to satisfy. M-D.

Joseph W. Clokey (1890–1960) USA

The Hill Country. Tone poem for two pianos 1950 (Flammer 1956; AMC) 45pp. My Old Home Town. The River Hills. Summer Evenings. This suite "is a sequence of mood memories of my birth place—the river hills of southern Indiana. The tunes, all of them original, are reminiscent of the tunes which I heard there as a child" (from the score). Tonal, with some modal treatment. MC. M-D.

Ulric Cole (1905–   ) USA

Divertimento 1971 (JF; AMC) 37pp. Transcribed by the composer from *Divertimento* (1932) for string orchestra. Toccata; Intermezzo; Finale: Fantasia. Neoclassic, freely tonal, many scalar figurations. The Finale is the most demanding movement. Thoroughly pianistic throughout with glissando conclusion. M-D.

Gilman Collier (1929–   ) USA

Collier studied at Harvard and Yale universities. His composition teachers were Paul Hindemith and Bohuslav Martinu.

Prelude and Fugue g (MS available from composer: 65 Larchwood Avenue, Oakhurst, NJ 07755) 20pp. Dedicated to the memory of Paul Hindemith. "The overall nature of the Fugue is a light ostinato. Every note is to be played detached unless specifically slurred or marked legato, and even the fortissimos should not be performed so loud as to obscure the contrapuntal writing" (from the score). Written for piano, four hands but the composer says: "I firmly believe that all piano-four-hand music should be played on two pianos when available." Strong neoclassic writing. M-D.

Overture, Variations and Epilogue 1980 (MS available from composer) 100pp. Overture: octotonic, flexible meters, fugal, glissandi, full parallel chords, extensive trills, centered around E–e. "Lovely to Look At"—Variations on a Song by Jerome Kern: melody ingeniously treated; contrasting variations, some rhapsodic; extensive dynamic range; material cleverly juxtaposed between instruments;

several simultaneous conflicting tempos; harmonics. Epilogue: wraps up most melodic material heard in rest of work. Freely tonal, neo-classic, strong Hindemith influence. Requires endurance. M-D.

Franz Constant (1910–   ) Belgium
Sonatine Française Op.32 1960 (CeBeDeM) 13 min.

Marius Constant (1925–   ) France, born Rumania
Psyche (Ric 2232). For two pianos and percussion, including vibraphone, tam-tam, bells, claves, bongo, marimbaphone, gongs, cymbals, temple blocks. All directions in French. Lengthy. Requires an advanced technique and familiarity with contemporary notation. D.

Barry Conyngham (1944–   ) Great Britain
Snowflake (UE 29082). For piano, electric piano, harpsichord, and celeste (one performer). Set of 4 parts.

Arnold Cooke (1906–   ) Great Britain
Cooke's study with Hindemith left a direct imprint on his style.
Sonata C 1938 (OUP) 18½ min. Bitonal, emphasis on harmonic structures; communicates a characteristically attractive gaiety that does not attempt to be profound. M-D.

David Cope (1941–   ) USA
Cope is Associate Dean for the Fine and Performing Arts at the University of California, Santa Cruz, CA 95064.
Glassworks 1979 (MS available from composer). For two pianos and computer-generated tape. Completed at the Stanford University Computer Music Center. Transparent textures though not always sparse. D.
Margins 1972 (CF). For two pianos, trumpet, cello, and percussion. 12 min. Contains some fascinating passages in which a lyrical duet for trumpet and cello is accompanied by jagged cacophony from piano and percussion. M-D.

Aaron Copland (1900–   ) USA
Leonard Bernstein has summed up Copland's influence on music: "Aaron is Moses." This says it all about the composer who has been so commanding, so vital, and so essential a figure on the American musical scene. His contribution to the two-piano medium has been considerable.
Dance of the Adolescent (Bo&H 1968) 24pp., 6 min. A movement from the ballet *Grogh* (1922–24), about a magician who could revive the dead and make them dance. In 1930 "Dance of the Adolescent" was reworked and became the first movement of the *Dance Symphony*. This two-piano version, made by the composer, is exuberant, invigorating, rhythmically inventive, and angular. With accomplished players it makes a fine effect. M-D.

Billy the Kid 1938 (Bo&H) 34pp., 16½ min. Suite arranged by the composer from his popular ballet score. The Open Prairie. Cowboys with Lassos; Mexican Dance and Finale. Billy and His Sweetheart [not in the symphonic suite]. Celebration after Billy's Capture. Open Prairie Again. This musical "horse opera" has no horses and is no opera but certainly is musical. Requires sensitivity and drive. M-D.

Danzón Cubano 1942 (Bo&H) 20pp., 10 min. Driving jazz and Latin American rhythms, propulsive, irregular phrasing. A lighthearted romp, much in the vein of *El Salón Mexico*. M-D.

El Salón Mexico (Bo&H 1943) 30pp. Arranged for two pianos by Leonard Bernstein. El Salón Mexico was the name of a dancehall in Mexico City. Sophisticated handling of popular music elements. Many changing meters. "The rhythmic intricacies may be greatly simplified if the performer remembers that the approach to these rhythms should be in terms of eighth-notes, rather than quarters" (from the score).

See: A. Brown, "Copland: El salón Mexico," *Music Teacher,* 55 (June 1976):17–18, for an analysis of this work.

H. Cole, "Popular Elements in Copland's Music," *Tempo,* 95 (Winter 1970–71):6–10.

Danza de Jalisco (Bo&H 1968) 4 min. Originally a chamber-orchestra work composed for the Spoleto Festival of Two Worlds; transcribed for two pianos by Copland in 1963. Energetic, engaging, percussive, varied meters. Full of cross-rhythms and hand-slaps. Requires a vivid performance. M-D.

Roque Cordero (1917–   ) USA, born Panama

Duo 1954 (PIC 1965) 24pp. The Allegro vigoroso is interrupted by an expressive Adagio, which grows to a *fff,* then subides to a *ppp* mysterioso. Serial, strong, and imaginative writing; hemiola device and fascinating rhythms add to the interest. Requires fine technique and excellent teamwork. M-D to D.

John Corigliano (1938–   ) USA

Music by Corigiliano has been performed by leading orchestras of the USA, and his reputation grows with each new work. He is a member of the composition faculties at Lehman College and the Manhattan School of Music, both in New York.

Kaleidoscope 1959 (GS 1964)5½ min. A study in contrasts of fast and slow, harsh and lyric, changing meters, varied tonalities and tone colors; neoclassic toccata style. Ideas are well developed even though there is much variation in rhythmic figuation from bar to bar. Brilliant climax. M-D.

Sérgio Oliveira de Vasconcellos Corrêa (1921–   ) Portugal
Corrêa studied composition with Camargo Guarnieri (1956–1968) and conducting under Martin Braunwieser, Hans Swarowski, and Simon Blech. He is a professor in the music department of the Arts Institute of the University of Campinas.

Dobrado 1963 (Da Suite Piratiningana) (Ric BR 3188 1972) 8pp. Freely dissonant around B♭, melodic interest shared by both performers, martial quality, strong accents. An effective short encore. Brilliant rhythmic drive required. M-D.

Gaetano Corticelli (1804–1840) Italy
Gran Sonata Brillante Op.12 (Ric).

Leland A. Cossart (1877–   ) Switzerland, born Madiera
Suite a Op.29 (Heinrichshofen).

Morris Cotel (1943–   ) USA
Cotel studied composition with William Bergsma, Vincent Persichetti, and Roger Sessions. In 1966 he won the American Rome Prize. He is a member of the composition faculty at the Peabody Conservatory in Baltimore.

Tehom 1974 (Midbar Music Press). For three pianos. Genesis I: 1. In the beginning, God created the heaven and the earth. 2. Now the earth was unformed and void, and darkness was upon the face of the deep; and the spirit of God hovered over the face of the waters. The deep— Hebrew, Tehom—the abyss. "The great beauty of the opening of Bereshith (the Hebrew word for the Book of Genesis; it means— literally—'in the beginning') has haunted me since childhood. The stark majesty of the ancient Hebrew contrasts strongly with its smooth English translation. The Hebrew is simple, direct, elemental and sublime. . . . In the beginning God created: The music begins with the material of the work swirling about, configurations called into being but chaotic and unarranged. The heaven and the earth: The music coalesces into two broad groups. One is metrically fluid and free; the other, durationally fixed and precise. Now the earth was unformed and void: the second group flares up in random configurations. And darkness was upon the face of the deep: and settles to the bass of all three pianos. And the spirit of God hovered over the face of the waters: chords, strummed inside pianos 1 and 2, float above the 'darkness' of piano 3 and hover quietly, fading away to nothingness" (notes from the composer). M-D to D.

Yetzirah 1979 (Midbar Music Press). For two microtonal pianos. 15 min. This work utilizes a 22-tone scale formed by two specially tuned pianos. A cassette tape of this scale is available from the composer for tuning, or tuning can be done with electronic equipment. Notation in cents is given in the score directions. *Yezira* is the Hebrew word for "creation," but also for "formation" and "composition." Based on a set of four pitches which are 3, 7, and 12 microtones apart. Thin textures, pointillistic, large sections unbarred, plucked strings, some sections "free," harmonics, much repetition of similar figuration, metronome markings for sections, some strings damped. Builds to a great climax, then dies away to nothing. Avant-garde. D.

Jean Coulthard (1908–   ) Canada

Sonata for Two Pianos "Of the Universe" 1979 (CMC) 15 min. Three movements. D.

Mildred Couper (1887–   ) USA

Dirge (New Music 1937, vol. 10; AMC). For two pianos, second piano tuned a quarter-tone higher than the first. This tuning increases the original 88 pitch levels to 176, expands the gamut by a quarter step, and emphasizes the amorphous character of the harmony. M-D.

François Couperin (1668–1733) France

Allemande à deux clavecins A (OUP; L'OL; Durand; Heugel; Augener). From the *Ninth Order,* in vol. II of Couperin's keyboard works published in 1716. One of the earliest works for two keyboards. Highly stylized dance form, brilliant and masterly, intricate ornamentation. The two parts are skillfully combined and equally demanding. Couperin was the first composer to transfer this conception to a full score. Int. to M-D.

La Juillet, La Létiville (Portrait) (OUP 1934). Published together. From the composer's *Troisième livre de pièces de clavecin,* 1722. "May be played on different instruments, but also on two harpsichords or spinets, i.e., the subject with the bass on one, and the same bass with the counter-melody on the other" (editor's note). Int.

Henry Cowell (1897–1965) USA

Celtic Set (GS 1941; AMC) 10 min. Reel; Caoine (a lament); Hornpipe. Contrasting moods and tempos, bagpipe imitation, contains a few surprises. Among the happiest and most exuberant works in the repertoire. M-D.

David Cox (1916–   ) Great Britain

Majorca (A Balearic Impression) (Elkin 1957) 8pp. Based on two traditional melodies of the Balearic Islands. Model of tasteful economy in length, ornamentation, and technical demands. Int. to M-D.

Michael Cox (1948–   ) USA

Toccata for Two Pianos and Percussion 1980 (MS available from composer: College of Fine Arts, Oklahoma Baptist University, Shawnee,

OK 74801) 25pp. Motoric, octotonic, fast repeated octaves, freely tonal, stunning conclusion. M-D.

Johann Baptist Cramer (1771–1858) Germany
Grand Duo Op.25 (Naderman; LC) 18pp. For two pianos or piano and harp. Allegro; Larghetto; Rondo: Allegretto. Charming, flowing, melodious. M-D.

Paul Creston (1906–   ) USA
Rumba—Tarantella (MCA 1953; LC) 6pp. Very fast, driving rhythms, chromatic, fun. M-D.

Bainbridge Crist (1883–1969) USA
Chinese Dance (CF 1941; LC) 9pp. Colorful even if obvious at places. Int. to M-D.

George Crumb (1929–   ) USA
"George Crumb, because of his constant seeking of new sonorities from both the keyboard and the interior of the piano, seems to occupy a position in the second half of the twentieth century analogous to that of Ravel, whose compositions expanded piano technique and whose music made the efforts expended in learning his works worthwhile" (Kenneth R. Gartner, "The Expansion of Pianism Since 1945," diss., New York University, 1979, p. 111).
Music for a Summer Evening 1974 (*Makrokosmos III*) (CFP 66590 1975). For two gently amplified pianos and percussion (two players). I. Nocturnal Sounds (The Awakening). II. Wanderer—Fantasy. III. The Advent. Hymn for the Nativity of the Star-Child. IV. Myth. V. Music of the Starry Night. The fivefold Galactic Bells / Song of Reconciliation. Crumb writes: "The combination of two pianos and two percussion instruments was, of course, first formulated by Béla Bartók in his sonata of 1937, and it is curious that other composers did not subsequently contribute to the genre. Bartók was one of the very first composers to write truly expressive passages for the percussion instruments; since those days, there has been a veritable revolution in percussion technique and idiom and new music has inevitably assimilated these developments. The battery of percussion instruments required for *Summer Evening* is extensive . . . including certain rather exotic (and in some cases, quite ancient) instruments. This kaleidoscopic range of percussion timbre is integrated with a great variety of sounds produced by the pianists.

"As in several of my other works, the musical fabric of *Summer Evening* results largely from the elaboration of tiny cells into a sort of mosaic design. This time-hallowed technique seems to function in much new music, irrespective of style, as a primary structural *modus*. In its overall style, *Summer Evening* might be described as either more or less tonal, or more or less atonal. The more overtly tonal passages can be defined in terms of the basic polarity F♯–D♯ minor. One other structural device which the astute listener may perceive is the isorhythmic construction of 'Myths,' which consists of simultaneously performed taleas (rhythmic patterns of differing lengths) of 13, 7 and 11 bars. I feel that *Summer Evening* projects a clearly-articulated large expressive curve over its approximately 40-minute duration. The first, third and fifth movements, which are scored for the full ensemble of instruments and laid out on a large scale, would seem to define the primary import of the work (which might be interpreted as a kind of 'cosmic drama'). On the other hand, the wistfully evocative 'Wanderer Fantasy' (mostly for the two pianos alone), and the somewhat atavistic 'Myth' (for percussion instruments) were conceived of as dream-like pieces functioning as intermezzos within the overall sequence of movements. The three larger movements carry poetic quotations which were very much in my thoughts during the sketching-out process, and which, I believe, find their symbolic resonance in the sounds of *Summer Evening*. 'Nocturnal Sounds' is inscribed with an excerpt from Quasimodo: ('I hear ephemeral echoes, oblivion of deepest night in the starred water'); 'The Advent' is associated with a passage from Pascal ('The eternal silence of infinite space terrifies me'); and the last movement 'Music of the Starry Night' cites these transcendently beautiful images of Rilke: ('And in the nights the heavy earth is falling from all the stars down into loneliness. We are all falling. And yet there is One who holds this falling endlessly gently in His hands.')"

The work explores virtually every expressive potential of the two instruments, individually and in ensemble. Enormous originality, imagination, and intellectual vitality are displayed. Creates a hauntingly beautiful atmosphere from the beginning and engages in a brilliant and musically satisfying exploration of sound and mood. In addition to performing traditional pianistic techniques, the pianist must pluck, strum, and dampen the strings; produce harmonics; strike the crossbeams by hand (be careful!); and lay paper sheets across strings. Thorough explanations are included. Other influences seen are Bach, Cage, Cowell, Debussy, Liszt, and Webern. A quote from the d♯ Fugue in Vol. II of the WTC is heard in the final piece. D. See: Review by Larry Lusk, *Notes*, 32/2 (December 1975): 393–94.

Ivo Cruz (1901–   ) Portugal, born Brazil

Pastoral (Sassetti 1956) 23pp. Ritornello: a festive choral introduction. Minuete: plaintive, much triplet use. Ritornello e evocação de Sarabanda: opening Ritornello idea returns transposed plus a tempo rubato Sarabande. Rigaudon e evocação de Siciliana: Siciliano serves as the B section between the Rigaudon. Ritornello final: a bright and cheerful closing, large chords, appealing. M-D.

Cesar Cui (1835–1918) Russia
Trois Morceaux Op.69 (Jurgenson 1906; LC). Intermezzo; Notturno; Alla Marcia. Expansive and effective pieces. M-D.

Robert Cundick (1926–   ) USA
Prelude and Fugue (CF). Prelude (one page) is slow and quiet. Four-voiced fugue has changing meters, quick tempo, and brilliant closing. M-D.

Michael Cunningham (1937–   ) USA
Dialogue Op.11a 1959 (Seesaw) 10pp. Neoclassic, freely tonal. Frequent interchange between instruments (as title suggests); ideas develop naturally; works to big climax; subsides and closes out *pp* on C tonality. Large span required. M-D.
Theater Music Op.58b 1974 (Seesaw) 56pp. Overture. Once upon a Time. The City Sleeps. Young and Idealistic Dreams. Innocent Love. The Story Continues. Whistling Song. Interlude. By the Waterfall. Sentimental Song. Dark Future. Lullaby. Children's Games. Yearning. Verbunkos. Interlude (in 5 episodes). Cynical Gavotte. Reprise. Village Dance. Afterthought. Short, attractive, freely tonal, contrasting, clever, colorful. One could select a group or perform the entire cycle. Int. to M-D.

Willy Czernik (1904–   ) Germany
Im Dämmerlicht. Eine kleine Differenz (Zimmermann 1959; LC). Published together, 12pp. Im Dämmerlicht: blues tempo, 3½ min. Eine kleine Differenz: perpetuum mobile, 2 min. Both pieces are clever and well conceived for the medium. M-D.

Carl Czerny (1791–1857) Austria
Although Czerny does not bring any startling innovations to the two-piano medium, his variations should be cited for their brilliant and imaginative treatment. His ornamentation requires a light-fingered facility, especially in the right hand. Each variation poses a different pianistic problem and is usually graceful and pretty. Czerny also arranged many orchestral works for two pianos.
Grand Polonaise Brilliant Op.18 (Cocks). With an accompaniment for a second piano, or for a quartet, both ad lib.
Première Grand Potpourri Concertant Op.38 (Cocks). For two pianos, six hands.
Second Grand Potpourri Concertant Op.84 (Cocks). For two pianos, six hands.

Six Grands Potpourris brilliants et Concertants Op.212 (Cocks). One of these is for two pianos, six hands.

Quartet Concertante C Op.230 1825 (Diabelli; LC). For four pianos. Sectionalized, brilliant display passages alternate with lyric sections. M-D.

Grandes Variations Concertantes pour deux pianofortes, sur un Thême de l'Opera, Montechi e Capuleti B♭ Op.285 (Cocks).

Grand Potpourri Concertant pour deux pianofortes Op.294 (Diabelli; NYPL).

Duo Concertant pour deux pianofortes B♭ Op.358 (Cocks). In a conservative Romantic vein, but requires a healthy dose of virtuoso fireworks. M-D to D.

Grand Duo brilliant concertant, pour Harpe et Piano ou Deux Pianos, sur des Motifs favoris de l'Opera, Linda de Chamounix, de Donizetti. . . , Op.719 by Carl Czerny, et Elie Parish Alvars, Op.63 (T. Boosey, 1840?; BrM).

10 Grandes Fantaisies Concertantes Op.798 (Cocks).

Second Grand Quartet Concertante Op. 816 (Cranz 1851). For four pianos.

D

Ingolf Dahl (1912–1970) USA, born Germany.

Quodlibet on American Folk Tunes (The Fancy Blue Devil's Breakdown)
(CFP 1957; AMC) 5½ min. For four players at two pianos. Based on
four old-fiddlers' tunes, one hillbilly song, and one cowboy tune combined in the style of a quodlibet. Much use of pentatonic scale; fast,
lean, tart; contrapuntal in a rhythmic as well as a linear sense. The
tunes go their way merrily, yet they have been brought into a convincing interrelation. Above all, this work is a rhythmic tour de force,
full of the bounciness of the fiddlers' tunes. M-D.

Luigi Dallapiccola (1904–1975) Italy
Dallapiccola's works are marked by great expressive vigor and sometimes
by boisterous and biting humor. The abundance of part writing and polytonal episodes generates harmonic webs.

Musica per Tre Pianoforti 1935 (Carisch 1936; facsimile of autograph new
edition 1954) 40pp., 15 min. Allegro, molto sostenuto: hammering,
chordal opening statement alternates between duple and triple
meters; frequent homophonic doublings between two pianos as the
third states a brief polyphonic episode. Un poco adagio; funebre:
opens with a mournful two-bar theme, over which the lowest three
notes on the piano resound; second theme is angular; the two are
combined as well as tossed back and forth among the instruments to
create tension and release; increases in intensity and finally returns to
opening mood of melancholy and solemnity. Allegramente, ma so-
lenne: a lengthy hammering of single tones using twelve-tone technique introduces this virile and spirited movement; salient
characteristics include rhythmic intricacy, polymeter; and frequent
patterns of statement and response; opening theme of second movement returns midway in this movement, followed by initial statements of first movement. Finale: combination of polyphony,
homophony, and superimposed triads generates dramatic fury and a
fiery closing. Requires three sensitive musical imaginations. M-D.

Jean-Michel Damase (1928–   ) France
Compliment d'anniversaire (EMT 872 1964) 16pp., 8 min. "Pour la Princesse Henri de Polignac." "Happy Birthday" opening theme, eight short variations. Dissonant, numerous meter changes, more "buffa" than serious. Would make a fine encore. M-D.
Sonatine (Salabert).

Paul Ekabovich Dambis (1936–   ) USSR
Sonata No. 4, Op.30 (USSR 1974) 47pp.

Georges Dandelot (1895–1964) France
Trois Valses (ESC 1939; Harvard University Library). Available separately. Valse Fantasque. Valse Rococo. Valse Romantique.

Nguyen Thien Dao (1941–   ) Vietnam
Bao Gio 1974–75 (Sal) 20 min. For two pianos and two percussion players.

Peter Maxwell Davies (1934–   ) Great Britain
Four Lessons for Two Keyboards 1978 (Bo&H) 11pp. Lento: sustained, plucked strings, chorale-like conclusion. Moderato: thin textures, plucked strings, rhythmic interest. Allegro: varied meters, trills, syncopation. Adagio: lyric, plucked strings, calm ending. Atonal writing throughout. The author notes in the score: "Although the *Four Lessons* were originally written for two clavichords, they may be played on two balanced keyboard instruments of any kind, alike or contrasting." The plucked-string effect is, however, invalid with an upright piano, harpsichord, or chamber organ. M-D.

John T. Davye (1929–   ) USA
Davye teaches at Old Dominion University in Norfolk, VA 23508. He received degrees from the University of Miami (Florida) and Ithaca College.
Sonatine 1978 (MS available from composer; SBTS) 10pp., 5 min. A monothematic five-part arch-rondo. Austero e dignitos: mixolydian on A; two-part song form (a b). Ballabile: dorian on A, darker mode, three-part song form (c d c). Dialogo: aeolian and dorian on A, darkest mode; two- and three-part counterpoint pitch order of last 32 bars in strict retrograde of first 32 bars. Ballabile: dorian on A, brighter mode; extension material of multifaceted polyphony. Austereo e dignitoso: mixolydian, brightest mode, ternary outline (e f g), cadenza-like material, coda. Somewhat in style of Ravel *Sonatine* but easier. Int. to M-D.

Emil Debusman (1921–   ) USA
Musica Rivelatore II (AME).

Claude Debussy (1862–1918) France

Debussy left fewer than twenty pedal marks in his entire piano music, and very few of these appear in his works for two pianos. But he did notate additional indications via long notes or long notes plus slurs. Debussy studied with a pupil of Chopin's, and he was imbued with the spirit of Chopin, who was his early inspiration. In many cases, Chopin's pedal marks may lead directly to Debussy, i.e., a subtle, fluctuating but considerable use of the damper and una corda pedals, often together. Debussy was interested in a graphic notation for the use of the pedals, and endorsed Marie Jäell's *Les Pedales du Piano*. However, in failing to use this system, he also regrettably avoided the considerable task of indicating his own conceptions by conventional means. Another great influence on Debussy was the Spanish pianist Ricardo Viñes (1875–1943), who introduced almost all of the repertoire of Debussy and Ravel. His playing was based on a subtle and complex use of the two pedals. He had some mysterious way of stroking the keys to produce an unusually evocative tone. Francis Poulenc, a pupil of Viñes, once said, "No one could teach the art of using the pedals, an essential feature of modern piano music better than Viñes." None of Debussy's pianos—a Pleyel, a Gaveau, a Bluethner, or a Bechstein—had a sostenuto pedal. However, there are places in many of his solo and two-piano pieces that can greatly benefit from its use.

Lindaraja 1901 (Durand; Joubert) 4½ min. This tone poem exhibits Spanish influence, winsome colors, and habanera rhythms. Ideas from this early suite turn up in later works such as *Soirée dans Grenade* and the prelude to *Pour le Piano*. M-D.

Danses 1903 (Durand) 22pp., 9 min. Originally for harp or piano with string orchestra. Arranged for two pianos by Debussy. I. Danse Sacrée. II. Danse Profane. M-D.

La Mer 1903–5 (Durand). Arranged for two pianos by the composer. De l'aube à midi sur le mer. Jeux de vagues. Dialogue du vent et de la mer. M-D to D.

Three Nocturnes (Durand 1909). 49pp. Arranged for two pianos by Ravel. Nuages. Fêtes. Sirènes: published separately. This original orchestral work has been translated into the two-piano idiom with independent artistry. Fêtes is unique in its realization of the fullest potentialities of two-piano sonority. For all its Impressionistic feeling, the music is classically precise, firm, and well-knit. This transcription ranks with the best original writing in the two-piano medium. D.

Prélude à l'après-midi d'un faune 1894 (Fromont, reduction for two pianos by the composer; GS) 10 min. This version has surprising depth and subtlety for a work that depends so much on orchestral color. Ravel made an arrangement for piano duet (Fromont) that is very effective on two pianos, although it may not be pure Ravel, for the American pianist George Copeland made a solo-piano version and may have helped Ravel with the duet version. The Debussy arrangement needs some thinning of the low-register tremolos and the addition of the original harp arpeggios. M-D.

En Blanc et Noir 1915 (Durand; H. Swarsenski—CFP 7286; IMC) 15 min. Written during World War I, this suite reflects Debussy's great depression and anxiety over the turmoil and also his eventually fatal illness. The title, citing the colors black and white, perhaps suggests a state of half-mourning. Avec emportment: dedicated to Serge Koussevitsky, it is a statement for those who would not, for supposedly physical or mental reasons, participate in the defense of France; waltz rhythm with cross accents. Lent Sombre: dedicated to the memory of a friend killed in the war; amid vague references to military bugle calls and the distant rumbling of guns, one hears snatches of *Ein feste Burg,* a symbol of the German threat; toward the end Debussy includes what he called a "pre-Marsellaise," to cleanse the air of the poisonous fumes spread by the Lutheran chorale, or rather what it represents; uses parallel motion, pentatonic scale, whole-tone scale, sevenths; moody and powerful but contains little cadential movement. Scherzando: dedicated to Stravinsky; calmer, with no warlike connotations but works too hard to be humorous. The entire suite is prophetic of later developments in two-piano writing by Bartók and Stravinsky.

See: Robert Orledge, "Debussy's Piano Music—Some Second Thoughts and Sources of Inspiration," MT, 1655 (January 1981):21, 23–27. Excellent discussion of the sources of the *Epigraphes antiques.*

Paolo Delachi (1874–1957) Italy
Prelude and Fugue g (Carisch).

Lex van Delden (1919–   ) The Netherlands
Ballet "Tij en Ontij" Op.52 1956 (Donemus) 24pp. One large movement with contrasting sections. Freely tonal, octotonic, flexible meters, imitation. Traditional pianistic treatment. M-D.

Norman Dello Joio (1913–   ) USA
Suite from Ballet "On Stage" (GS 1946). Overture; Pas de deux; Polka. A diverting set of tableaux that recaptures some of the delights of the parent score. A sparkling essay in folkish sophistication that can stand purely on its pianistic merits. M-D.

Aria and Toccata (CF 1955) 23 pp., 10 min. Adagio: calm. Poco più movimento: majestic and imitative; octave displacement in the subject. Allegro con ritmo. Secco, polytonal, full of rhythmic complexities, jazz influence. Neo-Romantic in color, neo-Baroque in form. Smartly laid out for both instruments, with melody and accompaniment evenly distributed; gratifying to perform. Interesting sonorities, conventional pianistic techniques, effective, MC. M-D.

Sinfonietta (LC) 47pp., 22 min. Arranged for two pianos by the composer. Slow but moving; Very fast; Slow; Fast. Beautifully conceived for the two instruments. Final movement returns to the last 16 bars of the first movement to round off the work. M-D.

Fantasy and Variations 1961 (CF) 24 min. A two-piano reduction by the composer from the original score for piano and orchestra. A two-movement work constructed from a four-note idea: G–F♯–B–C. First movement is a quiet Fantasy in three parts: Adagio; Allegro vivo; Adagio. The second movement begins in Piano II with the initial motive in reverse order: C–B–F♯–G; six variations of enormous scope follow; extremely brilliant ending. The composer said of this work: "My goal was music that would be exciting to listen to and demanding to play." D.

Claude Delvincourt (1888–1954) France

Bal Venitien (Durand 1936; LC) 66pp. Originally for orchestra, arranged for two pianos by the composer. Forlane; Passamezzo; Burlesca; Moresca; Tarentella. Light textured, Impressionistic. M-D to D.

Norman F. Demuth (1898–1968) Great Britain

Bolero (OUP 1928; LC) 7pp. Tonal; spirited; langoroso e espressivo midsection. M-D.

Habanera (OUP).

Notturno (Augener 1939; Br M).

Portrait of a Dancer (Elkin 1941; LC) 8pp. Light, graceful, chromatic. M-D.

Rhapsody (OUP 1926; LC) 5pp. Impressionistic; orchestral textures. M-D.

Rumba (Elkin 1941; LC) 7pp. Strong rhythms, chromatic. M-D.

Tango (Augener 1940; LC) 3pp. Ravel influence. Int. to M-D.

Paul Dessau (1894–1979) Germany

Quattrodramma 1965 (Bo&Bo) 31pp., parts. For two pianos, four cellos, and two percussionists. Serial, harmonics, pointillistic, subdivided rhythms, long trills, double glissandi, atonal, *ppp* closing. Three quotations from Sean O'Casey are given near the end. M-D to D.

E. Destenay (–   ) France

Chorale and Fugue Op.29 (Hamelle; LC) 34pp. Similar in style to Saint-Saëns. M-D.

Albert De Vito (1919–   ) USA
Contrasts (Kenyon 1977; AMC) 12pp. Flowing, parallel- and contrary-
motion chords, freely tonal around d-D, bright ending. Int. to M-D.

David Diamond (1915–   ) USA
Concerto for Two Solo Pianos 1942 (PIC 1953) 40pp. Allegro: striking
figuration bridges ideas into strong continuity; vigorous and driving;
many meter changes; this movement and the finale are strenuous and
dynamic affirmations, each with ideas requiring power and breadth of
presentation. Adagio: simple and reflective, noble quality, tender
beginning builds to big climax and subsides to calm conclusion. Allegro vivace: a trivial theme negates some of the effectiveness of the
finale; canonic staccato figures; splashing, effective "con tutta forza"
ending full of cascading scales. The formal outlines of this sturdy
work are vivid and concise; its rhythmic animation is sharp, if a
shade frenetic; and its lyric impulse is strong and shapely. The total
impression is one of expansive strength and brilliance. D.

Emma Lou Diemer (1927–   ) USA
Diemer teaches theory and composition at the University of California,
Santa Barbara, and also directs the Electronic Studio.
Homage to Cowell, Cage, Crumb, and Czerny 1981 (Plymouth 1983)
30pp. Uses harmonics, string glissandos, black- and white-key clusters, durational notation (play this bar for five seconds, etc.), rapid
tremolo on strings with palms of hands, patterns that are to be repeated as rapidly as possible, long tremolo patterns, and changing
meters. Strings are to be struck rapidly up and down with the
fingernails with the left hand placed lightly on strings to produce a
sound similar to that of a banjo. The notation furnishes a blueprint (at
times very precise) for planes of timbre that are extended horizon-
tally and interrelated in time. Vertical as well as horizontal sonorities
are exploited in a masterful manner. Diemer has an inner conception
of sound that generates the use of her own techniques. Fragments
come and go that seem to be inspired by the composers listed in the
title. A stunning work. Requires special expertise in the production
of the "inside the piano" effects. D.

John Diercks (1927–   ) USA
Diercks writes with a subtle, beautiful, and cool harmonic vocabulary that
nevertheless has much color and warmth.
From the Magic Circle (CSMP) 6pp. Builds interest through sheer continuity and lovely sound, direct in its atmospheric expression. Admirably structured, harmonics, generally quiet. Would add special color
to a program, MC. M-D.
Reminiscences 1971 (CSMP; SBTS) 6pp. Piano II is tuned a quarter-tone

lower than Piano I. Conjunct-motion melodies supported by Impressionistic sonorities. Hauntingly beautiful and effective. M-D.

Toward the Summer Land 1958 (CSMP) 20pp. 7 min. "The title derives from a theosophist-oriented painting Alan Hovhaness and I saw while waiting for a trumpet-reading" (letter from the composer, 14 October 1982). Flowing lines, colorful and exotic use of melodic and harmonic seconds. Oriental influence, tremolos, contrasting sections, warmly eloquent writing, MC. Much use of pedal. M-D.

Variations on a Flower Drum Song 1969 (CSMP) 4pp. For two prepared pianos. Preparation requires strip of rubber, bolts, narrow strip of metal, large nut, wooden sticks, masking tape, marble or small metal ball. Harmonics, plucked and strummed strings, long pedals. Fascinating and colorful sonorities, thin textures, Oriental influence. Attractive and appealing. M-D.

Jan van Dijk (1918–   ) The Netherlands

Trois Danses 1958 (Donemus) 13pp. Monte Carlo: syncopation, chromatic figuration, flexible meters. Alicante: blues influence; large span required. Biarritz: imitation, three eighths, three eighths, two eighths in 4/4 are exploited; works to an exciting climax. M-D.

Something 1962 (Donemus) 3pp. For "two piano players." Unusual notation, aleatory, avant-garde. M-D.

Henri Dillon (1912–1954) France

Concerto for Two Pianos Alone 1952 (Heugel 1955). First movement: busy SA. Adagio: twelve-tone accompaniment. Third movement: bitonal, octotonic, perpetual motion, linear counterpoint. Polytonal writing interspersed with lyric ideas. An altogether well-crafted work. M-D.

Grigoras Dinicu (1889–1949) Rumania

Hora Staccato (Roumanian) (CF 2281 1942) 13pp. Based on popular Rumanian rhythms. Clever and effective. M-D.

Hugo Distler (1908–1942) Germany

Sonata Concertante f, Op. 1 (Br&H 1931; Cornell University Library; NYPL) 32pp. Fluidity of movement from one idea to the next plus shows strong motivic fertility. M-D.

Konzertstück Op.20/2 (Br 1877). An arrangement by the composer of his string quartet, but it predates the final string version; it was premiered on two pianos in Stuttgart. Concise gestures, dynamic counterpoint, dazzling duo writing. Emphasizes continuously fluctuating rhythms and complete rhythmic independence of contrapuntal lines. Uses all of the scale vertically to create dissonant harmonies. M-D.

Friedhelm Döhl (1936–   ) Germany

Odradek (Moeck 1978). Playing score sheets.

Ernst von Dohnányi (1877–1960) Hungary
Dohnányi was an outstanding pianist who wrote fluently for his instrument in a Romantic virtuoso style. These pieces have a post-Brahmsian spirit about them.
Suite en Valse Op.39a (Lengnick 1948) 22½ min. Published separately.
    Valse Symphonique, 33pp.: extensive, chromatic, some bravura writing. Valse Sentimentale, 15pp: expressive, dolente; large span required. Valse Boiteuse, 20pp: shifting 3/4 and 2/4 meters; presto, eighth-note figuration in one instrument or the other. Valse de Fête, 40pp.: Introduzione—Andante con moto leads to Tempi di Valse— Allegro con brio, followed by Valse No. 1, Risoluto (Allegro deciso); No. 2, Un pochettino più mosso—lusingando—dolce; No. 3 (no indications); Coda, dramatic closing that recalls some earlier ideas. "Everything you ever wanted to know about the Valse." Some of the material is not strong, and the work must be carried off with great *élan* and brilliance to be effective. M-D.

Samuel Dolin (1917–   ) Canada
Concerto for Four "Queekhoven Revisited" 1977 (CMC). For two pianos and two percussionists, also playable by two pianos alone. "When played as a two piano piece, the sections indicated may be omitted. However both pianists may use some percussion instruments stationed beside them, a tom-tom, suspended cymbal, triangle, and wood block would add considerable colour when possible" (from the score). Moderato: large chords, fast figuration with some pointillistic usage, changing meters, dynamic extremes, fast repeated note for 4 seconds, secco, glissandi. Adagio: widely spread slow figures, repeated notes. [Untitled]: similar figurations and techniques as in first movement, harmonics, octotonic, large span and experienced ensemble pianists required. D.

Gustav Donath (1878–   ) Germany
Prelude and Fugue D (Lienau).

Franco Donatoni (1927–   ) Italy
Jeux pour Deux 1973 (SZ 7757).
Cinque Pezzi 1954 (Zanibon) 14 min. Tranquillo; Scherzoso; Notturno; Presto; Grave funebre.

Celius Dougherty (1902–   ) USA
Music from Seas and Ships 1941 (GS) 44pp., 14 min. Banks of Sacramento; Sea Calm; Mobile Bay. Inspired by sea chanteys. Pentatonic; facile keyboard style. M-D.

Pierre Douillet (–   ) France
Sarabande et Variations Op.21 (Br&H 1896; Cleveland Public Library;

LC) 19pp. Similar in style and pianistic treatment to the Saint-Saëns *Variations on a theme of Beethoven,* Op.35. M-D.

André Douw (1951–   ) The Netherlands

Go 1977 (Donemus) 15–20 min. Fast, repeated, changing patterns from beginning to end; *fff* and staccato without pedal (directions given on pg.34); crescendo to the end. Avant-garde. One might question if the piece is worth the effort. D.

John Downey (1927–   ) USA

Adagio for the Dead 1944 (AMC) 15pp. Chromatic and freely tonal. Works to large climax near middle of the piece and subsides to the end. Full chords, precipitando octaves, thick textures. M-D.

Sem Dresden (1881–1957) The Netherlands

Dansflitsen 1953 (Donemus) 14 min. Originally for orchestra, arranged for two pianos by the composer. Intrade—Alla polacca; Siciliano; Tempo di valsa; Passamezzo; Menuetto; Marcia funebre; Alla Tarantella. Freely tonal, MC sonorities. M-D.

Madeleine Dring (1923–1977) Great Britain

Three Fantastic Variations on Lilliburlero 1948 (Lengnick) 27pp., 9 min. Henry Purcell is supposed to be the composer of the seventeenth-century tune *Lilliburlero.* Three conventional variations in 4/4 with too much triplet use. Octotonic, MC. M-D.

Sonata 1951 (Lengnick) 43pp., 15 min. Drammatico e maestoso: E; long, extensive use of dotted and driving rhythms. Elégie: B; short, serene, changing meters. Allegro vigoroso: brilliant, motoric. Romantic overtones throughout, although less so in the last movement. Contains some outstanding two-piano scoring. M-D.

Tarantelle (OUP 1948) 3½ min. Jaunty rhythms, fast harmonic shifts. M-D.

Danza Gaya (Weinberger) 2 min.

Italian Dance (Arcadia) 2½ min.

Nostalgic Waltz (OUP) 3½ min.

West Indian Dance 1961 (Arcadia) 3 min.

These four pieces illustrate counterpoint, polytonality, clarity of phrase structure and form, as well as many aspects of neoclassic techniques in twentieth-century music. All are fun. Int. to M-D.

F. Percival Driver (–   ) Great Britain

Variations on an Original Theme (W. Rogers 1934; BrM; LC) 15pp. Chromatic Adagio theme followed by eight contrasted variations. Final variation requires fine octave technique. M-D.

Emilio A. Dublanc (1911–   ) Argentina

Norteña (Carlos S. Lottermoser 1945; IU) 11pp. Songlike, flowing, mainly tonal, a few meter and mood changes, glissando. M-D.

Pierre Max Dubois (1930–   ) France
Divertimento 1958 (Leduc) 17 min. Ouverture: chordal, octotonic, freely
   tonal, flexible meters, glissandi. Serenade: fast, lyric opening and
   closing sections, motoric midsection with chords and single notes in
   alternating hands; material is overworked. Villanelle: melodic, builds
   to climax, subsides. Carnaval: a contemporary jig full of glitter;
   Tango and Valse musette sections; clever, many effects. M-D.

Paul Dukas (1865–1935) France
L'Apprenti Sorcier, Scherzo d'après une ballade de Goethe (Durand 5314;
   UCLA) 18pp. Originally for orchestra, transcribed for two pianos by
   the composer. Highly effective. M-D.

Henri Duparc (1848–1933) France
Prelude and Fugue a (ESC 1903).

Hubert Du Plessis (1922–   ) Union of South Africa
Prelude, Fugue and Postlude Op.17 (Novello 1958; LC) 22pp. Prelude
   (Andante con moto): melodic. Fugue (Allegretto moderato): calm
   and serious. Postlude (Allegro): fast, bouncy. Chromatic and tonal.
   M-D.

Auguste Durand (1830–1909) France
Grand Duo Op.23 (Durand 7544; LC) 21pp. For piano and harmonium or
   two pianos. Allegro moderato; Thème; Variation; Andante; Finale.
   Franck and Saint-Saëns influence. M-D.

Jean Baptiste Durvenoy (1802–1880) France
Feu Roulant Op.256 (EBM). This "Rolling Fire" is a sparkling perpetual-
   motion recital piece. Still dazzling and attractive with running tunes
   everywhere. Int. to M-D.

Johann Ladislaus Dussek (1760–1812) Bohemia
Dussek's works display "significant pre-Romanticisms in his musical style
and piano writing" according to W. S. Newman. Dussek is an important
transition figure from Classic to Romantic style; his contribution needs
reexamination. Dussek possibly had the two-piano medium suggested to
him while he was studying with C. P. E. Bach.
Sonata F Op.26 (Rees, Madden—Schott 10507 1957) 31pp. Allegro; Larghetto; Rondo. First performed in London in 1790. The title page of
   the original edition states that the Sonata was written for "The Harp
   and Piano Forte or two Piano Fortes one with additional keys." The
   combination of harp and pianoforte was a favorite of the period. This
   work is one of the few in which the alternative of two pianofortes is
   mentioned. Editorial suggestions are in brackets. Charming rococo
   style with interesting harmony and pianistic texture. M-D.
Sonata E♭ Op.38 (Haslinger).

J. A. Jos. Duteil D'Ozanne (–   )
Suite Carnavelesque (Costallat).

Henri Dutilleux (1916–   ) France
Figures de résonances 1976 version (Heugel 1980) 13pp., 7 min. Note in
French. Four short contrasting sections, expressionistic, clusters,
harmonics, variable meters, ad libitum sections, pointillistic, colorful. Some knotty finger-breaking sections; requires ample technical
resources and large span. M-D to D.

Andrzej Dutkiewicz (1942–   ) Poland
Dutkiewicz graduated from the State Higher School of Music in Warsaw
and received his DMA from the Eastman School of Music. He is a
founder, a member, and the head of Group XX, which performs music of
the twentieth century.
Music for Two 1976 (AA) 13 min. Performance directions in English and
Polish. Chromatic lines, octotonic, repeated notes for indicated number of seconds, fast contrary-motion chords, dynamic extremes,
clusters, harmonics. Spatial notation; key signature used for part of
the work. Requires improvisation. An avant-garde work with real
musical possibilities when performed by experienced pianists who
have carefully worked out the ensemble problems. M-D to D.

Anton Dvořák (1841–1904) Bohemia
Slavonic Dances Op.46 (Simrock; IU has Nos. 1 and 2). All twelve dances
are published separately in the original two-piano version.

E

Anton Eberl (1766–1807) Austria

Prelude followed by Eight Variations, Op.31, on a March from the opera, *Raoul Barbe-Bleue* by Grétry 1804 (Gesellschaft der Musikfreunde, Q12702, Vienna). Eberl's only known work for two pianos. A brilliant introduction of 39 bars, full of sweeping scales, fast octaves and cadenza-like passages, precedes Grétry's theme of 16 bars. The two pianists toss various ideas back and forth. The variations are both ornamental and character-like. Eberl does not insist on easy recognition of the theme throughout all the variations. On several occasions Eberl performed, as did Mozart, at two pianos with Josephine Aurnhammer. He also performed these variations with Giacomo Meyerbeer on March 26, 1806, during a concert tour of Germany. M-D.

Friedrich Eckart (1919–   ) Germany

Kontrapunktische Variationen Op.7 (Hain Verlag).

George Edwards (1943–   ) USA

Edwards is a member of the composition faculty of Columbia University.

Double Play 1970 (APNM) Facsimile edition. 15 min. Proportional rhythmic relationships, pointillistic, highly organized, complex pianistic figures, fluid rhythmic patterns, expressionistic, frequent density changes. Absolute equality of parts, large span required. D.

Robert Braun Eilenberg (1873– ?) USA

Andante und Variationen—Quasi Fantasia Op.24 (B. F. Wood 1905; BrM; LC) 34pp. Andante espressivo theme is followed by contrasting variations, a fugue, and an expansive finale. Rambunctious writing in overblown nineteenth-century style. M-D.

Robert Elmore (1913–   ) USA

Swing Rhapsody (JF 1939; Southern Illinois University at Carbondale) 8 min. Inspired by Gershwin's *Rhapsody in Blue.* Sectionalized, blues influence, glissando closing. Requires a firm octave technique. M-D.

Georges Enesco (1881–1955) Rumania

Variations Op.5 1899 (Enoch; Br&H; Editura de Stat Pentru Literatura Si

Arta; LC) 15pp. for Piano I, 11pp. for Piano II. Dedicated to Edouard Risler and Alfred Cortot. Enesco, like the early Bartók, builds on Debussy's inspired style of piano sonority, adding qualities of his own that are often striking. Many octaves and skips, fugue-like closing. D.

Hans Ulrich Engelmann (1921–   ) Germany
Duplum Op.29 1965 (Tonos 1967) 34pp., 16 min. One movement, twelve-tone, involved, expressionistic, pointillistic, serialized dynamics, proportional rhythmic relationships, arm clusters. D.

Manuel Enríquez (1926–   ) Mexico
Enríquez studied at the Guadalajara Conservatory and the Juilliard School. In 1971 he worked at the Columbia-Princeton Electronics Music Center. He has been assistant concertmaster of the National Symphony Orchestra of Mexico and has taught composition at the National Conservatory there for a number of years.
Modulas para dos pianos (EMM 1967; IU) 16pp. In two large sections, twelve-tone, long trills, abrupt dramatic chords, long pedals with glissandi, aleatory sections, proportional rhythmic relationships. Number of seconds indicated for playing certain figures. Avant-garde. D.

Heimo Erbse (1924–   ) Germany
Sonata Op.3 1951 (Bo&Bo).

Pauline Erdmannsdoerfer-Fichtner (–   ) Germany
Thema mit 9 Umspielungen e (Emil Grunert).

Hermann Erler (1844–1918) Germany
Prelude and Gavotte Op.32 (R&E 1906; LC) 14pp.
Menuett Op.33 (R&E 1906; LC) 9pp.
These works are composed in classic style but liberally sprinkled with Romantic clichés. M-D.

David Ernest (1945–   ) USA
Ernest is a graduate of Duquesne University, Rutgers University, and the University of California at San Diego.
"P-2" 1971 (MS available from composer: c/o Music Department, York College of the City University of New York, 150–14 Jamaica Avenue, Jamaica, NY 11432). Includes performance instructions. Requires a wire brush and cloth or yarn mallets. Each page should take 30–45 seconds. Spatial relationships, indeterminate pitch, seconds, clusters, plucked strings, harmonics. Avant-garde. M-D.

Edwin Evans (1844–1923) Great Britain
Grand Sonata Op.26 (Lafleur).

Robert Evett (1922–1975) USA
Evett identified himself with the Baroque era and described his music as
well made and adhering to conservative principles.
Toccata and Two Fugues 1951 (ACA) 13 min.
Ricercare 1961 (ACA) 20 min.

F

Mario Facchinetti (1898–   ) Italy

Fantaisies 1952 (Hamelle) 12 min. Premiere Mouvement: imitation between instruments, octotonic, parallel chords. Romance: ostinato-like figures, added-note technique, melodic. Marche: rhythmic, fast octaves, syncopated scherzando section. Allegretto: waltz-like section alternates with a Più animato (Marche) section. Chanson Truculente: animated, fast scales, 2 with 3, freely tonal. M-D.

Richard Faith (1926–   ) USA

Concerto for Two Pianos (SP 1974) 22pp. Allegro deciso: abbreviated SA design. Andante, flowingly: romantic and introspective. Vivace: capricious rhythmic bite, Prestissimo closing. Good thematic construction, neo-Classic, terse and brilliant, unusual harmonic color, well conceived for the medium. Contains some involved ensemble problems. M-D.

Concerto No. 3 for Piano and Orchestra (MS available from composer: c/o School of Music, University of Arizona, Tuscon, AZ 85721) 43pp. Andantino, espressivo—Allegro; Lento, ma non troppo; Vivace. This two-piano reduction by the composer is highly effective. Faith's naturally unfolding writing is a joy to perform and a pleasure for the audience. M-D.

Variations and Presto 1976 (MS available from composer) 26pp. Andante: cantabile flowing modal theme, octotonic; Poco più mosso brings increased activity, flexible meters; tempo primo is more chordal, *pp* closing. Presto: rhythmic, thin textures, some long pedals, brilliant conclusion, large span required. Mood ranges from somber to lyrical to energetic; a winning sample of Faith's highly effective writing for the two instruments. M-D.

Leoš Faltus (1937–   ) Czechoslovakia

Prolog, Nenie e Paian 1970 (CHF) 12 min. Prolog: declamatory, interval of second used frequently; requires large span. Nenie: improvise for so many seconds around given figures, repeated clusterlike sonorities, black and white key glissandi together, chordal punctuation, dies away to *pp* with use of low trills. Paian: dramatic gestures, improvisation required based on given figuration, many glissandi, concludes with broad *fff* chordal chorale-like melody. Expressionistic. M-D.

Michel Fano (1929–   ) France
Fano studied with Boulanger and Messiaen. His acquaintance with Boulez from 1950 led him to a fundamental rethinking of music and composition, and the few instrumental works that he has not withdrawn date from this period. All his writing now is for the movies.
Sonate 1952 (SBTS) 15pp. Modéré; Tres lent. Totally serial. The series has no inversion, since the mirror form of the series corresponds to the retrograde form transposed up a half step. The exposition occupies the first five lines (two pages) of the score. Each line corresponds to one statement of the series or a polyphony of series. Dynamics and durations are organized. Six dynamic levels are used: *pp, p, mp, mf, f, ff.* Each dynamic series uses each of these values twice. D.
See: Richard Toop, "Messiaen/Goeyvaerts, Fano/Stockhausen, Boulez," PNM, Fall–Winter 1974:141–69 for a more complete analysis of this work.

Harry Farjeon (1878–1948) Great Britain
Rhapsody Op.70 (Goodwin & Tabb).
Vignettes Op.72 (Paxton 1932). Tone Picture. Pastoral Reverie. Published separately.

Giles Farnaby (1560–1640) Great Britain
For Two Virginals (OUP; Dover). In Vol. II of the *Fitzwilliam Virginal Book.* One of the earliest known works for two keyboards. 8 bars repeated, 2 phrases, each varied once. The second part consists of the same material with embellishment. All interpretive indications in the OUP edition are editorial. When played on two pianos the most delicate touch possible must be used. Int.

Reinhard Febel (1952–   ) Germany
Regionen (Edition Modern EM 2094 1979) 24 leaves in portfolio, ca. 20 min. Photostat. Preface in German.

Morton Feldman (1926–   ) USA
Feldman's music has, at its most characteristic, an arhythmic harmonic sensibility involving an element of choice far removed from the John Cage philosophy of "no-mindedness." Though one-sided in conception—much of it is very slow, very soft, and all evocatively timeless—its hypnotic qualities give it a true creative expressiveness. Feldman composes for the

sake of sounds, and the listener or performer may not always perceive a directed sense of motion. It is possible that Feldman's work was designed to reattract audiences largely put off by an extreme mathematical approach to music.

Projection III 1951 (CFP 6961) 3 graphs. "Relative pitch (high, middle, low) is indicated: ⊓ high; II middle; ⊔ low. Any tone within these ranges may be sounded. The limits of the ranges may be freely chosen by the player. Duration is indicated by the amount of space taken up by the square or rectangle, each box (⁞⁞) being potentially 4 icti. The single ictus, or pulse, is at the tempo of 72 or thereabouts. Dynamics are very low. Each pianist reads two parts simultaneously, with the lower part (◇) making of the piano a source of sympathetic resonance. Numbers in the piano parts indicate the amount of sounds to be played simultaneously" (from the score). Avant-garde. M-D.

Projection V 1951 (CFP 6962). For two pianos, three cellos, three flutes, and trumpet. Graphic notation; relative pitch indicated with limits of ranges freely chosen by performers; duration indicated by amount of space taken up by the square or rectangle. Numbers in the piano parts indicate the quantity of sounds to be played simultaneously. Trumpet plays into either of the two pianos. Avant-garde. M-D.

Extensions 4 1952–53 (CFP 1962). For three pianos. 21pp., 3 parts. Pointillistic, fast-changing dynamics, extreme range of keyboard exploited, pitch given but not time value. Absolutely precise ensemble required. M-D to D.

Intermission VI 1953 (CFP 6928 1963). For one or two pianos. 2pp. Chance composition. "Composition begins with any sound and proceeds to any other. With a minimum of attack, hold each sound until barely audible. Grace notes are not played too quickly. All sounds are to be played as soft as possible" (from the score). Contains 15 disparate sonorities on one page; performer may begin and end anywhere, having proceeded through the parts in any order. Avant-garde. M-D.

Two Pieces 1954 (CFP 6916) 4pp. Reproduced from holograph. To be played as softly as possible, harmonics, outer range of keyboard exploited. M-D.

Two Pianos 1957 (CFP 6939) 2pp. Durations are free. Slow, soft as possible, spare arrangements of sound events, much left to the choice of the performers. Large span required. Avant-garde.

Piece for Four Pianos 1957 (CFP). "As we proceed to experience the individual time-responses of the four pianists we are moving inexorably toward the final image where the mind can rest, which is the end of the piece" (from the score). Delicate textures and sonorities. Avant-garde. M-D.

Ixion (Summerspace—a Ballet) 1958 (CFP 6926a) 11 min. Arranged for two pianos by the composer. Graphic notation, a totally abstract sonic adventure. Avant-garde. M-D.

Vertical Thoughts I (CFP 6952 1963) 2pp. "Broken line indicates sequence of pianos. Each piano enters as the preceding sound begins to fade. The vertical line indicates a simultaneous sound. Dynamics very low throughout. Each sound with a minimum of attack. Grace notes to be played slowly (from the score). Avant-garde. M-D.

Two Pieces for Three Pianos 1966 (CFP) 5pp., 3 parts. Each sound in the first and second piano parts is held until it begins to fade. Dynamics extremely low throughout. Fascinating sonorities. Avant-garde. M-D.

False Relationships and the Extended Ending 1968 (CFP) 15pp. For three pianos, cello, violin, trombone, and chimes. "Durations for simultaneous and single sounds are extremely slow. All sounds are connected without pause unless otherwise notated. Dynamic level is extremely low, but audible" (from the score). Specific metronome marks are listed for many measures. Avant-garde. M-D.

Between Categories 1969 (CFP 6971) 9pp., parts. Photostat of MS. For two pianos, two chimes, two violins, and two cellos. "Durations of simultaneous and single sounds are extremely slow. All sounds are connected without pauses unless otherwise notated. The dynamic level is extremely low, but audible" (from the score). Changing meters, unusual subtle chordal sonorities throughout, avant-garde. Requires large span. M-D.

Five Pianos 1972 (UE 15499) 35–55 min.

Howard Ferguson (1908–   ) Great Britain

Partita Op.5b 1935–6 (Bo&H) 21 min. Grave—Allegretto pesante; Allegro un poco agitato; Andante un poco mosso; Allegro con spirito. Post-Romantic style, classical forms. Exists also in a version for piano and orchestra. "Each version was conceived for its own medium, so neither may be said to be an arrangement of the other" (composer's note). M-D to D.

Brian Ferneyhough (1943–   ) Great Britain

Ferneyhough is one of the most important young English composers. He has taught composition since 1973 at the Freiburg Academy of Music in Breisgau, Germany.

Sonata for Two Pianos 1966 (CFP 7120 1970) 34pp., 15 min. Highly organized serial writing that shows strong Webern, Boulez, and Stockhausen influence. Uses such devices as pointillism, proportional rhythmic relationships, dynamic indications on almost every note, harmonics, frequently changing meters, directed improvisation, long *ppp* trills in low register, ends *ppppp*. There are a few specific directions, e.g., "Whilst taking into account marked dynamics etc. this passage should be as 'colourless' and inexpressive as possible." Requires large span. Only for the most experienced and bold performers. Both parts are totally integrated. D.

George Fiala (1922–   ) Canada, born Russia
Sonata pour deux pianos 1970 (CMC) 18 min. Allegro non troppo; Berceuse; Arietta; Finale.

Jacobo Ficher (1896–   ) Argentina, born Russia
Three Hebrew Dances Op.69 (PIC 1964) 35pp. Wedding Dance; Mystic Dance; Hora. Based on folk music and dressed in a colorful contemporary garb, strong rhythms. A fine recital group. Requires facility in fast figuration and a well-meshed ensemble. M-D.

Michael Finnessy (1946–   ) Great Britain
Finnessy studied at the Royal College of Music in London and with Roman Vlad in Rome. He organized the Music Department at the London School of Contemporary Dance and lives in London.
Wild Flowers 1974 (Edition Modern 1782) 12 min.

Ernst Fischer (1900–   ) Germany
Zwei Klavier Plaudern (Schott 2443 1935; BrM; LC) 19pp. Glatteis . . . (Skidding Along); Perpetuum Mobile (Foxtrot). Colorful. M-D.

Irwin Fischer (1903–   ) USA
Ariadne Abandoned (ACA).
Burlesque (ACA).

Robert Fischhof (1856–1918) Austria
Trois Scenes Aragonaises (Dob).
Variations and Fugue on an Original Theme (Heugel).

Marius Flothuis (1914–   ) The Netherlands
Divertimento on a theme of van Kees Stokvis Op.28 1946 (Donemus) 11 min. Preludio; Tempo di Valzer; Intermezzo alla marcia; Rondo. Freely tonal, neo-Classic with touches of Gallic witticism. M-D.

Josef B. Foerster (1859–1951) Czechoslovakia
Nocturno Fantastico (Artia).

Zdeněk Folprecht (1900–1961) Czechoslovakia
Rondo Brillante Op.34 (CHF) 70pp. 3/4 in one to a bar, freely tonal, chromatic melodies, thin textures, dancelike, contrasting sections, large dynamic range, arpeggio figuration, subito *ff* marcato coda, virtuoso closing. This work is spacious, and, although it glitters in certain sections, a warm sound is required for its more restrained parts. M-D.

Jacqueline Fontyn (1930–   ) Belgium
Spirales (PIC 1974; IU) 31pp. Four untitled movements. Some unusual notation. Pointillistic, chord trills, dissonant, clusters, varied meters, dynamic extremes, tremolo chords between hands, carefully pedalled. Large span required. D.

Lukas Foss (1922–   ) USA, born Germany
Set of Three Pieces 1938 (GS; UCLA). Published separately. March, 13pp.: exciting, some imitation. Andante, 15pp.: long and flowing. Concertino, 31pp.: extensive and involved, various moods. All are freely tonal and exhibit MC sonorities. M-D.
Ni Bruit Ni Vitesse ("Neither Noise Nor Haste") (Sal 1972) 21pp. For two pianos and two percussionists. Careful explanations in English. Exploits sonorities on the keys and strings and requires in addition two cow bells, two Japanese bowls, and two triangle beaters. Percussionists play inside the pianos. Delicate percussive and timbre effects provide gamelan-like sonorities. Performers' activities provide much visual interest. Aleatory but hangs together remarkably well. M-D.

Paul Fournier (–   ) France
Toccata (Durand 1910; LC) 20pp. Originally for orchestra, arranged for two pianos by composer. Many repeated notes with melody clearly enunciated. Impressionistic. M-D.

Jennifer Fowler (1939–   ) Australia
Fowler studied at Perth University and then at the Electronic Studio of the University of Utrecht.
Piece for an Opera House 1973 (UE 29119). For two players on two pianos, or one pianist with tape recorder, or one pianist alone. 7–8 min.

Jim Fox (1953–   ) USA
Fox studied at Butler, De Paul, and Redland universities, working with Russell Peck, Phil Winsor, and Barney Childs. Presently he is instructor of electronic music and director of Redlands University Improvisational Ensemble.
Maybe Once or Twice 1974 (in *Score—An Anthology of New Music*, GS 1981) 6pp., 15–20 min. Figurations are notated and may be repeated a number of times. Figuration begins simply and increases in complexity. Coordination between instruments is necessary where indicated. Aleatory, avant-garde. M-D.

Jean Françaix (1912–   ) France
Huit danses exotiques 1957 (Schott 4984) 36pp., 10 min. Pambiche; Baiao; Nube gris; Merengue; Mambo; Samba lente; Malambeando; Rock 'n' Roll. Character of each dance subtly caught in each piece. Sophis-

ticated chromatic vocabulary throughout, rhythmically interesting.
M-D.

César Franck (1822–1890) France

Prelude, fugue et variation Op.15 (Durand). Transcribed for two pianos
by Franck, this work contains his style-prints everywhere: chromaticism, carefully worked out fugue, flowing lines. The Variation is a
repeat of the Prelude with varied figuration and is improvisatory. The
rhythmic and dynamic nuances require a free-and-easy give-and-
take. The success of this piece is largely due to the very pianistic
writing of the original version. M-D.

Les Eolides Poème Symphonique (Litolff 1489; Enoch; IU) 39pp. Arranged for two pianos by the composer.

Eduard Franck (1817–1893) Germany

Duo e Op.46 (Lienau 1883; BrM). Strong Mendelssohn and Schumann
influence. M-D.

Isadore Freed (1900–1960) USA

Carnival (TP) 13pp., 4½ min. Allegro: freely tonal around D, toccata style
contrasted with two short lyrical sections, frequent meter changes;
final cadence is a surprise. Would make a fine encore, brilliant and
exciting. Int. to M-D.

Hard Times (TP 1957; LC).Paraphrase on a folk theme. Modal, meter
varied, melancholy. Int.

Peter Racine Fricker (1920–   ) Great Britain

Four Fughettas Op.2 1946 (Schott 10124 1950) 17pp., 5 min. Moderato e
pomposo: octaves, chromatic, octotonic; requires large span. Capriccio: fast repeated notes, freely tonal, con forza chords. Lento: re-
citativo, cantabile sonorous lines, *pp* closing. Vivo: 6/8 scampering
mood, builds to climax, subsides and vanishes into a *pp*. Themes are
happily invented and handled with skill, but the fugues are short for
their ambitious expositions. Neo-Classic. M-D.

Sonata Op.78 1977 (Schott 1981). Thinner textures than Op.2 and more
clearly expressive. M-D to D.

Geza Frid (1904–   ) The Netherlands

Prelude and Fugue Op.23 1946 (PIC 1964) 9 min. Prelude: contrasting
sections, strong thematics, flowing sixteenths. Fugue: chromatic subject, evolves into toccata-like textures with some material returning
from the Prelude, glissando at end. M-D.

Ritmische Studies Op.58a 1959 (Donemus) 23pp. Seven contrasting
studies, each emphasizing and developing different rhythmic
figurations. Neo-Classic oriented, MC. M-D.

Music for S.D. Op.67 1963 (Donemus) 10pp. Contrasting sections, neo-Classic, octotonic, toccata-like closing, MC. M-D.

Dimensies (Dimensions) Op.74 1967 (Donemus) 10 min. Can be performed on three pianos, on two pianos, or on one piano with one pianist. Monologue; Dialogue; Le Fâcheux Troisième. Performance directions in Dutch and English. Chromatic glissandi with brush; clusters; tap on lid of piano; unusual sonorities. M-D.

Toccata Op.84a (Donemus 1973) 22pp., 10 min. Reproduced from composer's MS. Andante preciso introduction leads to the main body of the work, Allegro meccanico. A free cadenza appears in the middle of this section. Requires virtuoso technique. D.

Foxtrot 1975 (Donemus) 2½ min. In collection *Een suite voor de Suite*. Allegro molto, octotonic, neo-Classic, glissandi, appealing. Int. to M-D.

Ignaz Friedman (1882–1948) Poland
Suite E Op.70 (WH 1840 1917; IU; LC) 59pp. Tema con Variazioni; Choral; Finale. Brilliant traditional 19th century style handled effectively throughout, works to stunning conclusion. M-D to D.

Johannes Fritsch (1941–   ) Germany
Ikonen 1964 (Feedback 7104 1971). For three pianos. 10 min. Six sections are treated aleatorially between the instruments. Spatial notation. Expressionistic, pointillistic, strum glissandi on strings, extreme dynamic ranges, avant-garde. D.

Karl Fuegtistaller (–   ) Switzerland
Divertimento c Op.8 (Hug).

Sandro Fuga (1906–   ) Italy
Toccata (F. Colombo 128919).

Anis Fuleihan (1901–1970) USA, born Cyprus
Epithalamium (GS 1942; LC) 40pp., 12 min. Originally for piano and string orchestra, arranged for two pianos by the composer. The theme is a traditional Lebanese wedding song. Last of the 12 variations is an expansive finale. M-D.

The Bailiff's Daughter (CF 2550 1947; AMC; LC) 8pp. Based on a charming English ballad. Delightful and straightforward writing. Int.

Toccata (PIC 1965) 50pp. This is in reality a four-movement sonata. Introduction: fugal textures, angular lines, and persistent drive require granitic rhythm. Variations: 8 modal, Mediterranean influenced variations; No. 8, marked Barbaro, is a brilliant closing. Interlude: lovely syncopated theme, quiet and fluid, tranquil lyric lines supported by undulating chords. Fugue: complex but exciting 6-bar subject, percussive; requires steely fingers. D.

Disma Fumagalli (1826–1893) Italy
Sonata Op.26 (Ric).

Polibio Fumagalli (1830–1901) Italy
Divertimento Op.6 (Ric).

G

Pierre Gabaye (1930–   ) France

Récital Express (Leduc 1968) 9 min. Mise en Doigts: diatonic, octotonic, sudden dynamic changes, freely tonal. Valse Familiale: busy, chromatic, surprise ending. Toccata pour un "Bis": motoric, strong rhythms, somewhat similar in style to that of Jean Françaix, as is the whole suite. M-D.

Natalio Galan (1919–   ) Cuba

Intermedio Variado (Ediciones del Departamento de la Biblioteca Nacional "Jose Marti" 1960; IU; LC) 14pp. Originally the introduction to the second scene of the opera *El Paseo*, written in 1955. The two-piano version was composed in 1958. Theme and five highly rhythmic variations. Freely tonal, repeated chords and figurations, MC. M-D.

Janina Garścia (1920–   ) Poland

Mala Suite Op.18 (PWM 1961; LC) 11pp. Moderato opening leads to an Allegro with folk-like tune; Tempo di marcia; Scherzando; Cantabile; Tarantela. Charming tonal writing that is totally convincing. Int.

Eugen Gayrhos (–   ) Switzerland

Scherzo Diatonique Op.97 (Foetisch).

Heinrich Gebhard (1878–1963) USA, born Germany

Waltz-Suite (ECS 1929; AMC) 26pp. Seven contrasting waltzes in traditional idioms with the last one the most extensive. Sounds a little dated but carefully exploits the instruments throughout. M-D.

Rio Gebhardt (1907–   ) Germany

Artistique (Jazz-Novel) (Zimmermann).

Rolf Gehlhaar (1943–   ) Germany

Gehlhaar studied at Yale University, University of California, Berkeley, and was assistant to Karlheinz Stockhausen from 1967 to 1970.

Klavierstück 2—2 Boundaries 1970 (Feedback 7103) 17 min. Uses small glockenspiel or xylophone stick. Performance directions included. Notation is mainly spatial in the scale of 1 cm = 1.2 seconds. Tempo markings should be interpreted in reference to this basic tempo. "On page 5 the box above the system corresponds to a tempo scale of approximately 2 octaves, whose upper limit is as fast as possible! If, for example, the player's fastest tempo is approximately 12 attacks per second, then the notated tempo here is approximately 6 attacks per second" (from the score). Harmonics, clusters. Avant-garde. M-D to D.

Harald Genzmer (1909–   ) Germany
Sonata 1950 (Schott 4332) 32pp. Allegro; Tranquillo; Scherzando prestissimo; Moderato. Freely tonal, neo-Classic, well constructed. Traditional; easy on the ears for someone not overly fond of contemporary music. M-D.

Edwin Gerschefski (1909–   ) USA
Streamline Op.17 (CFE 1935; AMC) 5pp. Fast repeated notes, tremolo, motoric rhythms, glissandi, expansive conclusion. M-D.

George Gershwin (1898–1937) USA
Gershwin first sketched his concerted works for two pianos and published a number of them in that form. The two-piano writing reveals a great deal about Gershwin's thinking. All these pieces demonstrate the creative resourcefulness that marks the genius of Gershwin and makes him still the most "popular" American composer, especially outside the United States.
Rhapsody in Blue 1923 (Warner Brothers) 42pp. This version is more successful than the solo piano version although the orchestration is greatly missed in both. Ingenious rhythmic treatment, sparkling melodic and harmonic devices. The whole work abounds in extremely clever keyboard manipulations. M-D.
Concerto F 1925 (Warner Brothers). Original version for two pianos. Allegro; Andante con moto; Allegro con brio. Gershwin's compositional method (like that of Ravel and others) was to write out short scores on four staves before orchestrating the second part. This version works very well, and although it is flawed by some formal defects, it has proved to be one of the most popular works of the twentieth century. A secure technique and great rhythmic projection are needed for a proper performance of the three contrasting movements. M-D to D.
Second Rhapsody 1931 (Warner Brothers) 47pp. An initial "rivets" motif is stated at the beginning and is followed by development. After a rumba melody, the heart of the composition is reached with a blues song. A recapitulation of the opening section ends the piece. Although this work does not have the inspiration of the *Rhapsody in Blue,* it deserves more frequent hearings. M-D.

Variations on "I Got Rhythm" 1934 (Warner Brothers) 8½ min. Delightful, versatile salon writing at its best. The six variations—which include a Chinese version, a valse triste, and the blues—change the rhythm, structure, and melody of the original song. An effective performance work. M-D.

Elizabeth Gest (–   ) USA
Paraphrase on "Three Blind Mice" (EV 1939) 7pp. Attractive, clever, continuous variation treatment, *pp* closing. Int. to M-D.
Frere Jacques' Concert (JF 1956; AMC) 4pp. One piano has the tune while the other decorates; fun for all. Int.

David Gibson (1943–   ) USA
Gibson worked with Stanley Wolfe and Jacob Druckman
Three Pianos (Seesaw 1975) 15pp., 22½ min. Includes performance directions. "Pitches in the piece are given as a series of perfect fourths. The performers are to play all the semi-tones within the given perfect fourth randomly in the rhythms and tempos above the staves" (from the score). Figures are to be played by the number of seconds indicated above the score. Except for accents, dynamics are low. Damper and una corda pedals are depressed throughout the entire piece. Avant-garde. M-D.

Miriam Gideon (1906–   ) USA
Hommage à ma Jeunesse (To My Youth) 1935 Subtitled "Sonatina for two Pianos." (Mercury 1949; AMC) 25pp., 10 min. Allegretto; Pastoral; Allegro. Cheerful neo-Classic writing with strong linear and lyric lines. M-D.

Pia Gilbert (1921–   ) USA
Interrupted Suite (CFP 66677). For clarinet and three pianos. 10 min.

Gaetano Giuffre (–   ) USA, born Greece
Triptycus Byzantinus 1971 (Seesaw 1978) 57pp. D.

Philip Glass (1937–   ) USA
In Again Out Again 1968 (Dunvagen). For two pianos or electric keyboards.

Aleksandr Glazunov (1865–1936) Russia
*La Mer.*Fantaisie pour grand orchestra Op.28 (Belaieff 1890; BrM). Reduction for two pianos, eight hands, by the composer. Well laid out for the instruments, sectionalized, traditional treatment of musical material. M-D.
Fantasy f Op.104 1920 (Belaieff 459 1930; UCLA) 54pp. Molto tranquillo; Scherzo; Moderato. Rhapsodic and programmatic post-Romantic style, thick textures. M-D to D.

Reinhold Gliere (1875–1956) Russia
Six Pieces Op.41 (Jurgenson 1910; Philipp-IMC) 27pp. Prelude. Valse triste. Chanson. Basso ostinato (7/4). Air de ballet. Mazurka. Russian folk influence, traditional. M-D.
24 Morceaux Op.61 (Jurgenson). Published separately. 1. Prélude. 2. Six Variations sur un thème original. 3. Ostinato. 4. Soirée d'été. 5. Chant populaire. 6. Danse populaire. 7. Dans la forêt. 8. Les nymphes. 9. Nocturne. 10. Près du ruisseau. 11. Le génie de la forêt. 12. La chasse. 13. Prélude oriental. 14. Danse languide. 15. Muezzin. 16. Danse orientale. 17. Zourna. 18. Près d'une mosquée. 19. Au champ. 20. Le blé flottant. 21. Les bluets. 22. L'alouette. 23. Chant des faucheurs. 24. Le Vent. Grateful salon writing that seems a little dated, especially in Nos.3, 10–13, 21–23. M-D.

Benjamin Godard (1849–1895) France
Fantaisie Persanne Op.152 (Hamelle).

Leopold Godowsky (1870–1938) Poland
Godowsky was one of the greatest masters of counterpoint. His few works for two pianos are unique in their full use of the sonorities possible on paired keyboards.
Contrapuntal Paraphrases on Weber's "Invitation to the Dance" (CF 1922) 74pp.
Optional accompaniment of a third piano, 27pp. A large Romantic and involved but effective work. Melodious tunes are contrapuntally developed. At one place three previously stated themes are combined above a conventional waltz accompaniment. M-D.
Alt Wien (Old Vienna) (GS 1935; LAP) 6pp., 2½ min. Based on the motto "Whose yesterdays look backwards with a smile through tears." Effectively transcribed from the solo piano work. Thematic material excellently distributed between the two performers; contrapuntal. M-D.

Rolf Inge Godöy (1952–   ) Norway
Transfiguration für Zwei Klaviere 1975 (NMO 9215) 20pp. Moderato opening with chromatic lines in right hand over sustained chords in left hand; drops to *pp* arpeggiated sonorities; chromatic lines return and build to strong climax. Expressionistic, pointillistic; emotional element is thin. M-D to D.

Hugo Godron (1900–1971) The Netherlands
Pastorale 1953 (Donemus) 16 min. Fête: Tempo di Rumba. Nocturne: Andante doloroso. Rigaudon Latus: Allegro grazious, ben vivo. Colorful, MC, strong rhythms. M-D.
Sonate 1945 (Donemus) 23 min. Alla Marcia vivo; Andante; Allegro rit-

mico. Continues the Brahms pianistic tradition; has affinities with the Brahms *Sonata for Two Pianos* Op.34b. M-D to D.

Suite moderne 1941 (Donemus 1975) 17min. Andante; Intermezzo; Canzone; Rondo. Tonal, straightforward writing throughout, MC. Requires two experienced pianists. M-D.

Karel Goeyvaerts (1923–   ) Belgium

Sonata 1951 (Swets & Zeitlinger B.V., P.O. Box 810, 2160 SZ Lisse, Holland; SBTS) 12pp. Three untitled movements: Quarter note = 72; Eighth note = 84; Dotted quarter note = 56. "Written before Stockhausen's *Kreuzspiel* and finished before Boulez's *Polyphonie X,* this sonata was of decisive importance in laying the foundations for total serialism and 'point' (isolated note) writing" (Corneel Mertens, *The New Grove,* Vol. 7, p. 494). This sonata was probably the first totally serial structure, and it had great influence on Stockhausen, among others. Serial organization is extended to all aspects of the individual sound. The entire piece is a "cross-form," an *X,* in which material is retrograded from a central point at the end of movement II, and register and/ instrumentation are exchanged. In this case, the material is merely transferred from Piano I to Piano II, in imitation of the Ars Antiqua *Stimmtausch,* where the exchange occurred between equal voices.

See: Richard Toop, "Messiaen/Goeyvaerts, Fano/ Stockhausen, Boulez," PNM Fall–Winter 1974:141–69 for a more thorough analysis.

Richard Franko Goldman (1910–1980) USA

Le Bobino (PIC 1950; AMC; LC) 19pp. Burlesque in Three Scenes. Overture. Entr'acte. Le Jazz Cold. Inspired by a popular music hall, or vaudeville theater, in Paris. The suite attempts "to recapture some of the music of *Le Bobino* as it was in the 1930's" (from the score). The deliberate banality and wry humor of the music fall a little flat, but the work could be effective in a crisp, lively performance. M-D.

Otto Goldschmidt (1829–1907) Germany

Grand Duo Op.21 (Fritz Schuberth).

Duet for Two Pianofortes "When Spring Unlocks the Flowers, to Paint the Laughing Soil" Op.22 (Chappell 1886; BrM) 27pp. "This duet was written for, and first performed at, Sir Julius Benedict's Concert in June 1871 at the Floral Hall, Covent Garden Theater" (from the score). Contains a few charming moments, even if somewhat dated. M-D.

Duet Op.24 (Chappell 1886; BrM). Originally for harp, flute, clarinet, and double bass. Arranged for two pianos by the composer. Includes many harp figurations. Dated. M-D.

Fruehlingserwachen. Introduction and Allegro Giocoso (Br&H).

Forrest Goodenough (1918–   ) USA
Dance of the Apes (ACA) For four pianos.
Sonatine (ACA).
Suite (ACA).

Frederic Goossen (1927–   ) USA
Goossen is a member of the University of Alabama music faculty. Both of
the works below are big and powerfully expressive. They feature contrapuntal textures and display a palette that is broad in both style and color.
Their harmonic vocabulary ranges from traditional tonal materials to
polytonality, atonality, and free serialism. They are designed for virtuoso
pianists.
Double Concerto for Solo Pianos 1975 (MS available from composer: c/o
    Music Department, University of Alabama, University, AL 35486;
    SBTS) 44pp., 21 min. Facsimile edition. Non troppo allegro; Adagio;
    Allegro animato. D.
For Roy—Suite for Two Pianos 1980 (MS available from composer;
    SBTS) 49pp., 17½ min. Facsimile edition. Commissioned by the Ala-
    bama Music Teachers Association in memory of Roy McAllister.
    Prelude—Free but broad: widely spread chords in one instrument
    punctuated with octotonic lines in the other; pianos freely coor-
    dinated in one section; rapid tremolo effects with interval of 9th.
    Waltzes—con moto: chromatic, octotonic, tempo changes, some
    Ravel influence. Elegy—con moto: clear textures, intense. Inven-
    tion—Allegro marcato e risoluto: imitative, repeated octaves and
    chords, syncopation, brilliant conclusion. D.

Eugene Goossens (1893–1962) Great Britain
Rhythmic Dance (Curwen 1928) 17pp. Originally composed for perfor-
    mance on the pianola. To be "played strictly *a tempo* throughout"
    (from the score). Perpetual motion throughout except for an expres-
    sivo e cantabile (with a good swing) mid-section. Strong rhythms,
    glissandi, freely tonal. Large span required. M-D.

Henryk Mikolaj Gorecki (1933–   ) Poland
Toccata 1955 (PWM 1975) 14pp. Allegro e molto ritmico. Octotonic,
    works to an imposing climax, motoric motion throughout. The pillars
    and buttresses of its architecture are thin and strong. M-D.

Alexandre Edouard Goria (1823–1860) France
Duo de Concert sur Belisario Op.27b (Schott).
March Triomphale Op.91 (CF; Schott; NYPL).

Louis Moreau Gottschalk (1829–1869) USA
Gottschalk possessed a stage personality that was able to move audiences

and critics to hysterical acclaim. His strengths lay in his combining Creole and Afro-American tunes and rhythms with showmanship and bravura performances. In the past few years we have come to realize that he was one of the most original American artists of the nineteenth century.

La Nuit des Tropiques 1858 or 1859 (UCLA). Symphony for orchestra and additional band, arranged for two pianos by John Kirkpatrick with grateful borrowings from the unfinished arrangement for two or three pianos by N. R. Espadero. 28pp. Andante; Allegro moderato. Retains the Gottschalk stylistic glitter throughout. Composed under the inspiration of the friendly Antilles. John Kirkpatrick, in a short but penetrating study of Gottschalk's music, wrote that this symphony "demonstrates what a good piece he could write when he wanted to—it impresses one as perhaps the only time he really tried—the poetic atmosphere throughout is admirably realized—the line has surprising expansion."

Ses Yeux Op.66 1865 (in *The Piano Works of Louis M. Gottschalk,* 5 volumes—Arno Press).

Grand Tarantelle Op.67 1868. (in *The Piano Works of Louis M. Gottschalk,* 5 volumes—Arno Press; Eugene List—Bo&H 1963) 7 min. A large, one-movement, exuberant virtuoso piece. It still retains its power to charm and delight. M-D.

Morton Gould (1913–   ) USA.

Bolero Modern (EBM 1938) 12pp. Based on "Ay! Ay! Ay!" The bolero accompaniment is contained in Piano II, melody in full chords in Piano I. Gradual crescendo from beginning to end (Ravel influence), works to large climax. Requires plenty of octaves. M-D.

Boogie-Woogie Etude (Belwin-Mills 1943) 13pp. Transcribed from the solo-piano version by the composer. "Fast, driving tempo (Steely hard)" (from the score). Catchy. Requires fine octave technique. M-D.

Dark Eyes (H. Flammer 1937; LC) 15pp., 3½ min.

Dialogues (Chappell) 22 min. Originally for piano and string orchestra, transcribed by the composer for two pianos. Recitative and Chorale; Embellishments and Rondo; Dirge and Meditation; Variations and Coda. Dodecaphonic procedures used. M-D.

Hoodah-Day (H. Flammer 1937; LC) 16pp., 3 min. A fast and brisk setting of a sea chantey. M-D.

Interplay (American Concertette) 1943 (Belwin-Mills) 13 min. Originally for piano and orchestra, arranged for two pianos by the composer. With drive and vigor: extremely rhythmic. Gavotte: a short, light dance. Blues: in a slow, nostalgic mood. Very fast: a brilliant, rapid finale. M-D.

La Cucaracha (H. Flammer 1937; LC) 12pp., 4½ min. A spiffy rumba. M-D.

Pavanne (Belwin-Mills). Transcribed for two pianos by the composer.

Rumbalero (CF 1934; LC) 11pp. Effective Cuban dance based on attractive rhythms and tunes. M-D.

Théodore Gouvy (1819–1896) France

Gouvy's style is similar to that of Saint-Saëns but without the latter's polish.

Scherzo B♭ Op.60 (Costallat; BrM) 21pp. Allegretto: fanciful, a few key and mood changes. M-D.

Lilli Bulléro, Variations sur un air Anglaise G♭ Op.62 (Simrock; BrM) 17pp. Andante espressivo opening leads to a Più lento, then to the theme Un poco maestoso; five contrasting variations. M-D.

Marche E♭ Op.63 (Richault; BrM) 21pp. Much glitter with frequent use of octaves and chords alternating between the hands. Alkan-inspired. M-D.

Sonata Op.66 (Costallat; BrM; LC) 39pp. Largo maestoso: d, contrasting sections. Adagio cantabile: B♭. Allegro vivo: D. Pianistically effective, but the composer's craft is thin at the seams of sections. M-D.

Phantasie g Op.69 (Br&H 1882; BrM) 15pp. In three distinct movements: Grave—Allegro molto moderato; Adagio (attaca); Alla Breve. Orchestrally conceived. M-D.

Divertissement Op.78 (K&S 1886; BrM; LC) 15pp. Andante con moto; Lento—Allegro vivace. Overly sectionalized. M-D.

Hermann Graedener (1878–   ) Germany

Sonata Op.18 (M. Brockhaus; LC) 43pp. Allegro moderato; Non troppo lento; Finale—Allegro molto. Shows strong influence of both Brahms and Reger. M-D.

Percy Grainger (1882–1961) USA, born Australia

Blithe Bells (GS). A free ramble on the aria "Sheep May Safely Graze" by J. S. Bach. M-D.

Children's March: Over the Hills and Far Away 1916–18 (GS) 29pp. Uses marimba mallets to strike the strings. "This 2 piano edition can be used together with wind instruments, etc., in chamber music performances" (from the score). Harmonics. M-D.

Country Gardens (GS; Schott) 7pp., 2 min. English Morris dance tune. Grainger's most popular piece. Int. Also available for two pianos, eight hands (GS; LC). Easy to Int.

Eastern Intermezzo (GS). "Composed for small orchestra, 1898 or 1899. Dished-up for 2 pianos July 15–16, 1922" (from the score). Repeated notes and chords, oriental influence. Int. to M-D.

English Dance, Two Musical Relics of My Mother. 1899–1909 (Schott 4175 1924; LC) 25pp. For two pianos, six hands. Int. to M-D.

English Waltz (Schott 5336; LC) 18pp. Last movement of *Youthful Suite* for orchestra, arranged for two pianos by the composer. A delicious setting, glissandi. M-D.

Green Bushes (Passacaglia) (Schott 3923 1923) 15pp. For two pianos, six hands. Transcribed by the composer from an orchestral work based on an old English folk song. Piano I is played by one pianist, Piano II by two. Clever and fun. Int. to M-D.

Handel in the Strand "Clog Dance" (Schott 5230; LC) 12pp. Includes a few snatches of Handel's "Harmonious Blacksmith." Displays Grainger at his most delightful breezy self. M-D.

Hill Songs I, II (GS).

In a Nutshell (GS) Suite. Arrival platform humlet; Gay but wistful; Pastoral; The Gum-Suckers: march; Spoon River. Int. to M-D.

Lincolnshire Posy (Schott 5085; LC) 28pp. Originally for a military band, arranged for two pianos by the composer. A setting of six English folk tunes. M-D.

Molly on the Shore (Schott 5334; LC) 16pp. An Irish reel. Int. to M-D.

Shepherd's Hey (Schott 5235; LC) 8pp. A fetching tune and good time for all. Int. to M-D.

Two Musical Relics of My Mother (GS 1924; LC) 9pp. Hermund the Evil: Faeroe Island Dance. As Sally Sat a-Weeping. English folk songs. M-D.

Renata de Grandis (1927–   ) Italy
Toccata a Doppio Coro Figurato 1964 (Gerig).

Arthur de Greef (1862–1940) Belgium
Menuet Varié (Heugel 1913; LC) 8pp. Originally for string orchestra, arranged for two pianos by the composer. Cadenza is much more difficult than the rest of the piece. M-D.

Sonata 1928 (Schott).

Ray Green (1909–   ) USA
Dance Sonata (AME).

Hymn Tune Set (AME 1962; AMC) 7pp. Sweet Prospect. Sweet Solitude. Sweet Joy. Modal; clever and varied treatment of tunes. Effective individually or as a set; excellent service music for church. Int.

Jig for a Concert (AME 1953; AMC). Driving and vigorous, modal, incessant fourths, octotonic, imitation, effective. M-D.

Scotch! Sonatina (AME 1962; LC) 7pp. Folk tune inspiration, glissando closing. Int.

Cestmir Gregor (1926–   ) Czechoslovakia
Introdukce a Toccata 1976 (CHF) 20pp. A short Allegretto lyric introduc-

tion leads directly to the Toccata, which is interspersed with contrasting materials. Fast moving full chordal octaves bring the piece to a rousing conclusion. Neo-Classic and freely tonal. M-D.

Alexander Gretchaninov (1864–1956) Russia

Deux Morceaux Op.18 (USSR) 22pp. Poème: expressive, lyric and melodic, antiphonal effects. Cortège: strong march, needs good octaves. M-D.

Geoffrey Grey (1934–   ) Great Britain

Three Pieces 1964–67 (Lopes Edition) 12 min.

Edvard Grieg (1843–1907) Norway

Complete Works (CFP). Instrumental Music, Vol. 7: Two Piano, Original Compositions and Arrangements.

Variations on an Old Norwegian Romance Op.51 (CFP 2494 1890) 46pp., 23½ min. Romantic, traditional and effective pianistically, many large open intervals. Contrasting variations and a brilliant finale that concludes *pp.* M-D.

Second-Piano Accompaniments to Sonatas by Mozart (GS). Published separately: K.189h, 545, 475, 457, 494, 533. These accompaniments seem to "gild the lily." Int. to M-D.

S. van Gronigen (–   ) The Netherlands

Suite Op.11 (Br&H).

Cornelis Wilhelmus de Groot (1914–   ) The Netherlands

Apparition 1960 (Donemus) 5 min. Opens with driving rhythmic figures; a colorful mid-section Meno, ma non troppo lento is expressive and free (rubato). Opening section ideas return. Ends with secco molto marcato punctuated chords, freely tonal. M-D.

Cloches dans le matin 1972 (Donemus) 4pp. Descriptive, long pedals, Impressionistic. Int.

Fantaisie sur deux études de Fr. Chopin (Donemus 1973) 12pp., photostat. Combines both Chopin etudes played simultaneously; clever, even if a little contrived. M-D.

La patineuse. "Sjoukje Dijkstra-wals" 1963 (Donemus 1973) 17pp., photostat, 3½ min. Waltzlike; folk song materials freely treated. M-D.

Rudolph Gruen (1900–1966) USA

Scherzo a Op.4a/2 (AMP 1936) 11pp. Fast, rollicking, traditional. M-D.

Humoresque Op.14/2 (AMP 1935; AMC; LC) 13pp. Changing meters, flowing sixteenth notes, chromatic, octotonic, scherzo elements, rubato, faster final section. M-D.

Camargo Guarnieri (1907–   ) Brazil

3 Danzas (Ric).

Carlos Guastavino (1914–   ) Argentina
Tres Romances (EAM 1951) 51pp. Las Niñas. Muchacho Jujeño. Baile. Highly chromatic, constant modulations, thick textures. Virtuosic. M-D to D.
Se Equivocó La Paloma (Ric BA10993 1954; LC) 7pp. Folk-like tune; cadenza mid-section; opening idea returns at ending. M-D.

Juan Guinjoàn (1931–   ) Spain
Cinco Estudios 1968 (Alpuerto). For two pianos and percussion. 10 min. Hermetic, complex, and knotty from every point of view. Runs the gamut from dynamic violence to delicacy. D.

David W. Guion (1895–1981) USA
Guion was a chronicler of musical Americana. His music is clever and whimsical, always accessible, but sophisticated. He noted in his score that it required "the technical skill and artistic finish of the concert pianist."
The Harmonica Player (GS 1926; LC) 7pp. Good rhythmic encore, based on an original melody in folk style. M-D.
Sheep and Goat Walkin' to the Pasture (GS 1936) 2½ min. Cowboys' and old fiddlers' breakdown. A real rip-snorting tune interlaced with fetching rhythms. A superb encore. M-D.
Shingandi (Ballet Primitif) 1930 (GS 1945; AMC; NYPL; LC) 40pp., 20 min. Story dictates music and describes the sacrifice required to bring peace between two warring African tribes. Colorful if somewhat dated. Full chords, glissandi, modal, strong rhythms. M-D.
See: Steve Buchanan, "The All-American Appeal of David Guion," *Clavier* 21 (January 1982):20–25.

Cornelius Gurlitt (1820–1901) Germany
Eight Melodious Pieces Op.174 (GS 1619; Augener 1891; BrM). Eight progressive duos. Traditionally tuneful. Int.
Three Rondos Op.175 (GS; Augener 1891; BrM) D; E♭; e. Published separately. Int.
Fantaisie sur un air original E♭ Op.176 1890 (Augener). For two pianos, eight hands.
Ländliche Bilder (Rustic Pictures) Op.190 (Augener 1893; LC). For two pianos, eight hands. The Start. Arrival in the Country. O'er Hill and Dale. Evening at the Inn in the Wood. Country People Tilting at the Ring. The Chase. Under the Village Lime Tree. Return to the Town. Published separately. Int.
Two Character Pieces (R&E). Capriccio. Valse.

Jacques Guyonnet (1933–   ) Switzerland
Guyonnet studied with Boulez in Darmstadt and lectures in contemporary music at the Geneva Conservatory.

Polyphonie II 1961 (UE) 10pp., 5 min. Many rhythms and tempo changes. Avant-garde. D.

Polyphonie III 1964 (UE 13550) 23pp., parts. For two pianos, flute, and viola. Explanations in French, German, and English, including placement of the instruments. Highly organized (pitch, dynamics, etc.), harmonics, expressionistic, percussive treatment of the pianos, dynamic extremes, shifting meters, pointillistic, avant-garde. D.

Joseph Guy-Ropartz (1864–1955) France

Piece b 1898 (Durand; BrM) 24pp. Sectionalized, highly chromatic, Franck influence. A large work requiring well-developed pianism. M-D.

Elizabeth Gyring (1886–1970) USA

Theme and Variation 1952 (AMC) 18pp. Theme and six contrasting variations. Final variation is most extensive and difficult. Freely tonal with much chromatic usage, expressionistic influence. Requires advanced pianism. D.

Two Marches (ACA). For two pianos, timpani, and triangle.

H

Polo De Haas (1933–   ) The Netherlands
Orgella (Donemus 1975) 14pp. For two pianos, eight hands. Photostat of
    MS. Explanations in English. Metronomes used in performance, re-
    sulting in "maddening end" (from the score). Graphic notation, alea-
    tory sections, parts of works by Bach and Beethoven, improvisation,
    gliding and rolling clusters. Pianists should wear T-shirts with
    "Orgella" in big letters, front and back. The visual is as important as
    the aural. Avant-garde. M-D.

Johannes E. Habert (1833–1896) Germany
Sonata Op.90 (Br&H).

Reynaldo Hahn (1875–1947) France
Caprice Mélancolique 1897 (Heugel; LC) 7pp. Poetic, flowing, subtle, and
    picturesque. A nostalgic little salon piece. M-D.
Le Bal de Béatrice d'Este (Heugel 1905). Suite. Arranged by the com-
    poser for two pianos from the suite for wind instruments, two harps,
    and piano. M-D.
Le Ruban Dénoué (Heugel 1916; LC) 50pp. A suite of twelve waltzes.
    Conventional harmony, rhythm, and pianistic idiom. M-D.
Pour Bercer un Convalescent 1915 (Heugel 1916; University of Louis-
    ville) 11pp. Andantino sans lenteur; Andantino non lento; Andantino
    espressivo. Cool chromatic writing, generally quiet, lovely lines. Int.
    to M-D.

Alexei Haieff (1914–   ) USA, born Russia
Sonata 1945 (Chappell 1954) 15 min. Three contrasting movements writ-
    ten in a combined Romantic and neo-Classic style. Freely tonal,
    large-scale, linear, slim thematic material, accented chords, strong
    rhythms, flexible meters, fast repeated figures, driving coda. D.

Mihaly Hajdu (1909–   ) Hungary
Tre Pezzi 1971 (EMB 1977 Z7986) 16pp., 8 min. Preludio: Allegro, ben
    ritmico; thin textures, motoric, much inversion of lines between in-
    struments, very rhythmic. Intermezzo: Andante moderato, poco

rubato; Impressionistic, parallel chords, clusterlike sonorities accompany disjunct melody. Rondo: Vivace; toccatalike figure in alternating hands, syncopated chords and melody, Bartók influence. M-D.

Aleš Hájek (1937–   ) Czechoslovakia
Sonata 1966 (CHF) 16pp. Directions in Czech. Aleatory, sections in blocks, repeated figuration, clusterlike sonorities, avant-garde. M-D.

Cristobal Halffter (1930–   ) Spain
Halffter has been director of the Madrid Conservatory since 1964. Since the mid-1950s he has used serial techniques.
Processional (UE 15995). For two pianos, winds, and percussion.
Formantes (Movil) Op.26 1961 (MS available from composer) 8 min.
    See: H. Riley, "Aleatoric Procedures in Contemporary Piano Music," *Musical Times,* April 1966:311–12, for an analysis of this work.

Rodolfo Halffter (1900–   ) Mexico, born Spain
Halffter's early works are strongly influenced by Manuel de Falla, with whom the composer studied in 1938. He began using twelve-tone techniques in 1953.
Música para dos pianos Op.29 1965 (EMM) 43pp. Reflected Images: contrasting character (maestoso, impetuoso, tranquillo), proportional rhythmic relationships, serial, dramatic. Cyclic Rotations: changing meters; row is further distilled; sustained writing contrasted with percussive figuration. D.

Calvin Hampton (1938–   ) USA
Hampton is organist at the Calvary Episcopal Church in New York. He has been active in bringing keyboard instruments into the electronic-music age.
Catch-up (CFP 66175 1970). For four pianos, or for two pianos and tape recorder. Versions 1 and 2: 2 playing scores, each 4pp. Performance instructions. A conductor would be helpful. Piano II can be tuned ¼ tone flat. Version 1 may be performed live (when four pianos are available) or recorded in two-channel stereo. Version 2 is performed live against the taped performance of Version 1 and enters at the second measure. Avant-garde notation, aleatory. Letters $\boxed{A}$, $\boxed{B}$, etc., are not rehearsal letters but indicate patterns of related texture occurring at different times in the two versions. Fun for all. M-D.
Triple Play (CFP 66176). For two pianos and ondes martenot, four hands. 7½ min.

Lou Harrison (1917–   ) USA
Concerto in Slendro (CFP 6610 1978) 11 min. For two tackpianos, violin, celesta, and percussion. The title refers to Indonesian modes. The

Far East has inspired Harrison to write some of his finest music. This work has many extraordinary appealing and luxurious sounds. M-D.

Tibor Harsányi (1898–1954) France, born Hungary
Prière (Salabert 1929). Atonal, spontaneous and resourceful writing, some harmonic delicacy. M-D.
Piece (Salabert). Atonal, energetic. Alternates a Tempo di Valse with a Fox-Trot. M-D.

Karl Hasse (1883–1960) Germany
Variations Op.1 (J. M. Reiter-Biedermann 1908; LC) 30pp. Theme, eight variations, and Fugue. In Reger style. M-D.

Paul Hassenstein (1843–1927) Germany
Three Duos Op.43 (C. Simon; Br&H).

Roman Haubenstock-Ramati (1919–   ) Poland
Catch Two 1970 (UE 14881). For one or two pianos. 8–15 min. 10 pages with 2 strips of graphics per page. Instructions in English and German. The player selects one strip prior to performance and plays only one strip per page. Constructed so that the first five pages mirror the second five. Player begins with any leaf and continues in order, as in the classical round or catch. Graphic notation but with specific interpretation of the figurations. Aleatory, avant-garde. M-D.

Charles Haubiel (1894–1980) USA
Miniatures (Composers Press) 10 min. A Mystery. Madonna. Gayety. Shadows. Snowflakes. Festival. Int. to M-D.
Suite Passacaille 1935 (Composers Press) 23 min. Allemande: serious (available at AMC). Menuet: graceful. Sarabande: stately, in Phrygian mode. Gavotte: pompous and brilliant. Neo-Classic style. M-D.

Herbert Haufrecht (1909–   ) USA
Square Set (AMP 1972) 31pp. Originally for string orchestra, arranged for two pianos by the composer. Reel. Clog Dance. Jig Time. Composed as a result of Haufrecht's travels to the Catskill Mountains. Folk tunes included "Ta-ra-ra-Boom De Ay" and "Wilson's Clog." The I and V chords in "Jig Time" simulate the push and pull of an accordian. Light-hearted writing. M-D.

John Haussermann (1909–   ) USA
The following scores are also available directly from the composer: Highland Towers, Apt. 2000, 1071 Celestial Street, Cincinnati, OH 45202.
Prelude and Fugue Op.4 (Senart 1934; LC) 20pp. Neo-Classic style, thick textures in the Prelude. Fugue works to big climax. M-D.
A Pastoral Fantasie Op.5 (Senart 1934; LC) 17pp. Flowing, glissandi, colorful. M-D.

Waltz for Two Pianos Op.33/1,2 (ACA). Available separately. Both of these waltzes have thin textures, are freely tonal, and build to effective closings. No.1 is a little more difficult than No.2. M-D.

John Hawkins (1944–   ) Canada
Etudes for Two Pianos 1974 (CMC) 48pp. No.1: exploits a limited group of intervals—tritones, major and minor sixths, major sevenths, and minor ninths; gradually gains in intensity and speed with constantly shifting gears, before slowly dissipating to upper-register tinklings. No.2: uses a static background to set off a foreground of misfit stops and starts. No.3: pits one pianist's 5/4 against the other's 4/4, while an ostinato chord pattern in one contrasts with the other's basically lyrical passages; *pp* coda. The pieces are basically studies of rhythm and pitch relationships. D.

W. Battison Haynes (1859–1900) Great Britain
Prelude and Fugue Op.6 (K&S 1882; BrM) 9pp. Strong Mendelssohn influence. M-D.

Doris Hays (1941–   ) USA
Hays, born in Chattanooga and now living in New York, is an outstanding pianist. She has composed extensively.
If 1972 (Seesaw). For two pianos and tape, 4pp., 7½ min. Consists of four tape sections and three piano sections, with the tape running continuously. Piano I begins each section, and Piano II enters freely. Any fragment may be repeated any number of times. Clusters, pointillistic, avant-garde. M-D.
Only 1981 (MS, tapes, slides, and film on rental from composer, 697 West End Avenue, New York, NY 10025). For one or two pianos, one or more tapes, optional slides, and optional 8mm film. 8–9 min. Can use some improvisatory skills. M-D.

Maximilian Heidrich (1864–1909) Germany
Suite Op.58 (Leuckart).

Anton Heiller (1923–1979) Austria
Toccata d 1946 (UE 11644) 27pp., 7 min. Fast running figures in 9/8 are juxtaposed against a staccato-like subject; textures become weightier on the way to the brilliant conclusion. Challenging virtuoso piece, faintly dissonant. M-D to D.

Irwin Heilner (1908–   ) USA
Boogie-Woogie Rhapsody (ACA).

William Hellerman (1939–   ) USA
Hellerman is a free-lance composer/performer and Executive Director of The Composer in Performance, Inc., New York. He has composed exten-

sively with electronic sound and written for various instrumental ensembles, expanding into dance and theater-related works as well as the visual arts.

Round and About 1970 (Merion 1980). For any two or more instruments. Chart. 10–13 min. Detailed performance instructions. "This piece is a canon based on the imitation of sound-objects and performance actions instead of pitched melodies. The notation specifies kinds of sounds and approximate speed of performance. The imitation will not be exact. The maximum number of different parts is seven" (from the score). Avant-garde. M-D.

Circle Music 2 1971 (Merion 1980). For any two or more players. Chart. 18 min. "*Capital letter* events are to be given a fixed unvarying definition, identical for all players, that will hold for each trip through the circles. *Lower case* events are never to sound exactly the same as capital letter events" (from the score). Avant-garde. M-D.

Circle Music 3 1971 (Merion 1980). For six players. Chart. 21 min. "Circle Music 3 is a performance construction. Only relationships are established. Any performance events and any approach to over-all form consistent with the relationships used to construct the figure may be employed. The over-all form is based on the interaction of two circle systems. In order that the symmetric nature of the construction be realized, all performances should be primarily polyphonic" (from the score). Avant-garde. M-D.

Everett Helm (1913–   ) USA

Eight Minutes for Two Pianos (AMC) 17pp. Easily Moving: flowing arpeggios, melody in octaves, Impressionistic. Quarter note = 72–76: rhythmic, fast scales, some legatissimo and cantabile sonorities. Song: octotonic melody, parallel chords, bitonal closing. Half note = 72: syncopated chords in one piano against octotonic melody in the other. Freely tonal. M-D.

Eugene Hemmer (1929–1977) USA

Introduction and Dance 1949 (AME 1955; AMC) 12pp. Andantino tranquillo Introduction, many fourths, freely tonal around D; short bridge leads directly to the Dance. The recurring theme in the Dance is adapted from the Appalachian folk song "The Devil's Ten Questions." Glissandi, strong rhythms, fiddle tuning "fifths," tremolo chords at ending, cheerful, attractive. Int.

Dance Sonata 1953 (AMC). Through the Maze; The Initiation; The Revelation; In Celebration.

Gerard Hengeveld (1910–   ) The Netherlands

Suite (PIC 1971) 40pp. Allegro ma non troppo: exuberant, full of quartal and secundal chords. Movement di blues: lives up to its title. Lento—

Allegro: jazz and other dance influence. Dissonant, bold and powerful, intricate rhythms, 40pp. of dynamite. Large span required. M-D.
Seven Sonatinas (Book 1) (B&VP).

Hans Henkemans (1913–   ) The Netherlands
Sonata 1943 (Donemus 1950) 59pp., 23½ min. Four brilliant contrasting
and eclectic movements. Early Beethoven style characteristics
mixed with compositional techniques popular in the 1940s, freely
tonal. Requires complete musicianship. D.

Adolph von Henselt (1814–1889) Germany
If I Were a Bird Op.2/6 (Harcourt Brace). Arranged by the composer,
with slight alterations by unidentified editor. Int. to M-D.
Romance b Op.10 (Br&H 1919) 3pp. Lyric, slow, melodic. M-D.
Duo Op.14 (Cranz). After *Duo* for piano and cello.

Hans Werner Henze (1926–   ) Germany
Divertimenti 1964 (Schott 5444) 57pp. Four weighty movements. Dissonant, much activity for both players, misnamed. D.

Henri Herz (1803–1888) France
Grandes Variations de Concert sur un thème des"Puritains" (Bellini)
"Hexameron" variations. Written in conjunction with Liszt and Thal-
berg. See more complete entry under Liszt.
Duo du Couronnement Op.104 (Schott).
Grand Duo sur les Huguenots Op.208 (Schott).

Henri Herz (1803–1888) and **Jacques Simon Herz** (1794–1880) France
Variations and Rondo Brilliant Op.16 (Schott). *Second grand Duo concertant sur les Marches favorites d'Alexandre et de La Donna del
Lago* Op.72 (Schott 4333 18?; LC) 13pp. Theme, three variations,
expansive finale. Brilliance with dated harmonic usage. M-D.

Heinrich von Herzogenberg (1843–1900) Germany
Theme with Variations D♭ Op.13 (Dob 1895). Pleasant and mild but not
terribly impressive. M-D.

Hans Joachim Hespos (1938–   ) Germany
Tja: Für Zwei Pianisten 1981 (Harrassowitz C2HES0000017) 4pp.
Graphic score, mostly text. Explanations in German.

Kurt Hessenberg (1908–   ) Germany
Fantasie Op.19 1938 (Müller 1263) 13 min. Basically Classical in style but
contains Wagnerian elements in dramatic passages. M-D.

Jacques Hétu (1938–   ) Canada
Hétu teaches at the University of Quebec in Montreal. In 1978 he wrote:
"The essential is not to try to find a completely novel way of organizing

sounds but rather to discover one's own way of perceiving music. To me, true originality is more authentic than eccentric" (*Jacques Hétu, Compositeurs au Quebec,* No. 10, Centre de musique Canadienne, Montreal). *Sonate* Op.6 1962 (Berandol) 13 min. Allegro; Adagio; Vivace. Shows influence of Bartók and Hindemith by expanded tonality. Uses a vocabulary that is both contemporary and personal. Exploits contrasting sonorities. Well organized but slightly contrived. M-D.

Ernst Heuser (–   ) Germany
Pastoral Theme with Variations and Tarantella Op.50 (R&E).
Easy Variations on an American Folk Song (Dip, Boys, Dip the Oar) Op.68 (K&S 1909; LC). Int.

Ethel Glenn Hier (1889–   ) USA
Bells of Asolo 1940 (AMC).
Theme and Variations 1938 (AMC) 24pp. Theme and ten contrasting variations. Last one is the longest and contains subsections. Post-Romantic style. M-D.

Edward Burlingame Hill (1872–1960) USA
Jazz Studies 1922–38 (GS; LC; LAP has No.1). Four excellent examples of improvised jazz; well crafted. M-D.

Jackson Hill (1941–   ) USA
Hill received his doctorate from the University of North Carolina at Chapel Hill and studied composition there with Roger Hannay. He has also worked with Iain Hamilton. In 1977 he studied in Japan and has made a speciality of Japanese traditional music. He is chairman of the Music Department, Bucknell University, Lewisburg, PA 17837.
Tōrō Nagashi 1977 (Lanterns of Hiroshima) (MS available from composer) 10 min. "Tōrō Nagashi is the ceremony of sending lighted candles placed on small rafts downstream and out to sea to symbolize the return of human spirits to earth. At dusk in Hiroshima on the 6th of August each year, candles are set afloat in the Ota-Motoyasu river beside Peace Memorial Park to commorate the 60,000 lives that were lost in the atomic blast of August, 1945" (from the score). Freely sectional, Impressionistic, pentatonic, colorful, pointillistic influence, effective throughout. Improvisation required; some "notes need not be struck absolutely together." Exploits resources of both instruments in a highly musical manner. M-D.

Ferdinand Hiller (1811–1885) Germany
Hiller's Romantic style was strongly influenced by Mendelssohn.
Duett über Luetzows Wilde Jagd von Carl M. von Weber Op.108 (Schott 20450; LC; Oberlin Conservatory Library) 15pp. A Vivace chromatic

scalar introduction leads to the first main section, Allegro energico. Four other sections follow, each exploiting contrasting mood and figuration. Dated but fun to play. Int. to M-D.
Grand Duet Op.135 (R&E; Novello).

Lejaren Hiller (1924–   ) USA

Fantasy for Three Pianos 1951 (MS available from composer, c/o Department of Music, State University of New York at Buffalo, Buffalo, NY 14214; SBTS) 71pp., 16½ min. "In 1951, I was asked by three young Venezuelan pianists who had formed a trio to write a composition for them, thus adding something to an obviously very limited repertory. I did so, but by the time I finished this piece, the group had broken up and so that ended immediate performance possibilities. The one salvage job I did at the time was to score it as the finale of my *Symphony* No. 1, still an unperformed composition.

"The problem, as I saw it, was essentially one of how to justify the presence on the stage of three pianos and how to have the three pianists kept busy doing things that are not just doublings for sonority. The texture of the composition, consequently, is frequently quite busy and comprises multiple theme combinations. Overall, this single movement composition is in sonata form in B-flat minor, to which is attached an extended coda in G major. Though basically tonal, it is also rather modal in cast (flattened leading tones, and so forth). It pretty much concludes the early period of my music writing, during which I was most concerned with learning traditional compositional know-how.

"*Fantasy for Three Pianos* was finally performed for the first time in Buffalo in April 1976" (note from the composer). Allegro; Moderato: full chords, tremolo, extended arpeggio figuration, fast octaves, strong triplet chords lead to final climax. M-D.

Suite for Two Pianos and Tape 1966 "A Triptych for Hieronymus" (TP rental catalog; AMC) 19 min. Part of a larger work called *A Triptych for Hieronymus,* for dancers, actors, film, slide projections, tape, and orchestra. The *Suite* is not merely a transcription of excerpts but a piece with its own reasons for existence. The three movements, each of which is made up of one or more subsections, are played without pause: I. Retrospect: Animal Dance; Estampie. II. Circumspect: Carnival Time; Sonata a Cuatro; Magician's Waltz; Vox Humana; Grand Parade. III. Prospect: Intrada. Tape cues have been transcribed into the score. The loudspeakers for the left channel may be placed relatively nearer to Piano I, the loudspeaker for the right channel nearer to Piano II. An alternate plan is to place the four sound sources (two pianos, two tape tracks) in the four corners of a square room. A third performer is required to operate the tape recorder. Much parody; clever craft infused with sonic mischief; perhaps too long. M-D.

A Cenotaph for Two Pianos 1971 (MS available from composer). "Webster's dictionary states that a cenotaph is 'an empty tomb erected in honor of some deceased person; a monument erected to one who is buried elsewhere; as a *cenotaph* in Westminister Abbey. "A *cenotaph* his name and title kept"—Dryden'.

"When Frina and Kenwyn Boldt asked me if I could write a composition for two pianos for them, I happened to be thinking about how all academically respectable authorities on music have condemned the interval of the perfect fifth, chains of parallel fifths and most of all, triads major and minor, as absolutely inadmissible to today's compositional vocabulary. Consequently, I decided to write a work comprised of nothing but perfect fifths, chains of parallel fifths and triads. Every sound in this score is doubled by at least one fifth and most of them are triads as well. Hence the title—among other things, this is a cenotaph in honor of our dearly departed friends. It is in one movement played *pietrosamente* ($\flat$ = 60). It possesses a symmetrical archform assembled from eighteen-bar components. It is also a symmetrically constructed array of vertical sonorities, F over B in the first half, B over F in the second part" (note from the composer).

Paul Hindemith (1895–1963) Germany

Two pianos are an ideal medium for Hindemith's contrapuntal style.

Quartet 1938 (Schott). For clarinet, violin, cello, and piano. Transcribed by the composer for two pianos. 24 min. Mässig bewegt; Sehr langsam; Mässig bewegt—Lebhaft. This transcription has been made in a straightforward way and may be enjoyed by two skilled players. A comparison of this score with the original will show that much of the transcription is very literal, and a little unimaginative in places. M-D to D.

Sonata C 1942 (Schott 3970) 42pp., 16 min. Facsimile, easy to read. Chimes: majestic opening, canonic figure, chord-chimes toll melody over orchestral bells in Piano II. Allegro: four subjects, rhythmic bite necessary. Canon: free recitative based on a fourteenth-century literary quotation, "This World's Joy," leads to final Fugue. With two players the opposing rhythms take on more character. The phrasing of the work must be primed toward the rhythmic shape of the line. Strong neo-Baroque posturings; clear, if a little crowded, tonality; animated counterpoint; generally transparent texture. D.

Voizech Hlaváč (1849–1911) Czechoslovakia

Suite f (Br&H 1882; BrM) 20pp. Prélude; Scherzino; Nocturne (based on

Chopin Nocturne Op.55); Valse (mixes Chopin Valses Op.64/2 and Posthumous in e); Eglogue; Finale zu Chopin Op.25/2 (Etude f). M-D.

Emil Hlobil (1901–   ) Czechoslovakia
Sonata Op.55 1958 (CHF 497) 55pp., 19 min. Allegro vivace; Grave; Allegro con brio. Rich in ideas, many musical motifs, freely dissonant but basically tonal, strong dynamic contrasts, neo-Classic. M-D.

R. Bruce Hobson (1943–   ) USA
Sonata 1971 (Mobart; AMC) 43pp., 18 min. One large movement. Proportional rhythmic relationships, changing meters, expressionistic, restless, emotional excitement, tempo fluctuations, fast dynamic changes, Bartók and Berg influence. Large span required; only for the most experienced ensemble pianists. D.

Edwin Michael Hoffman (–   ) USA
March Mock Heroic (AMC 194?). For piano and organ or two pianos. 26pp. "Based on 'Marching through Georgia' and an Indian-like quality representing the essence of 'America the Beautiful' " (from the score). The major ideas seem to struggle constantly! M-D.

Heinrich Hoffmann (1842–1902) Germany
March, Novelette and Waltz Op.103 (Br&H 1890?). For two pianos, eight hands. Each piece is published separately. Late nineteenth-century traditional style. M-D.

Oskar Hoffmann (–   ) Germany
Fantasia appassionata Op.20 (Rieter—Biedermann).
Toccata and Fugue Op.32 (W. Gebauer).

Alexis Hollaender (1840–1924) Germany
Theme and Variations Op.15 (Lienau).
Variations on a Theme of Schubert Op.61 (C. F. Kahnt 1905; LC). A simple waltz theme is treated to fourteen variations followed by a Tempo di Menuetto that concludes with a furious flourish. M-D.
Ländler Op.64 (Stahl 1908; LC) 34pp. Eight contrasting pieces in an overblown nineteenth-century Romantic style. M-D.

Karl Höller (1907–   ) Germany
Toccata, Improvisation, and Fugue Op.16 (Leuckart).

G. Augustus Holmes (–   ) Great Britain
Fantasia on "Les Cloches de Corneville" by R. Planquett (J. Williams 1893; BrM). For two pianos, eight hands.

Gustav Holst (1874–1934) Great Britain
The Planets Op.32 (Curwen 1979). Arranged by the composer for two

pianos; foreword by Imogen Holst. Mars; Venus; Mercury; Jupiter; Saturn; Uranus; Neptune. Published separately. The faster-moving parts are the most effective. M-D.

Eduard Horn (1881–   ) Germany
Duo Op.5 (K&S).

Anthon van der Horst (1899–1965) The Netherlands
Sonata in modo conjuncto Op.51c 1951 (Donemus) 14 min. Poco andante; Poco adagio, possibile; Finale (doppio movimento). A modulazione section appears four bars before the Finale. A Cadenza and Epilogo are part of the Finale. Freely tonal, octotonic; has an affinity with Max Reger's style. M-D to D.

Zoltan Horusitzky (1903–   ) Hungary
Sonata 1973 (EMB Z.7320 1975) 30pp. Andante con moto: expressive opening leads to Più mosso, molto agitato with sweeping gestures; other sections gradually return to character of opening sections; *ppp* closing. Adagio: develops a brooding chromatic idea; Impressionistic. Allegro vivace: strong rhythms; octotonic; mixed meters (3/8 + 2/8 + 3/8 in a Vivace con bravura section and 3/16 + 2/16 + 3/16 Presto possible) conclude this exciting movement. MC. M-D.

William Hoskins (–   ) USA
Elegy and Toccata (ACA 1961) 11pp. Adagio, molto sostenuto: quiet sonorous legato chords grow into tremolo figurations and return to opening chords. The Age of Iron: thunderous toccata with fast-moving octaves, chords, and trills; freely tonal. M-D.
Queensboro Suite (ACA 1964) 28pp. Scherzo: "Social Whirl," Allegro amabile, freely tonal, 5/8, numerous tempo and mood changes, octotonic, white-key clusters, fairly thick textures. M-D.

Patrick Houlihan (1953–   ) USA
Houlihan is a product of the University of Mississippi and Florida State University.
Contrasts 1977 (MS available from composer: c/o Music Department, Mississippi Valley State University, Itta Bena, MS 38941) 7 min. Two untitled movements. "My aim in writing *Contrasts* was to produce a rather simple piece; simple, that is, to the listener. Short, clearly recognizable motives comprise all thematic material, and the formal structure is quite easily perceived. Each motive is treated primarily, though not exclusively, in one piano part. The material of each part is contrasted with that of the other through much of the work. Also contrasted are the roles of the two parts. The listener must decide in each passage whether one part accompanies the other

or if the two are equal in significance" (letter to the author, March 31, 1981). Expressionistic, strings struck with bass drum mallet, length of sections indicated by number of seconds, clusters. M-D.

Alan Hovhaness (1911–   ) USA
Hovhaness has drawn consistently from a single tradition, that of Armenian modal music and its traditional instruments and related lore. He uses a great deal of repetition or variation of melodic lines as well as the polyphonic intermingling of figures and arabesques.
Mihr Op.60/1 1946 (Merion) MS reproduction. Flexible meters, keys, and tempos. Mihr is an ancient Armenian fire god. Imitates a kanoon (zither) orchestra. Percussive, repeated notes. Solo sections for each piano. M-D.
Vijag Op.37 (CFP 6559 1964) 9pp., 4½ min. Captures the "spirit of an old Armenian Festival." A plaintive song grows from a rapid figure that is repeated, with slight variations, throughout the piece. Single melodic line, toccatalike continuous sixteenth notes are divided between hands. Piano I holds damper pedal down throughout the work and creates a drone. Requires good finger dexterity. M-D.
Ko-Ola-U Op.136 (CFP 6530) 3 min. Hovhaness' six months in Hawaii in 1962 as composer-in-residence gave him the opportunity to study Polynesian chants and mythology. This piece is a contemporary homage to the Ko-Ola-U Mountains. White keys throughout, duplets in Piano II against triplets in Piano I (with pedal held throughout), quartal harmonies, polytonal, clusters. Int. to M-D.
O Lord, Bless Thy Mountains Op.276 (ACA).

Egil Hovland (1924–   ) Norway
Varianti Op.47 1964 (NMO 8538) 15 min. Uses plectrum on strings, fingertips to create glissandi on strings. Some unusual notation. Twenty variants on a twelve-tone row, a compendium of contemporary piano styles. The reason for the designation *variants* is that these are not *variations* in the usual meaning of that word. The variants are on loose sheets and can be played in any order but the variant marked omega is always the conclusion. Explores freely the latent possibilities of a series with regard to a varied treatment of intervals, rhythm, meter, dynamics, and sound. Some tempos measured in seconds. Tempo regulated by dynamics in variant 8: the repetition is performed *ritardando* with the volume decreasing from *fff* to *ppp*. It is repeated many times until *ppp* is reached. D.

Mary Howe (1882–1964) USA
Berceuse (BMC).
Castellana (Romansca on Spanish Themes) (AMC) 42pp. Originally for two pianos and orchestra. Arranged for two pianos by the composer. Sectionalized; Spanish rhythms and lush harmonies. M-D.

Three Spanish Folk Tunes 1926 (BMC; AMC; LC) 7pp. each. Available separately. Habanera de cinna. Spanish Folk-Dance. Petenera (Folk Song). Somewhat dated but contain a certain amount of charm. Int. to M-D.

Herbert Howells (1892–1983) Great Britain
Polka 1951 (Novello) 12pp. Freely tonal, varied and contrasted sections, rubato, octotonic, strong rhythms. M-D.

Karl Hoyer (1891–   ) Germany
Fantasie und Doppelfuge (Leuckart 1914; LC) 27pp. Active writing throughout with energetic fugue subjects, bombastic conclusion. M-D.

Hans Huber (1852–1921) Switzerland
Huber's eclectic style shows strong influences of Brahms, Liszt, and Schumann.
Sonata B♭ Op.31 (Br&H; LC). An expansive Langsam section leads immediately to an Allegro con fuoco. Virtuoso writing. M-D to D.
Improvisations Op.64 (Etudes on an original theme) (Rieter—Biedermann; BrM). 23 contrasting improvisations (short variations) on the main idea. Melodious and well worked out. M-D.
Sonata II E♭ Op.121 (Br&H 1905; LC) 72pp. Three expansive movements. In Reger style. M-D to D.
Sonata giocosa Op.126 (Steingraber 1908; LC) 52pp. Four large movements with the finale a Perpetuum mobile. Much chromatic usage. M-D.

Johann Nepomuk Hummel (1778–1837) Austria
Introduction and Rondo E♭ Op.Posthumous No.5 (Br&H; LC) 11pp. Colorful; uses chromaticism (especially chromatic scale) to exploit vast expressiveness of upper range of keyboard; bold harmonic usage especially in modulations; lyric melodies that do not lend themselves to development; frequent brilliant passages. Dynamic energy, somewhat Schubertian in manner. Feeds the auditory nerves and caresses the intelligence. M-D.

Richard Hunt (1930–   ) Canada, born Great Britain
Merkabah 1973 (CMC) 59pp., 12 min. The composer describes this piece as a study in "stereophony," giving the pianists identical material with only limited changes in rhythm and dynamics. Takes off on occasional Impressionistic flights, with these flurries of activity broken up by static, "sound piece" passages. Could use basically stronger material. Harmonics, plucked strings. "Dynamic marks refer more to *touch* than actual sound" (from the score). Pianos

should be placed symmetrically at the extreme left and right of stage with both lids removed. M-D.

Ilja Hurnik (1922–   ) Czechoslovakia
Fantasie (CHF 1980) 39pp., 11 min. Impetuoso: declamatory opening punctuated with octaves and running octotonic figures, leads to Grazioso: 9/8, more lyric than lilting; moves to Marcia: marcato, pompous and jiglike; a più vivo buoys up the conclusion. The piece is an exploration of timbral and coloristic effects. M-D.
Stravinskiana (CHF 1969) 28pp.
Two large sectionalized movements: Marcia; Allegretto. Exploits all the neo-Classic characteristics of Stravinsky and Hindemith. Embraces tonality, lyricism, and contemporary sounds. There is much frantic business that never seems to jell. M-D.

Karel Husa (1921–   ) Czechoslovakia
Eight Czech Duos 1955 (Schott 4779 1957) 36pp., 18 min. Although originally written for piano four-hands, the composer suggests the two-piano idiom as also appropriate for performing these works. Overture. Rondeau. Melancholic Song. Solemn Procession. Elegie. Little Scherzo. Evening, Slovak Dance. Unusual rhythmic patterns; melodies derive from Czech folk music. Moods vary from pensiveness to exuberance. Int. to M-D.

Peter Huse (1938–   ) Canada
Sonata for Two Pianos 1962 (CMC) 15½ min. Adagio; Andante; Allegro; Largo. A highly organized work with unusual directions for performance: "with love, with power, with power and love, with love and power, with a passion for action." Final instructions are "may be repeated ad infinitum." Thin, pointillistic textures. M-D.

I

Jacques Ibert (1890–1962) France
La Licorne ou The Triumph of Chastity (Editions Françaises de Musique).

Toshi Ichiyangi (1933–   ) Japan
Two Existences 1980 (Schott SJ1004) 19pp.

Vincent d'Indy (1851–1931) France
D'Indy's style was greatly influenced by his teacher, César Franck.
Symphony on a French Mountain Air Op.25 (Hamelle). Arranged for two
    pianos, six hands, by the composer; one player at piano A, two
    players at piano B. Complex, severe, and intellectual writing. M-D
    to D.

Manuel Infante (1883–1958) Spain
Trois Danses Andalouses 1921 (Salabert) 14 min. Ritmo. Sentimento.
    Gracia. Based on characteristic rhythms and the Andalusian scale,
    which is the Phrygian mode with a raised third. Colorful; appealing
    Spanish dances with a flare and occasional lyric melodies; pianistic.
    Ritmo is the most effective. M-D.
Musiques d'Espagne 1941 (Salabert). Suite on Spanish themes. Exciting
    Impressionistic recital literature. M-D.

Yoshiro Irino (1921–   ) Japan
Music for Two Pianos 1963 (Ongaku No Tomo) 16pp., 8 min. Fast chang-
    ing meters, twelve-tone, expressionistic, clusters, contrasted sec-
    tions, *pp* conclusion. M-D.

Charles Ives (1874–1954) USA
Three Quarter-Tone Piano Pieces 1923–24. Possibly derived from piano
    pieces of 1903–4 (G. Pappastavrou—CFP 66285) 26pp., 11 min. Piano
    II is tuned ¼ tone higher than normal pitch. Largo: atmospheric,
    haunting, primarily diatonic. Allegro: jazzy dance tune sounds very
    twangy with these tunings; rhythms contrasted on "split" between
    the two pianos. Chorale: combines wit with serious exploration. "My

Country 'Tis of Thee" appears in frantic fragmentation side-by-side with microtone remembrances of four-voice chorale style. Augmented and syncopated chords, ragtime elements, alternating melodic tones between the pianos. M-D.

See: George Pappastavrou, "Ives Quarter-Tone Pieces," *Clavier,* 13 (October 1974):31–32.

Harry Perison, "The Quarter-Tone System of Charles Ives," CM, 18 (1974):96–104.

Judith Tick, "Ragtime and the Music of Charles Ives," CM, 18 (1974):105–13.

Calcium Light Night 1907? (Merion 1964). For two pianos, six winds (piccolo, oboe, clarinet, bassoon, trumpet or cornet in B♭, and trombone), and two drums (snare drum and bass drum). Arranged and edited by Henry Cowell in collaboration with the composer. 2½ min. Slow march time. "Accel. and cresc. little by little until turning point, measure 34; slowing and decres. little by little from measure 44 to end" (from the score). Pianos are used primarily for color and rhythmic drive. Some clusterlike sonorities. M-D.

J

Najla Jabôr (–   ) Brazil
Pandemônio 1952 (OMB) 5 min. No.3 from *Suite of 3 Movements*. Originally for solo piano; transcribed for two pianos by the composer.
Fantasia Oriental 1957 (OMB) 6 min.
Um Burrinho vendedor de agua 1972 (OMB) 2 min. Originally for solo piano; transcribed for two pianos by the composer.
Branca de Nive 1973 (OMB) 2 min. Transcribed by the composer for two pianos.
Somente . . . saudate: valsa No.2 1973 (OMB).

Frederick Jacobi (1891–1952) USA
Four Dances from the Prodigal Son (AMC 1946). Polka: rhythmic drive, octaves, chromatic mid-section. Polonaise: con bravura, sudden key shifts, delicate chromatic triplets, cadenzalike sweeps near end, single line high register conclusion. Waltz: strong tonal feeling with modulatory freedom. Tarantella: lighthearted, good frolicking conclusion. M-D.

Maurice Jacobson (1896–   ) Great Britain
Ballade (Elkin 1939) 23pp. One movement. Varied sections, tempos, and moods. Short-winded themes seem to go nowhere. M-D.
Fantasia on a Theme by Tallis (Curwen).
Prelude to a Play 1939 (Lengnick).

Solomon Jadassohn (1831–1902) Germany
Jadassohn was once a well-known theorist and composer.
Chaconne Op.82 (K&S).

Pal Járádnyi (1920–1966) Hungary
Sonata (EMB 2839 1948; BrM) 40pp.

Zoltán Jeney (1943–   ) Hungary
Desert Plants (EMB Z8310 1978) 36pp. For two pianos or two prepared pianos. Note in Hungarian and English for piano preparations. Pointillistic, notation given in terms of seconds, highly organized, dynam-

ics serialized. Similar in style to John Cage's *Etudes Australes* for solo piano. "The material used to prepare the piano and the distribution of it over the required strings can be selected freely, but corresponding notes on the two instruments have to be prepared in the same way" (from the score). Avant-garde. D.

Alden Ferriss Jenks (1940–) USA
Marrying Music 1979 (MS available from composer: 1201 Ortega St., San Francisco, CA 94122) 18 min. One movement. M-D.

Joseph Joachim (1831–1907) Germany
Ouvertüre zu Shakespeare's Heinrich IV (Simrock 1902; LC) 39pp. Originally for orchestra; arranged for two pianos by Johannes Brahms. Beautifully laid out between the instruments. The two performers have equal assignments. M-D.

Svend Aaquist Johansen (–) Denmark
Songs in Between Op.5 1970 (MIC). For two pianos, soprano, and tenor.

Roy Johnson (1933–) USA
Variations 1972 (MS available from composer: c/o School of Music, Florida State University, Tallahassee, FL 32306) 32pp. Cantando theme followed by six contrasting variations. An Interlude appears between variations 3 and 4. Neo-Classic, well constructed, effective writing. M-D.

André Jolivet (1905–1974) France
Hopi Snake Dance (P. Noël 1953) 28pp.

Marinus de Jong (1891–) Belgium
Habanera Op.62 (CeBeDeM 1963) 16pp., 6 min. Facsimile score. Colorful and lively; nineteenth-century style. M-D.

Léon Jongen (1884–1969) Belgium
Campeador 1935 (CeBeDeM) 9 min.
Divertissement en forme de variations sur un thème de Joseph Haydn 1958 (CeBeDeM) 15 min.

Erik Jørgensen (1912–) Denmark
Quintet 1962 (MIC). For two pianos, two percussion players, and double bass.

Rafael Joseffy (1852–1915) Hungary
Märchen—Scherzo Fantastique (Prochazka 1884; LC) 23pp. Dedicated to Theodor Thomas. Cheerful, bright, molto vivace. Requires fleet fingers. M-D.

Wilfred Joseph (1927–) Great Britain
Doubles Op.85 (B. Ramsey 1979). Twice 22 doubles on two themes by

two composers for two pianos. This work "left us in no doubt that we were hearing a major contribution to the repertoire. Josephs' juxtaposition of Mozart and Rameau (the A minor Rondo K.511 and La Poule) provided a fascinating *mélange* of echoes and influences as well as a marriage of dazzling incongruity. Given such deliberate oddity the result amounted to something far more expressive and suggestive than mere mockery. *Doubles* is surely a beautifully rewarding work with Mozart's closing bars forming an oddly moving epilogue" (Bryce Morrison, M&M, January 1979, p. 49). This "double formula" has generated a work demanding enormous energy from two fine pianists to meet the composer's outpouring of brilliant music, and to "point up" the subtle humor. M-D to D.

Werner Josten (1888–1963) USA, born Germany
Jungle (Symphonic Movement) 1928 (AMP 1940; AMC) 32pp. Arranged for two pianos by the composer. Sectionalized; varied sonorities, tempos, and textures; Impressionistic; programmatic influence. M-D.

A. Junkelmann (–   ) Germany
Andante with Variations Op.22 (Br&H).

Paul Juon (1872–1940) Germany, born Russia
Sonata c Op.221 (after Sextette Op.22) (Lienau; ECS; LC) 79pp. Moderato; Tema. Andantino quasi Allegretto: theme and variations 1–5. Menuetto: variations 6 and 7. Intermezzo: variation 8 plus Largo coda. Finale—Allegro non troppo. Broad nineteenth-century gestures; Brahms influence. D.
Jotunheimen ("Northland" tone poem) Op.71 (Lienau 1924; ECS; Northwestern University) 40pp. Colorful, dramatic, chromatic, sectionalized, long trills, glissandi, restful *ppp* closing. Late Romantic style that is sometimes stronger on craft than inspiration. M-D.

K

Pal Kadosa (1903–   ) Hungary
Since 1945 Kadosa has been professor and dean of the piano faculty at the
Liszt Academy in Budapest.
Sonata Op.37 1946 (EMB Z3665) 68pp. Allegro impetuoso; Andante;
  Vivace. Extensive work in Bartók style (although Kadosa studied
  with Kodály). Vigorous and robust, thorough exploitation of the in-
  struments. M-D to D.

Mauricio Kagel (1931–   ) Germany, born Argentina
Metapiece (Mimetics) (UE 1961) 13pp. folded into one long accordian-like
  page. Can be performed as solo, by two pianos, as piano duet, or with
  other instruments. Includes detailed explanation. Diagrammatic notation in part. Stones can be placed on the strings and/or on the
  keyboard. Kagel asks the player to slap with the free hand, the palm
  of the hand pressing a note simultaneously with the playing of that
  note, to provide a percussive clap that will enhance the note played.
  Many clusters and pointillistic figurations. Avant-garde. D.

Jouni Kaipainen (1956–   ) Finland
Kaipainen studied composition at the Sibelius Academy under Aulis Salli-
nen and Paavo Heininen. His compositions include several large works.
"Ladders to Fire" (Concerto for two pianos) Op.14 (Finnish Music Information Centre) 21 to 24 min. The title is a quotation from a novel by
  Anais Nin. The main idea is textural polarity between the two pianos
  and subsequent tension between the players. This polarity takes different forms in each of the three movements. Passionate polarities:
  introduction, three expositions, three canons, and a developing section; the introduction, as well as each of the expositions, presents
  first a wild and sharp form of the textural polarity, then undergoes a
  process of relaxing the tension to zero point, i.e., a point where both
  players actually "do the same thing." Emotive expansion: contains
  much of the same material as the first movement, but the textural
  polarity lies deeper in the music; and although a situation of two
  rivals is also present here, the main concept of this movement is

101

much more cooperative than that of the first; this movement is more like a rest between two dramatic movements, between a development and a recapitulation; in the chorale section, the gradually increasing exaggeration of the "strange" elements is to be done clearly and totally, giving time for things to happen. Sequential solutions: open form, consists of six sections, the first five of which may be performed in any order; the sixth must always be performed as the finale; each section represents one single "solution" to the problems that have come forth during the playing of the first two movements, and thus it is the players' duty to put these "solutions" in an order that reflects their idea about the macrostructure of the piece. Proportional rhythmic relationships, clusters, some graphic notation. Both pianos should have a sostenuto pedal. Improvisation required. Further instructions in English footnotes and in the text. Avant-garde. D.

Hermann Josef Kaiser (1938–   ) Germany
Pas de Deux 1961 (Edition Modern 1124) 15 min.

Sharon E. Kanach (–   ) USA
Spontaneous Dialogue 1978 (ACA) 26pp., 19 min. Staccato sempre; Slow; Rather fast. Fast chromatic figuration, clusters with block of wood, chain to be placed in upper range of piano, pianists must tap on the wood underneath keyboard with knuckles. Harmonics, string glissandi, pointillistic, avant-garde. D.

Udo Kasemets (1919–   ) Canada, born Estonia
Since around 1960 Kasemets has been interested in chance operations, investigations of new timbres and new performance methods, tape composition, and particularly the area of mixed-media invention. He is music critic for the Toronto *Daily Star*.

$\sqrt[5]{5}$——— 1962–63 (Berandol 1969) 8 min. For two performers using two pianos and selected percussion instruments. An essay in piano (and percussion) sonorities. Players can choose the sequence of the happenings and have much freedom in interpreting the information provided in the parts. Despite this apparent freedom the work is rigidly organized, its form being derived from various operations with the number 5. Essentially graphic notation, though use is made of many conventional symbols. 25 second-long pages, each containing five 5-second blocks of musical events. Avant-garde. D.

Howard Kasschau (–   ) USA
Country Concerto for Young Pianists (GS). Good introduction to concerto form. Int.

Lucjan M. Kaszycki (–   ) Poland
Expositions 1964 (PWM 1970; LC) 11pp. Tempo ad libitum, ma maestoso;
Lento; Allegro; Possible presto. Contrasting movements; tremolo
chords between hands repeat certain sections for number of seconds
indicated; conventional and unconventional notation. M-D.

Dieter Kaufmann (1941–   ) Germany
Boleromaniaque (Edition Reimers). No. 12 in Avanti series, Olympic
games for keyboard instruments.

Hugo Kaun (1863–1932) Germany
Suite im alten Stil Op.81 (Heinrichshofen).
Suite Op.92 (Zimmermann 1913; University of Louisville; LC) 63pp. Mär-
kische Heide; Abendstimmung; Menuett; Nachtgesang; Aus Grosser
Zeit. Extended work in style similar to Max Reger. Requires endur-
ance (for performer and audience!). D.

Roland Kayn (1933–   ) Germany
Divertimento 1955 (SZ 8821 1982) 37pp.

Wendell Keeney (1903–   ) USA
Spanish Capriccio (JF 1935: LC) 13pp. Allegro introduction leads to sec-
tion based on "La cucaracha"; followed by "Boleras Sevillanas."
Brilliant conclusion requires fine technique. M-D.
Mountain Tune (GS 1936; AMC) 11pp. Catchy folk tune handled color-
fully. Kind of a mountain "hoe-down"! Int. to M-D.

Frederick S. Kelly (1881–1916) Austria
Theme, Variations, and Fugue Op.5 (Schott 1913; BrM).

Rudolf Kelterborn (1931–   ) Switzerland
In 1968 Kelterborn became professor of composition and music analysis
at the Zurich Musikhochschule and in 1969 editor-in-chief of
Schweizerische Musikzeitung. He has appeared as guest conductor in
Switzerland and Germany.
Sonata (Br 3505 1959) 11½ min. Toccata I: punctuated chords contrasted
with linear section. Ritornell: relaxed and flowing. Toccata II: brilliant motoric octotonic triplets. Serial; changes of tempo are also
subject to serialization. Both melody and harmony are derived from a
basic tone row, with intervals of minor seconds and major sevenths
used as mainstays. M-D to D.

Talivaldis Kenins (1919–   ) Canada, born Latvia
Concertino for Two Pianos Alone 1956 (CMC) 44pp., 13½ min. Allegro
non troppo; Adagio espressivo; Molto animato e scherzando. Well
written, idiomatic and pianistically effective rather than musically

satisfying, in a contemporary vein although not extremely dissonant. The third movement is written in a toccata-like motoric style. M-D.

Folk Danse, Variations and Fugue 1963 (CMC; University of Toronto) 16pp. For two pianos, eight hands. Carefully laid out for all parts. The folk dances and variations are short and sectionalized. The simple fugue subject is not overly worked. Attractive and MC. Int.

Harrison Kerr (1897–1978) USA
Dance Suite (ACA). For two pianos and five percussionists.

Jan Willen Kersbergen (1857–1937) The Netherlands
Variations and Fugue on No. 1 from "Eriks Liederschatz" Op.5 (R&E).

Ella Ketterer (　　–　　)
Grand Caprice Hongroise, Etude de Concert Op.7 (Schott).
Marche Orientale Op.92b (Schott).

Eunice Lee Kettering (1906–　　) USA
Rigadoon (GS 1970) 11pp. Thin textures, octotonic, clever syncopation, tuneful, *pp* closing. M-D.

Piet Ketting (1904–　　) The Netherlands
Preludium, Interludium e Postludium 1969–71 (Donemus 1977) 50pp., 18 min. Preludium: lengthy and exciting Agitato movement; two main ideas divided between the two instruments, who vie with each other to gain dominance; full range of keyboard exploited. Interludium: Lento; players exchange pianos; plucked strings; Impressionistic sonorities; no barlines; great rhythmic freedom; octaves and large chords. Postludium: players return to original positions; staccato fugue subject and countersubject lead to all types of fugal treatment; prestissimo ending; powerful demands on both players. A large dramatic work, dissonant, clusters, quartal harmonies, traditional figuration, octaves. D.

Aram Khatchaturian (1903–1978) USSR
Suite 1948 (CFP 4738; K 3585; MCA) 32pp., 10 min. Ostinato: melody against a three-note ostinato. Romance: lyric, Armenian characteristics. Fantastic Waltz: flashy, effective. In the style of the Rachmaninoff suites but lacking their harmonic vigor and brilliant effect. Colorful, extrovert writing. M-D.

Bruno Kiefer (1923–　　) Brazil, born Germany
Vendavais: Prenúncios 1971 (OMB) 9 min.

Wilhelm Killmayer (1927–　　) Germany
Paradies 1972 (Schott ED6694 1977). For piano three hands, or two pianos, 15pp. Instructions in German only. Ostinato in bass through-

out (300 bars), one gradual crescendo from beginning to end, freely tonal around E♭, imitation. Chords grow in size to clusterlike proportions, with the fourth hand gradually assisting (if necessary); MC. M-D.

John King (1953–   ) USA
Notes from Underground (the mousehole) (Pembroke 1978) 30pp. Facsimile edition. "Duration is proportional only where seconds are given. Box notation is to be played from left to right, within the duration indicated by the arrows. If the boxes are divided by dotted lines then those sub-sections are to be played from left to right, but may be separated by spaces. All clusters are chromatic. When one piano plays two systems simultaneously, the top system is to be superimposed into the lower system, within the indicated duration" (from the score). Pointillistic, proportional rhythmic notation, dynamic extremes, expressionistic, avant-garde. "It goes without saying that both these *NOTES* and their author are fictitious. Nevertheless, people like the author of these notes may, and indeed must, exist in our society, if we think of the circumstances under which that society has been formed" (at end of score). D.

Theodor Kirchner (1823–1903) Germany
Kirchner was a disciple of Robert Schumann.
Variations on an Original Theme Op.85 (Hofmeister 1888; LC) 28pp. Andante theme followed by ten contrasting variations. Requires mature pianism. M-D.
7 Waltzes Op.68 (CFP 2468 1889).

Yayoi Kitazume (1945–   ) Japan
Inner Space 1978 (Japan Federation of Composers) 13pp. Facsimile score. One page of performance directions. " 'Inner Space' is derived from the title 'Oku no Akima' (literally 'a vacant room in the rear') given to a piece of sculpture by Masayuki Nagare. 'Inner Space' in my work, however, refers to the inner music of the composer, the performer, the audience. . . . To listen to the 'inner music' means to listen to the intervals between sounds, even to pry into the minutest crevices between sounds. Conversely it also means to listen to the vast and boundless spatial sounds. In this work sounds weave an invisible 'thread' as elastic as rubber bands. Sometimes they flag widely or at other times they become so thin and twisted, swaying as if they would break any second" (from the score). Expressionistic, avant-garde. D.

Giselher Klebe (1925–   ) Germany
Sonata Op.4 1952 (Schott 4292) 27pp. Con moto: busy and spirited. An-

dante con grazia: dances lightly; moves directly to Vivo: boogie-woogie, many seventh and ninth chords. Technically expert, fearfully contrived, willfully complex. M-D to D.

John Klein (1915–   ) USA
Three Dances 1943 (AMP 1946; AMC; LC). Jig Waltz: changing meters, freely tonal, more jiglike in outer sections, waltzlike mid-section. Stoop Dance: flowing melodies, mild dissonances, surprise ending. Whirl: motoric rhythms, chromatic octaves, trills, fast distantly related harmonies, *pp* ending. Attractive. M-D.

Richard Rudolf Klein (1921–   ) Germany
Overture, Recitativ and Rondo (Möseler 18.503).

Iwan Knorr (1853–1916) Germany
Knorr lived in Russia a number of years. He became director of the Frankfurt Conservatory in 1908.
Variations and Fugue on a Russian Folk Song Op.8 (Br&H). Effective salon style. M-D.

Frederick Koch (1923–   ) USA
Two Impressions for Two Pianos Op.27 (Seesaw 1972) 15pp. Sophistication. Excitement. Freely tonal, contrast of mood and tempo between movements. Octotonic in one piano, chords in the other; MC. M-D.
12/12 1974 (Seesaw 1976) 27pp. Twelve contrasting sections using techniques such as striking string with timpani mallets, stopping strings, sweeping string with fingertips, plucking strings. Aleatory sections, clusters, avant-garde. M-D.

Charles Koechlin (1867–1950) France
Suite Op.6 (Leduc 1899; LC) 15pp. Four movements. Flowing, strong melodic writing, colorful harmonic usage. M-D.

Rezsö Kokai (1906–1962) Hungary
Sonata 1949 (EMB 1971 Z6546) 64pp. Allegro ostinato: quiet opening leads to vigorous (tutta forza) rhythmic section with glissandi and fast-moving chromatic chords; more lyric mid-section with thinner texture provides expected contrast. Andante variato: strongly contrasted variations that exploit many aspects of piano technique; variety of influences: Debussy, Bartók, Busoni, to mention a few. Presto finale: rhythmic triplets interspersed with freely tonal chords, rondo character. The whole piece displays a tendency to build passages or sections out of germ cells of one, two, or three intervals. M-D.

Barbara Kolb (1939–   ) USA
Kolb was the first American woman composer to receive the Prix de Rome.

Spring River Flowers Moon Night 1974 (Bo&H 1982). For two pianos with instrumental ensemble or prerecorded tape. 20 min. Inspired by an eighth-century Chinese poem, in six continuous movements. Instruments heard on the tape in addition to electronic sounds include: chimes, vibraphone, marimba, mandolin, and guitar. Lyrical, light, sensitive and emotionally descriptive; organic progressions of sonic growth and decay, tension and relaxation. A lovely spellbinding work that recalls George Crumb's style in some aspects. Uses conventional playing as well as percussive effects produced by plucking strings. D.

Heinrich Konietzny (1910–   ) Germany
Toccatina 1969 (Simrock 2940) 10pp. A fast and dissonant work with much syncopation; bitingly hilarious; basically in 5/8; many hammered sevenths. M-D to D.

Thomas Koppel (1944–   ) Denmark
Concert Héroique Op.22 (MIC). For three pianos, choir, and wind machine.

Peter Jona Korn (1922–   ) USA, born Germany
Deborah Suite 1956 Op.32 (Nymphenburg 1974; UCLA; AMC) 11pp. Air: pastoral, flowing; centers around c. Presto Ostinato: octotonic, imitative, works to large climax. Largo Ostinato: bitonal chordal sonorities in one instrument with octotonic figuration in the other, mildly dissonant. M-D.

Arkadie Koughell (1896–   ) USA, born Russia
Slavonic Rhapsody (Barger & Barclay 1957; AMC) 23pp. Contrasting sections, modal, freely tonal, octotonic, tremolo chords. M-D.

Boris Koutzen (1901–1966) USA, born Russia
Sonatina 1947 (Gen 1078). One movement in contrasting sections, flexible meters, atonal. M-D.

Henri Kowalski (1841–1916) France
Salute à Pesth, Marche Hongroise de Concert (Schott; GS).

Hans Kox (1930–   ) The Netherlands
Diabolus Feriatus 1956 (Donemus 1978) 31pp. Photostat. Ballet for two pianos. Homo Scientia Furiosus; Intermezzo; Homo Lubidinosus; Intermezzo; Homo Narcissus; Epilogo. Highly chromatic, moves between tonality and atonality with shades of bitonality and polytonality. Requires technical flexibility and emotional variety from both players. M-D to D.

Leopold Koželuh (1748–1818) Czechoslovakia
Sonata Op.19 (Lemoine). Well written, melodious, attractive. Int. to M-D.

Anton Krause (1834–1907) Germany
Sonata E Op.17 (Br&H).

Johann Ludwig Krebs (1713–1780) Germany
Konzert für zwei Cembali a (B. Klein—DVFM 1966; UCLA) 38pp. Editorial addditions in parentheses. Allegro; Affettuoso; Allegro. Imitative; octotonic; flowing Affettuoso has numerous ornaments. Effective Baroque writing. M-D.

Ernst Krenek (1900–   ) USA, born Austria
Krenek's evolution as a composer mirrors the development of twentieth-century music in general.
Basler Massarbeit Op.173 1960 (Br3510) 6 min. Six short pieces based on a twelve-tone row and its inversion and retrograde form, rigorously organized. Contains complex metrical units, harmonics, secco style, fastidious textures. Only for the most adventurous pianists. D.
Doppelt Beflugeltes Band (Tape and Double) Op.207, 1969–70 (Br) 22 min. For two pianos and tape. One piano is prepared with a light metal chain stretched over the strings and serves as a timbral buffer between the normal piano and the electronic sounds. Many fragmentary effects strung together. D.

Joachim Krist (1948–   ) Germany
Kreuzwege 1976 (Feedback 7503 1978). For piano quartet. 22 leaves in portfolio, photostat. Four copies needed for performance.

Emil Kronke (1865–1938) Germany
Kronke was an ardent admirer of Liszt. He edited over 200 of Chopin's works.
Symphonic Variations on a Nordic Theme Op.14 (Steingräber 1907; LC) 29pp. Theme and ten variations in Lisztian style. M-D.
Suite Op.42 (Schott 1908; LC) 51pp. Festivo; Vivo leggiero, con delicatezza; Romanze; Carnaval. Virtuosic. M-D to D.
Little Suite Op.73 (K&S 1910; LC) 19pp. Melodie; Gavotte; Valse noble; Gondoliera; Scherzo-Caprice. M-D.
Concert Variations Op.80 (Symphonic Ballade) (Leuckart 1912; LC) 39pp. Theme and ten variations. M-D to D.
Lyric Pieces Op.94 (K&S 1914; LC) 15pp. Hymne; Menuett; Albumblatt; Walzer; Scherzo. M-D.

Gail Kubik (1914–   ) USA
In 1964 Nadia Boulanger summed up Kubik's style as follows: "The instrumental combinations: very original, and the forms clearly define them. In the rapid movements, full of indomitable energy, music tinkles, titters, toddles or runs at high speed. . . . The composer gives to each

instrument the opportunity to come out in all its brightness. . . . The slow movements, often confidential, meditative, tranquil, the peace of open spaces. Therein dwells a penetrating, intimate, moving poetry.

"The perspicacious listener will also perceive that a music so 'natural' has nothing to do with any form of *laisser aller*—of carelessness, unconstraint or lack of selectivity—but presupposes a keen *esprit de finesse* and the faculty of discrimination and economy. . . . This music, for instance, will seem to reveal the composer's personality in a light vein. But these scores are more than that. . . . To be able to be gay and light has a much deeper significance than that revealed at first sight. For in these [scores] are pages of great and meditative poetry. There is a time to be serious and grave. In a word, to make a music of this depth with such a skill and wit shows real understanding and taste" (from record jacket notes, Orion ORS 80372, recordings of *Symphony for Two Pianos* and *Prayer and Toccata*).

Symphony for Two Pianos 1949–79 (PIC 1981) 63pp., 43 min. Moderately slow; moderately fast, gracefully. Slowly, sadly. With vigor. Introduction: Fast, with great energy (theme, three variations, and finale). Has a leisurely quality, its ostinatos and melodic references often being carried to a considerable length. Basic texture is homophonic with melody and accompaniment distinctly separate. Melody appears in brief snatches, ideas often reshaped (not really transformed) by the adding of different beginnings or endings. Harmony is polytriadic with its frequent suggestion of two simultaneous background chords against a melody that subscribes to one of them or outlines a third chord. Kubik's triads, although juxtaposed, can all be heard because of their transparently wide spacing. This work began as two movements from Kubik's *First Symphony* in 1949 and was reworked and assumed its present state in 1979. M-D to D.

Song and Scherzo (PIC).

Prayer and Toccata 1969–79 (MS available from composer: P.O. Box 192, Claremont, CA 91711). For two pianos and organ. 44pp., 15 min. Quietly. Fast, gaily, with spirit. More tightly organized than *Symphony for Two Pianos*. Here the accompaniment tends to be more affected by the thematic content. Often the two pianos are cast in a supportive role, adding colorful tints, rival rhythms, or a form of commentary with respect to the organ. Two or three ideas permeate the *Prayer,* while a persistent rhythmic cell underlies the *Toccata*. The *Toccata* accumulates meaningfully, moving energetically and relentlessly toward climaxes of textual complexity, before evanescing just before the conclusion. This neo-Classic work was originally written in 1969 for organ and chamber orchestra. The rewriting for two pianos and organ was completed in 1979. M-D.

Jos Kunst (1936–   ) The Netherlands
Stenen Eten (The Stone-Eaters) 1965 (Donemus) 5 min. Performance directions in Dutch and French. Two untitled movements. Proportional notation, clusters, fast tremolo. Pointillistic, extreme dynamic range, avant-garde. D.

Meyer Kupferman (1926–   ) USA
Sonata (Frank). Three movements—FSF, surges with controlled intensity. The middle movement, a set of variations, is particularly well wrought. M-D.

Ladislav Kupkovic (1936–   ) Yugoslavia
Clavierübung 1977 (SBTS; MS available from composer: Ruhmkorff-strasse 17, 3000 Hannover 1, W. Germany). For four pianos. 8 min. Brilliant keyboard display with alternating chords, contrary and parallel scales, classic cadences, juxtaposition of keys, fugal polytonal textures, neo-Classic. Instruments are treated soloistically and sometimes orchestrally. Basically tonal with "foreign" keys briefly introduced. Would "bring down the house" when effectively performed. Recorded on EMI-Electrola 1C 066-45 424. M-D.
Requiem für Meine Selbstmörder 1978 (SBTS; MS available from composer) 41pp., 20 min. In seven sections, untitled except for No. 6, Tempo de Polka. Piano II plays first section solo. Freely tonal, strongly contrasted moods. Contains a great variety of traditional figuration made slightly contemporary sounding by expanded tonal concepts, clever syncopation. M-D.
Happy-End 1976 (MS available from composer). For four pianos. 45 min.

L

Josef Labor (1842–1924) Austria
Capriccio Big Ben (UE).
Fantasy on an Original Theme Op.1 (UE).
Scherzo in the Form of a Canon Op. 2 (UE).

Theodore Lack (1846–1921) France
The following pieces are all written in an elegant salon style.
Saltarelle Caprice Op.35 (Durand).
Duo Symphonique Op.65 (IMC; BrM 1883).
Cabaletta Op.83 (GS; Durand).
Sonatine Op.129 (K.F. Heckel).
Marquise, Menuet Op.271 (Schmidt).

J. Ladd (–   ) New Zealand
Diversions (Price Milburn).

Paul-Emile Ladmirault (1877–1944) France
Brocéliande au martin (Sal). Refined and lyric writing. M-D.
Suite Bretonne (Sal). Available separately. Danse de l'Epée. Rondo.
    Scherzo.

Henry Lahee (1826–1912) Great Britain
Duo sur Stabat Mater de Rossini (Schott).

Cecily Lambert (1915–   ) USA
The Fisher's Hornpipe (BMC 1945; AMC; LC) 11pp. A colorful and free
    adaptation of an old New England folk tune. Int.

Walther Lampe (1872–1964) Germany
Lampe studied piano with Clara Schumann.
Theme und Variationen Op.2 (Simrock 1901; LC) 15pp. Theme (Andante
    espressivo), eight variations, and a Finale. In Brahms style, effec-
    tively worked out. Worth investigating. M-D.

Serge Lancen (1922–   ) France
Promenade 1961 (Editions Françaises de Musique; LC) 3 min. Short,
    salon style, simple melody, similar to Poulenc. Int.

Alcides Lanza (1929–   ) Argentina

Plectros I 1962 (Bo&H) 6 min. For two players at one or two pianos. Instructions for clusters, plucked strings, etc. 2 pages of directions for 4 pages of musical notation. Avant-garde. M-D.

Trio Concertante 1962 (Bo&H) 5 min. For any three instruments. Three groups of nine fragments (three in each group) are to be treated according to the directions in the score. Each fragment has a different tempo indication. Expressionistic, pointillistic, avant-garde. M-D.

Plectros IV 1974 (Bo&H). For two pianists of the opposite sex with percussion and electronic sounds. 15 min. Scores (three needed) and tape on rental. "A mixed media composition. Music and musical instruments are seen as antiques in the future. In a robot civilization human loving attitudes will find new *raison d'être* thanks to the sheer beauty of music. The cast includes a robot customer (pianist I), a robot attendant (pianist II) and Eric, a toy robot. The pianists must be of opposite sex. Two assistants are required: one for the lights and toy robot, the other for the electronics. A concert performance (with no acting) is possible, from 1 minute to 14½ minutes" (from the score). Mixture of conventional and graphic notation; performers use stopwatches for synchronization. The pianists play some percussion. Both the electronic tape and the written score contain quotes from Robert Schumann's music, with modifications (*Andante and Variations* Op.46 and *Fantasy* Op.17). Further directions in the score. Avant-garde. M-D.

Angel E. Lasala (1914–   ) Argentina

Danza de la China Querendona (Ric BA 10344 1960; LAP) 7pp. Two with three, flowing and expressive, climactic mid-section, much use of pedal, a few added-note chords. M-D.

Payada (Ric BA 10928 1953) 10pp. Driving rhythms contrasted with cantando melodies, freely tonal. M-D.

Fernand de la Tombelle (1854–1928) France

Fantaisie (Costallat).

Prelude et Fugue a (Durand; BrM; SBTS) 15pp. Dedicated to the composer's teacher, Saint-Säens, but inspired by Franck. M-D.

Max Laurischkus (1876–1929) Germany

Three Duos Op.7b (Simrock: Br&H).

Angelo Lavagnino (1909–   ) Italy

Sonatina (Carisch 1949) 18pp., 16 min. Entrata (Ironico-molto moderato). Inno vesperale (In nativitate domini): slow, serious, fugal. Parodia in Boogie-Woogie (Allegro dinamico): lively and rhythmic. Freely tonal, dissonant, quartal and quintal harmony. M-D.

Mario Lavista (1943–) Mexico

Piece for Two Pianists (EMM). One pianist remains completely silent but is required "to communicate this silence to the listeners." Avant-garde. M-D.

Henri Lazarof (1932–) USA, born Bulgaria

Lazarof has taught at UCLA since 1962.

Intonazione (AMP 1972) 16pp., 12 min. Fragmented musical ideas, clusters, semi-serially organized. Tempi and dynamics highly contrasted, bombastic with some Impressionistic effects, silences cleverly exploited. Simultaneous black- and white-key glissandos. Exploits extreme ranges of keyboard. Difficult ensemble problems. D.

Gustav Lazarus (1861–1920) France

Three Pieces Op.39 (Simon 1899). Ländler. Scherzo. Valse Lente. Published separately. Max Bruch influence. M-D.

E. Markham Lee (1874–1956) USA, born Great Britain

Five Sketches (Galaxy).

Noël Lee (1924–) USA

Fantaisie Autour D'ut 1952, rev. 1974 (AMC) 20pp., 10 min. Adagio: cantando line in Piano I, long pedals in Piano II. Allegro molto: rhythmic, thin textures, requires span of ninth; Adagio opening idea returns at closing. Written in an accessible style that is based on the free use of the twelve tones around a center, propelled by striking dissonances and energetic rhythms, a well-shaped form. D.

Benjamin Lees (1924–) USA

Sonata 1951 (Bo&H) 46pp. Allegro giocoso: angular melodies, brisk rhythmic chords, harmonically witty, chats along merrily, octotonic. Adagio semplice: expressive, linear. Allegro: fugal. Freely tonal, rich textures. The work is gratefully free from any touch of pretentiousness or sentimentality and is idiomatic throughout. Clear-cut textures, rhythms, and expressiveness are coupled with energetic forcefulness. M-D.

Etudes for Piano and Orchestra 1974 (Bo&H) 20 min. Two-piano reduction by the composer. Steady, rather quickly. Simply, leisurely. Briskly, with authority. Not too fast. Quickly. Alternates between thrust and intense lyricism. Virtuosic, large span required. D.

Ton de Leeuw (1926–) The Netherlands

Sonata (Donemus 1950) 44pp., 21 min. Moderato appassionato; Minuet; Lento; Allegro non troppo. Large, demanding, polytonal work reminiscent of early Schönberg, intervallic use of seconds and fourths reminiscent of Bartók. Small motifs woven together make for complex textures, atonal. No meter signatures, but full of changing meters. D.

René Leibowitz (1913–1972) France, born Poland

Explanation of Metaphors Op.15 (Boelke-Bomart 1950) 27pp. Revised version for two pianos, harp, percussion (two players), and narrator. Percussion required: suspended cymbal, bass drum with pedal, triangle, and tamtam. Narration uses *Sprechstimme* technique with indicated time values and approximate pitch relationships. Serial, expressionistic, pointillistic, dynamic extremes, harmonics, frequent tempo changes, changing meters, tremolo, quasi-cadenza passages; works to enormous climax. Requires performers experienced in the style. M-D.

Kenneth Leighton (1929–   ) Great Britain

Scherzo 1950 (Lengnick) 19pp., 4 min. Strong rhythms, modal, melodic, contrapuntal, impressive conclusion. M-D.

Vlastimil Lejsek (1927–   ) Czechoslovakia

Invence 1962 (CHF) 13pp. Allegro vivace, neo-Classic, contemporary Alberti bass, broken octaves, a few changing meters, freely tonal. M-D.

Toccata 1977 (CHF) 12pp. Same style as *Invence* but with more key changes; exciting coda. M-D.

Timothy T. Lenk (1952–   ) USA

Fore and Aft 1976 (AMC) 2 min. Facsimile. Prelude: chordal with plaintive melody. Counterpoint: canonic, melody full of triplets, tonal. Would make a nice program opener. Int.

Jacques Lenot (1945–   ) France

Fuge, Dilecte Me (Sal 1979) 9pp.

Daniel Lesur (1908–   ) France

Fantaisie 1962 (Ric 2201) 28pp., 7 min. One movement. Rhapsodic, contrasting sections, fast broken-chord passages, skips, MC. M-D.

Contre-Fugue 1970 (Choudens) 8pp., 3 min. Sustained fugue subject is carried in one instrument while the other comments in a pointillistic style. M-D.

Passacaille (Billaudot). Refined and lyric writing. M-D.

Mischa Levitzki (1898–1941) USA, born Russia

Valse Tzigane Op.7 (H. Flammer 1936; LC) 8pp. In a light salon style; effective. M-D.

Peter Lewis (1932–   ) USA

Capriccio Concertato 1960 rev.1962 (AMC) 12pp. "To dramatize even more the dialogue between them, the two pianos should be set apart

at a convenient distance" (from the score). An atonal Adagio introduction leads to the main body of the work, à capriccio, ritmico:
quasi-staccato, pointillistic, flexible meters, extensive dynamic
range. Thoroughly enjoyable, but only with two first-rate pianists.
M-D to D.

Sergei Liapunov (1859–1924) Russia
Ballade Op.2 (Bo&Bo 14607; LC). Originally for orchestra, arranged for
  two pianos by the composer, 26pp.
Prelude Pastoral Op.54b (Zimmermann 1914).

Bruno Liberda (1953–   ) Germany
Turn Slowly (Blues) (Ariadne 79004 1979). For two–three pianos. 3pp., 1
  leaf. Preface in German and English.
Twist (Ariadne 79003 1979) 3pp., 1 leaf. Preface in German and English.

Charles A. Lidgey (–1924) Great Britain
Ballade f♯ Op.3 (Br&H).

György Ligeti (1923–   ) Hungary
Drei Stücke für zwei Klaviere 1976 (Schott 6687) Facsimile edition, 20pp.,
  16 min. Monument: develops block chords, stiff, static, addition and
  subtraction of dynamic levels, no crescendo or decrescendo.
  Selbsportrait: "Self portrait with (Steve) Reich and (Terry) Riley
  (with Chopin in the background)": witty, repetitive, intricate rhythmic configurations played rapidly and continuously, combines
  Riley's technique of repeating models and Reich's phase shift with
  Ligeti's own method of overlapping networks and "over-saturated
  canons"; Chopin hovers near the end when rhythmic layers unite into
  a joint presto unisono that suggests the character of the presto from
  Chopin's Sonata b♭, Op. 35. Bewegung: difficult to read the MS.;
  flowing, lustrous moving colors; uses some material from Monument
  and an eight-part canon "folding like a telescope" and acting as a
  common coda for all three pieces. All three pieces are essentially
  light in character yet they reflect the unusual level of musicality and
  technical assurance characteristic of Ligeti. He attempts to make the
  music appear three-dimensional, like a hologram suspended in imaginary space, through the differentiation of dynamic planes. M-D to D.

Magnus Lindberg (1958–   ) Finland
Lindberg studied at the Sibelius Academy under Paavo Heininen. He has
composed pieces for chamber ensemble and orchestra as well as electronic music.
Play 1 1979 (Finnish Music Information Centre) 10 to 15 min. Proportional
  notation, 20 sections entitled Movements, Routes, Prisms, Figures
  and Points, and Closure. Includes performance directions in English.

Performers decide form of the piece. "No dynamics are written due to the fact, that the interpreters will have the freedom to underline and balance the sections according to the decisions they make about the whole piece" (from the score). Avant-garde. D.

Dinu Lipatti (1917–1950) Rumania
Trois Danses Roumaines 1943–45 (Salabert) 44pp. Vif: in 7/8 (2 + 2 + 3). Andantino: in 2/4. Allegro vivace: in 2/4. Athletic and rhythmic; folk melodies are harmonized with dissonant chords; fast figurations. M-D to D.

Franz Liszt (1811–1886) Hungary
Liszt performed two-piano music (either two-piano compositions *per se* or piano concertos) with almost every important pianist of his day. He was an inveterate reviser and arranger of his own and other composers' works. Most of his original pieces exist in multiple versions and show in their various reworkings a progressive expansion and refinement of his musical conceptions. S. numbers refer to Humphrey Searle's catalogue listing in *The New Grove,* 1981.
Beethoven's 9th Symphony S.657 1851 (Schott).
Concerto Pathétique e S.258 1856 (Br&H 2277; GS 1534) 51pp. Allegro energico—Andante sostenuto—Allegro trionfante. A bold one-movement form similar to a symphonic poem in three contrasting sections. Exploits many pianistic problems. Brilliant sonorities, cadenza passages, orchestral effects, theme transformation, subdivided by tempo changes. Although the score is unusual in that it has no programmatic background, it displays the same unique pianistic approach that distinguishes Liszt's more-familiar piano works. Virtuosic throughout. M-D to D.
A Symphony to Dante's "Divina commedia" S.648 1856–59 (Br&H).
Fantasy on themes from Beethoven's "Ruins of Athens" S.649 1848–52 (Joseffy—GS 1915) 39pp., 11 min. This short, brilliant work, is one of the most effective Liszt ever arranged for two pianos, with both parts meshed masterfully. For sheer charm, he never surpassed what he achieved in this brilliant and altogether lovable piece. M-D.
A Faust Symphony S.647 1856 rev. 1860 (Schuberth 1863) rev. 1870.
Hexameron. Grand Variations de concert sur un thème des "Puritains" (by Bellini) S.654 (Schuberth 1870) 20 min. Written by Liszt, Herz, and Thalberg, the original version was composed for solo piano and included variations by Czerny, Herz, Pixis, Thalberg, Chopin, and Liszt. This set appeared in 1835 under the title of *Hexameron,* alluding to the six co-composers. The work may have been intended as a memorial to Bellini, who died in 1835 at the age of 33 soon after the performance of his last opera. Liszt, who had composed the in-

troduction and the finale, subsequently arranged the piece for two pianos, at that time omitting the variations by Chopin, Czerny, and Pixis. The work is reminiscent of all the grandeur and flamboyancy characteristic of this period. The most interesting fact about this potpourri is that the most musically effective of the variations were written by those mere "empty virtuoso composers," as we regard them today—Thalberg and Herz. It must entertain and dazzle, make the hair stand on end, and raise the roof. The entire piece is an extraordinary mastodonic survival of the "pianistic" past. M-D to D.

Hungarian Fantasia S.123   1852 (GS 1056; CFP 1187a; UE; Philipp-Durand) 15½ min. This work uses the same material as the *Hungarian Rhapsody* No.14. It is undeniably effective and contains much ingenious technical detail. Liszt intended it to be a brilliant instrumental concert piece with dazzling colors. M-D.

Réminiscences de Don Juan S.656 arranged 1841 published 1877 (Br&H; E. Szegedi—EMB Z7810   1978) 50pp., 16 min. The EMB edition contains a preface in Hungarian, German, and English. A breathtaking transcription by Liszt in most brilliant fashion for paired pianos. Structurally more cohesive and technically more brilliant than the original solo version. The antiphonal potential of the two instruments is magnificently exploited in this version (the second), especially in the "La ci darem la mano" section. D.

Réminiscences de Norma S.655 arranged 1841 (Schott 1874) 12½ min. "The most difficult passage in the solo version of the *Norma* Fantasy (the "Guerra chorus" theme, jumping from various registers of the piano) is kept intact in the first piano part of the two-piano version, while the second piano reinforces the material in a way that is impossible in the original version. Simplification was certainly not Liszt's primary motive for rewriting this music. No one who hears the climactic moment in the two-piano version of the *Norma* Fantasy, wherein the themes from the opening and closing scenes of the opera are combined, can be satisfied with the similar passage in the solo version. What Liszt implied in the latter is fully realized in the two-piano setting, where a rich bass part can support the contrapuntal interweaving of the two themes" (from record jacket Connoisseur Society CS2039).

Spanish Rhapsody S.254 arranged by Busoni (Belwin-Mills 9511; GS; Siloti—K&S; CFP) 15 min. This arrangement of Liszt's solo piano work enhances its effectiveness. Following a short cadenza for the pianist, a series of variations emerge based on the "Folies d'Espagne" theme. They build to a strong climax and then subside into a lively Jota aragonese. A piano cadenza leads to the second theme, which is developed before the first Jota tempo returns. These two contrasting themes are worked together with increasing excitement and lead to a dramatic statement of the "Folies d'Espagne." Lisztian fireworks close the piece. D.

Totentanz (Dance of Death) S.652 (EMB; Sauer—CFP; K; Br&H; Paragon) 17 min. This set of variations on Dies Irae (Day of Wrath) was planned in 1838, finished in 1849, and revised in 1853 and again in 1859. Liszt creates an unearthly atmosphere of mingled horror and fantasy. The virtuosity of the piano parts underscores the grotesque and savage character of the entire work. Glissandos, but no excessive technical demands in this highly effective work. M-D.

Twelve Symphonic Poems (Br&H) Vol. I: Ce qu'on entend sur la montagne, S.635. Tasso, S.636. Les Préludes, S.647. Orpheus, S.638. Prometheus, S.639. Mazeppa, S.640. Vol. II: Festklänge, S.641. Heroïde funèbre, S.642. Hungaria, S.643. Hamlet, S.644. Hunnenschlacht, S.645. Die Ideale, S.646. Liszt transferred the orchestral sound to the two keyboards in a marvelous manner in these pieces. M-D.

Wanderer-Fantasia S.653 1850 or 1851 (Joseffy—GS; UE; Cranz) 22 min. Liszt took a great deal of interest in this piece, since both the piano writing and the form of the work show a strong affinity with his own aims. He did not change the formal construction of Schubert's work, but only enriched the transition to the second subject with a cadenza. The form is that of a sonata in four movements played without pause: Allegro con fuoco—Adagio—Presto—Allegro. The slow movement is a series of variations on Schubert's own song *Der Wanderer* Op.4/1 (D.493) composed in 1816. M-D to D.

George Lloyd (1913–   ) Great Britain
Aubade (UMP).

Larry Lockwood (1943–   ) USA
Quartet 1976 (MS available from composer: 302 West 79 Street, New York, NY 10024). For two pianos and two percussionists. 16 min. Two movements. M-D.

Norman Lockwood (1906–   ) USA
Sonata (ACA).

Theo Loevendie (1930–   ) The Netherlands
Voor Jan, Piet en Klaas 1979 (Donemus) 5 min. For two pianos, eight hands. Voor Jan: Lento, serious, slow chromatic melody. Piet: Allegro molto, ostinato-like figures, octotonic. En Klaas: Tranquillo, small melodic figuration, clusters, MC. M-D.

Josef Loew (1832–1886) Germany
Allegro brilliant Op.325 (GS).
Serenade Op.489 (Br&H 1884; BrM; LC).

Ruth Lomon (1930–   ) USA, born Canada

Lomon performs as a member of the two-piano team, Lomon and Wenglin, which has introduced an international collection of compositions by women composers. She lives in Cambridge, MA, where she teaches composition and piano.

Triptych 1978 (AMC) 8pp., 7 min. Dark as the dawn (Presto; Solemn—Andante); Aria; Aura. Piano I has seven prepared notes. These strings should be muffled (damped) by spreading strips of masking tape on them. For Piano II place a music stand to the left of the keyboard and suspend a triangle and two finger cymbals of different pitches from it. Strings are strummed and played with a leather mallet; some notes are played by tapping a clave stick on the piano brace. Black- and white-key clusters. Sensitive expressionistic writing, colorful and effective. M-D.

Federico Longas (1895–   ) USA, born Spain

Jota Aragonesa (Ric BA 9723   1957) 7pp. Would make an exciting encore. M-D.

Alessandro Longo (1864–1945) Italy

Theme with Variations Op.30 (Rahter; University of Louisville) 33pp. Introduction, Theme, six variations, Pause, Finale (Fugato). Late nineteenth-century style. Fugato is effective if a bit contrived. Both performers are busy most of the time. M-D to D.

Six Piccole Suite Op.38 (Ric).

6 Unterhaltungen Op.39 (Ric). Variations on Ah, vous dirais je, Maman. Gavotte. Easy Suite. Etude. Idyll. Theme with Variations.

Nikolai Lopatnikoff (1903–   ) USA, born Estonia

Arabesque 1941 (AMP 1948) 4 min. Arranged by the composer from the second *Russian Nocturne* Op.25 for orchestra. Essentially neo-Classic in style. Int. to M-D.

Mark Lothar (1902–   ) Germany

Danza della palle Op.79/3 (Bo&Bo 1973) 15pp. Prestissimo leggiero (possible). Salon style, sprinkled with measures of 2/4 in chromatic waltz figuration, glissandi, handclaps, much use of tremolo. M-D.

Erik Lotichius (1929–   ) The Netherlands

Sonata 1981 (Donemus) 12 min.

Alain Louvier (1945–   ) France

Études pour Agresseurs (Leduc 1977) Book 4. The title refers to the entire series of etudes the composer has written, the others being for solo piano and solo harpsichord. Includes definitions in French, English, and German. "Studies should be understood in the musical rather than in the didactical meaning" (from the foreword). Vol. 1, 32pp.

Study 19: develops strong dynamic contrasts; play it on two pianos placed some distance apart, to underscore the stereophonic type of writing. Study 20: requires a careful choice of touch and almost imperceptible transitions between instruments. Study 21: a chase (canon) between two (or three) pianos; indications of seconds must be followed strictly. Study 22: a Divertimento. Vol.2, 32pp., 24½ min. Etude 23: For 32 Aggressors upon the "Triangle" by Pascal. The 32 "Aggressors" consist of 20 fingers, four palms, four fists, and four forearms. Clusters indicated by many different signs. Other signs used are for harmonics, transposable sounds, chord kept up by tremolo, accelerate—slow down, highest and lowest sounds possible, slurred chords. Also includes the mathematical triangle (table) by Pascal on which the work is based. Rhythmic complexities are reminiscent of Boulez. Only for the Kantarsky brothers? Avant-garde. D.

Pierre Luboshutz (1891–1971) USA, born Russia
The Bat—a Fantasy on Themes from Johann Strauss's Die Fledermaus (JF 1951) 34pp. Traditional harmony; brilliant and effective concert piece. M-D to D.

Raymond Luedeke (–   ) USA
Krishna (Seesaw). For two pianos and five percussion instruments.

Otto Luening (1900–   ) USA
The Bells of Bellagio (CFP 1973) also contained in *Scores—An Anthology of New Music* (GS 1981; AMC) 11pp. For two or three players at one, two, or three pianos. Full score for one piano only. Many ways to perform the piece: parts 1 and 2 alone; 1 and 3 alone; 2 and 3 alone; all at one piano; all three together, etc. Two short pieces (Hail!; Farewell) portraying the sounds of bells. Damper pedal held throughout each piece; no key signature; canonic usage is important; polytonal. Three levels of difficulty involved. Could provide a dramatic interlude on a recital. Int. to M-D.

David Lumsdaine (1931–   ) Australia
Lumsdaine studied at the Sydney Conservatory, Sydney University and at the Royal Academy of Music in London. In 1970 he was appointed lecturer in music at Durham University.
Flights 1967 (UE 29046 1975) 3pp., 10 leaves, 20–23 min. A collection of material from which the players prepare their own sequences of "grounds" and "flights." Performance directions difficult to understand. Requires plenty of imagination. Chance composition. Contains some very sensitive sonorities and beautiful sounds. D.

Signe Lund (1868–1950) Norway
Valse de Concert Op.40 (WH) 7pp. M-D.

Don-David Lusterman (–   ) USA
Sonata 1954 rev. 1955 (AMC).

Witold Lutoslawski (1913–   ) Poland
In his works of the 70s and 80s, Lutoslawski has developed a method of indeterminant counterpoint in which the composer plans the form as a whole while minor details are left, in place, to the performer.
Variations on a Theme by Paganini 1941 (PWM 1949) 21pp., 6 min. Based on the famous Caprice a, No.24. Theme, eleven variations, coda. Translucent texture; brilliant, tritone combinations; chromatic coloring; bold atonal harmonies. One of the most effective twentieth-century works for this medium. M-D to D.
Miniature (Ars Polona).

Charles Samuel Lysberg (1821–1873) Switzerland
Lysberg was a pupil of Chopin.
La Baladine Caprice Op.51 (CF; BrM) 7pp. Salon style. M-D.
Fantasy on "Don Juan" Op.79 (Hofmeister).
Fantasy on Motives from the "Magic Flute" Op.121 (Hofmeister).
Les Bruits des champs, Idylle symphonique Op.134 (Hofmeister).

M

Robert McBride (1911–   ) USA
Punch and the Judy (ACA) 8 min.

John McCabe (1939–   ) Great Britain
Basse Dance 1970 (Novello 1974) 40pp., 11 min. No ritardandi or ac-
celerandi are allowed; harmonics used. The only metrical license
taken should be that written in the music (pauses or commas), and
the basic pulse should always remain exactly the same throughout.
Strong rhythms, clusters, twelve-tone influence. M-D.

Teo Macero (1925–   ) USA
One-Three Quarters (CFP 66178 1970) 11pp., parts. 8 min. For two
pianos, piccolo/flute, violin, cello, trombone, and tuba. One piano is
to be tuned down a ¼ tone; strings play up or down a ¼ tone at
specific indication. Tremolando, octotonic, dramatic arpeggiated gestures, syncopation, chromatic chords. Extreme registers exploited;
short sections are repeated. Colorful sonorities. M-D.

George F. McKay (1899–1970) USA
Dancing in a Dream (Novelette) (Delkas 1945; AMC; LC) 5pp. Graceful
and charming melody accompanied with syncopated figuration. Int.

Priscilla McLean (1942–   ) USA
Residing and composing presently in Austin, Texas, McLean is co-
director, with her husband, Barton McLean, of the American Society of
University Composers' National Radio Series. She and her husband tour
performing their own live and taped electronic music as The McLean
Mix.
Interplanes 1970 (A. Broude 1978; also in vol.5 of the American Society
of University Composers published by European American Music;
AMC) 35pp. Two untitled contrasting movements. Expressionistic,
dynamic extremes, flexible meters, motivic development. Unveils a
remarkable canvas of pianistic sonority in carefully notated and easy
to read facsimile score. "A restless dramatic atmosphere pervades
the first movement, as two strong, divergent personalities with their
own planes of music complete for dominance. In the second move-

ment the individuals merge into one broad, complex atmosphere out of which melodies, motives, and arpeggios emerge and fade, moving as from one large integrated instrument. This work, inspired by Charles Ives' *The Unanswered Question,* is a collage of superimposed contrasts" (from jacket notes on *Advance Recordings* FGR-196). For experienced ensemble players only. D.

Colin McPhee (1901–1964) USA
Balinese Ceremonial Music 1934 (GS 1940; AMC; LC). Published separately, 5 min. each. Pemoengkah. Gambangan. Taboeh Teloe. Authentic transcriptions from percussion ensemble (gamelan) by an outstanding ethnomusicologist. Duple rhythm becomes monotonous; limited scales. Transparent and subtle heterophonic music. M-D.
See: Colin McPhee, "Five-tone Gamelan Music of Bali," MQ, XXXV, April 1949, 250-81.

Jan Maegaard (1926–   ) Denmark
Three Choral Preludes Op.58 1974 (MIC). Arranged for two pianos by the composer.

Jakad Major (1858–1925) Hungary
Concert Fantasies Op.67 (Béla Mery). In the Romantic tradition of the nineteenth-century German School. M-D.

Arthur Malawsky (1904–1957) Poland
Toccata et Fugue en forme de variations (PWM 1949).

Gian Francesco Malipiero (1882–1973) Italy
Dialoghi I 1956 (Ric 129401 1957). "Con Manuel de Falla (in memoria)." Originally for small orchestra, transcribed for two pianos by the composer. 11 min. Melodies consist of combinations of motives and ideas that are molded into long phrases. Development of musical material through free association and constant variation in what the composer calls a "free conversation" that produces a cumulative formal structure. M-D.
Dialoghi II 1956 (Ric 129402) "Between Two Pianos." 29pp., 8 min. Light, transparent counterpoint that never obscures the main melodic ideas. Extended concept of tonality with chromaticism, sharp dissonances; borders on atonality. Somewhat esoteric but certainly expressive. Much interplay between instruments. M-D.

Riccardo Malipiero (1914–   ) Italy
Nuclei (SZ 1966). For two pianos and three percussionists. 15 min.

Michio Mamiya (1929–   ) Japan
Three Movements Op.2 1952 (Ongaku No Toma Sha 1968) 30pp., 13 min.
    Vivace: fast triplet passages intended to provide a sense of speed.

Andante: derives from the rhythm of a rice-planting song from northern Japan, expressive rhythm used midway through this movement is altered slightly and used as the third theme of the rondo in the third movement, Allegro, which is pleasant and light. Style suggests Bach and Poulenc as major influences. M-D.

Ursula Mamlok (1928–   ) USA
Children's Suite No. 2 (ACA).

Luigi Manenti (1899–   ) Italy
Fantasia (EC 1962) 34pp. A large one-movement atonal work in contrasting sections; linear. M-D.
Moto Perpetuo (EC 1959) 16pp. Busy, dissonant, rhythmic. M-D.

Leopold Damrosch Mannes (1899–1964) USA
Petite Suite (Senart).

Franco Mannino (1924–   ) Italy
Serie 1964 (Ric 130904) 18pp., 6½ min. Twelve-tone, complex. Three-page Lento introduction moves into a fast and driving Moderatomente mosso for the rest of the work. M-D.

Luc-André Marcel (1919–   ) France
Concert pour deux pianos 1964 (EMT) 71pp., 24 min. Photograph of MS. Allergo: agitated and excited. Andante: sustained, lyric. Presto: propulsive. All movements relate to a B-A-C-H motif; disjointed octotonic writing between the instruments creates a polytonal atmosphere; overextended. D.

Tera de Marez Oyens (1932–   ) The Netherlands
Sonatina 1961 (Donemus) facsimile, 25pp. Allegro: playful, nonlegato, rhythmic. Andante: quiet, nocturne-like. Allegro deciso: facile and acrobatic. Quartal and quintal harmonies, freely tonal. M-D.

Franco Margola (1908–   ) Italy
La Ginevrina; fantasia in tre tempi per due pianoforti 1951 (Bongiovanni) 40pp., 16½ min. Andante svero; Adagio assai; Allegro. Lengthy, atonal, octotonic, angular melodies. D.
Notturni e Danze (Carisch 1958) 15pp. Six sections, thin textures. Int. to M-D.
Sonata Pianistica per due mani destre (Bongiovanni 1969) 16pp., 10 min. Con brio; Doloroso; Vivace. Could be performed on one instrument but is easier to manage with two. Neo-Classic, freely tonal. M-D.

Jean Marie (1917–   ) France
Le Tombeau de Carrillo (Jobert).

Gino Marinuzzi (1920–   ) Italy
Partita a (Carisch).

Igor Markevitch (1912–   ) France, born Russia
Partita 1931 (Bo&H). Originally for piano and small orchestra, arranged
    for two pianos by the composer. 17 min. Ouverture; Choral; Rondo.
    Anti-tonal canonic and serial writing in the outer movements, strong
    writing in Choral somewhat similar in mood to the Andante religioso
    of the Bartók Piano Concerto III. M-D.
    See: Alex de Graeff, "Partita for Piano and Small Orchestra," *Tempo*
    133/4, September 1980, 39–43.
L'Envol d'Icare 1932 (Bo&H). For two pianos and percussion. Originally
    a ballet, 24 min. Seven movements.
    See: Clive Bennett, "Icare," *Tempo* 133/4, September 1980, 44–51.
Le Nouvel Âge 1937 (Bo&H). Originally a sinfonia concertante for or-
    chestra, 23 min. Auverture; Adagio; Hymne.

Wladyslawa Markiewiczowna (1900–   ) Poland
Suite 1936 (PWM 1975) 25pp., 8 min. Toccata; Intermezzo; Rondo rus-
    tico. Freely tonal, glissandi, triplets in Piano II with four 16ths in
    Piano I. All three movements well conceived for the medium. Final
    movement more tonal than the first two. Attractive musical syntax.
    Carefully fingered, requires well-developed pianists. M-D.

Henri Martelli (1899–   ) France, born Corsica
Sonate Op.64 1946 (Schott ME 60-6569 1951). Three movements. Neo-
    Classic, much decoration and interweaving of themes. Each part
    makes a musical entity. M-D.

Frank Martin (1890–1974) Switzerland
The reputation of Martin, one of Switzerland's foremost composers, is
based upon a relatively few works that constantly reappear in the concert
repertoire. But this remarkably gifted composer produced a large oeuvre
in a musical language that, while of his time, is uniquely his own. He
totally assimilated various modern musical languages, from Debussy and
Ravel to de Falla and Schönberg, and used them as vehicles for wholly
personal yet very disciplined poetic expression.
Two Pieces (Overture and Fox Trot) 1924 (GS 1976) 31pp. Written during
    a period when American jazz was sweeping Europe, these pieces are
    fascinating as a document of the serious attitude that European musi-
    cians adopted toward a completely American idiom. They are among
    the most spirited of Martin's early works. They require a firm rhyth-
    mic control and a large hand span. M-D.
Etudes for Two Pianos 1955–56 (UE 13012 1969) 46pp., 20 min. Facsimile
    of MS. Transcribed by Martin from *Etudes for String Orchestra*.

Overture; Etude I—pour l'enchainment des traits; Etude II—pour le rythme; Etude III—pour l'expression; Etude IV—pour le jeu fugue ou "chacun et chaque chose à sa place." Distinctive harmonic treatment in that triads, conspiciously frequent, support and enrich melodies that use the whole chromatic scale. All twelve notes of the chromatic scale are arranged in such a way as to exploit their tonal implications. Fresh and grateful writing with influences of Hindemith, Ravel, and Shostakovitch. M-D.

Jean-Louis Martinet (1912–   ) France
Prelude et Fugue C (Heugel 1949) 10½ min. Dissonant and complex, harmonically banal, slight musical value, but from a purely keyboard point of view, it has a certain brilliance. M-D.

Bohuslav Martinů (1890–1959) Czechoslovakia
Martinů's natural feeling for folk-like syncopations and for repeated harmonic patterns gives a fascination to these works.
La Fantaisie 1929 (ESC 7641 1969) 29pp. One movement. Neo-Classic, toccata style, dissonant and pungent sonorities, passages between the pianos a half-step apart, virtuosic. Contains a bubbling stream of nervous cross-rhythms and some unpredictable, magical moments of special spiritual insight. D.
Trois Danses Tchèques 1949 (ESC 7564) 53pp., 15 min. Allegro; Andante; Allegro (non troppo). Original melodies by the composer, who manipulates them ingeniously, keeping the character and zestful rhythms of Czech native folk dances prominent. Brilliant two-piano writing; large span required. M-D.

Tauno Marttinen (1912–   ) Finland
Kukon Askel Op.100 1975 (Finnish Music Information Centre). Twelve-tone fantasy with contrasting sections and clusters. The *ppp* Lento conclusion finally settles on F♯. Requires strong octave technique. M-D to D.

Giuseppe Martucci (1856–1909) Italy
Fantasy d Op.32 (Ric 1889).
Theme and Variations E♭ (Ric 1902).

Joseph Marx (1882–1964) Austria
Castelli Romani (UE 8233 1930) 30 min. Originally for piano and orchestra; arranged for two pianos by the composer. Villa Hadriani. Tusculum. Frascati. Picturesque writing; many tempo and mood changes. Requires bravura pianism. M-D to D.

Daniel Gregory Mason (1873–1953) USA
Birthday Waltzes Op.2 (BMC).
Prelude and Fugue Op.20 (JF 0292) 11 min. Originally for piano and

orchestra; arranged for two pianos by the composer. Rather sterile writing but contains a few spots of real ingenuity. The closing of the Fugue is very Lisztian in pianistic treatment. M-D.

Scherzo Op.22b (CF 1931) 27pp. Chromatic, driving rhythms. M-D.

Divertimento Op.26a (CF 1927; LC). March. Fugue. Published separately. Mid-section of March is a colorful Trio. M-D.

Jan Masséus (1913–   ) The Netherlands

Variaties op een theme van Brahms Op.1 1948 (Donemus 1976) 28pp., 12 min. Photostat. Theme is from the Brahms Romanze Op.118/5, followed by nine variations. No. 9 is the coda and contains a fugato that leads to a brilliant conclusion. M-D.

Schubert-variaties Op.2 1950 (Donemus 1976) 12 min. Photostat. Theme and four variations. No. 4 has many contrasting parts and provides an extensive coda to the whole work. MC. M-D.

Symphonische fantasie Op.7 1947 (Donemus) 5 min. Adagio introduction leads to Allegro energico: fugal, octotonic. Andante tranquillo, followed by Adagio, Allegro (Capricioso), Andante, and Allegro assai. Each tempo change presents a change of mood and figuration. MC. M-D.

Balletto Piccolo Op.27 1955 (Donemus) 8 min. Tango; Wals; Blues; Etudietta; Barcarolle; Rumba. Bi-tonal, neo-Classic, thin textures, MC. M-D.

Bruce Mather (1939–   ) Canada

Sonata for Two Pianos 1970 (MS available from composer: c/o Department of Music, McGill University, P.O. Box 6070 Station A, Montreal, Canada H3C 3G1) 15 min. Recorded on McGill University Records 77002. A rarefied dialogue, mostly quiet. Transparent piece with repeated notes, fast flurries, and other events in exquisite array. Dynamics and pitch relations fully explored. D.

Georges Mathias (1826–1910) France

Mathias studied piano with Chopin and Kalkbrenner.

Allegro Symphonique (Heugel).

Yoritsune Matsudaira (1907–   ) Japan

Portrait 1968 (SZ) 20 loose leaves for Sections I-IV, 22 for Section V. Aleatory, avant-garde. M-D to D.

Johann Mattheson (1681–1764) Germany

Sonata g (Hin 311a 1960) 13pp. French overture leads to fast diatonic scales and tremolo figuration. Lacks originality. Requires effective finger dexterity. Int. to M-D.

Suite g 1704–5 (Hin 311b 1960) 10pp. Allemande; Courante; Sarabande; Gigue. Little or no imitation. A rare example of Baroque suite form in ensemble literature. No editorial markings. Mattheson's table of ornaments from his *Vollkommene Capellmeister* is reproduced. Makes an excellent program opener, has real charm. Int. to M-D.

William Matthews (1950–   ) USA
Matthews studied at Oberlin College, University of Iowa, Yale School of Music, and the Institute of Sonology in Utrecht, Holland. He is presently a member of the music faculty of Bates College, Lewiston, Maine.
Ferns 1976 (ACA; SBTS) 16pp. Also available in a solo version from ACA. This piece evolves from a single hexachord (D♭, E♭, A, D, G♯, A♯ upwards) and various permutations. Extensive use is made of the whole-tone scale and the set of intervals generated by such scales (major seconds and thirds, the tritone, minor sixths and sevenths). These scales and the source hexachord are all very symmetrical—like the leaves of ferns. The form is articulated by varied occurrences of the opening gesture, which is a straight whole-tone scale through five notes. This compelling piece pays homage to both the "process music" textures of Steve Reich and the "night music" imagery of Bartók. Delicate and colorful writing that requires great sensitivity from the performers. One simple preparation is necessary for each instrument: for Piano I, a strip of masking tape should be put across the strings of the top octave; for Piano II, a rubber eraser should be placed between the two lowest strings (A and B♭) to produce a dull thud. D.

Tilo Medek (1940–   ) Germany
Lesarten 1967 (DVFM 1977).

Nicolas Medtner (1880–1951) Russia
Russian Round-Dance Op.58/1 (Augener) 6 min. Cheerful bucolic themes set against a carillon-like background. Int.
Knight Errant Op.58/2 (Augener 1946) 44pp. SA design, three strongly market themes fully worked out with the development section containing an effective fugue based on the first subject. Late nineteenth-century Romantic style. M-D.

Louis de Meester (1904–   ) Belgium
Variations 1947 (CeBeDeM) 15 min.

Chiel Meijering (1954–   ) The Netherlands
Ace 1978 (Donemus) 15pp., photostat, 5 min. Long trills, extreme dynamic range, proportional rhythmic relationships, pointillistic, serial influence, repeated sections, clusters. Fluctuates between a vapory post-Impressionistic and a brittle post-Expressionistic style. Some avant-garde techniques. D.

Arne Mellnas (1933–   ) Sweden
Fragile 1973 (Edition Reimers) 2pp. No. 13 in Avanti series. One page of directions in English and Swedish. Consists of nine sections each lasting about one minute. A shorter version is possible. Low dynamic level *(ppp-p)*, aleatory. "*Fragile* should be performed in rather dim lighting. Special light arrangements are to be desired: a dim spotlight covering the musician's space on the stage, stand-lights, or candles" (from the score). Avant-garde. M-D.

Jacques de Menasce (1905–1960) USA, born Austria
Divertissement sur une Chanson d'Enfants (CF).

Felix Mendelssohn (1809–1847) Germany
Symphony I c Op.11 (Busoni—Br&H 1253). For two pianos, eight hands. Efficently managed. M-D.
The following works, all originally for piano and orchestra, have been arranged for two pianos by the composer. For a discussion of each, see MFPO, pp. 189–90.
Capriccio Brillant b Op.22
Rondo Brillant E♭ Op.29
Serenade and Allegro Giocoso b Op.43
Duo Concertant en Variations Brillantes sur la Marche Bohémienne from the Melodrama Preciosa de C. M. de Weber Op.87B 1833 (Kistner ca. 1849; LC) 14½ min. For two pianos with optional orchestral accompaniment. It was jointly composed by Mendelssohn and Ignaz Moscheles. Mendelssohn wrote the Introduction and the first two variations, Moscheles the third and fourth, and they shared efforts in the extended Finale. Chromatic runs, chords, and octaves; brilliant and effective writing. Tuneful, occasionally wistful and playful, charming, and witty. M-D.

Gilberto Mendes (1922–   ) Brazil
Mendes lives in São Paulo and writes for some of the leading newspapers and musical periodicals of Brazil. In his music he uses texts by Brazilian concrete poets.
Blirium C9 (Ric NMB 13 1965). For one, two, or three keyboard instruments, or for three, four, or five different instruments of the same family. Percussion instruments of indeterminate sounds may be added to any of the above arrangements. 4 pages of performance instructions, 2 pages of notation. 13 groups of melodic fragments are treated aleatorially; avant-garde. M-D.

Pierre Menu (1896–1919) France
Fantaisie dans l'ambiance espagnole (Durand).

Usko Merilainen (1930–   ) Finland

Papillons 1969 (Finnish Music Information Centre) 17 min. Mutatio mas-
cula: fast toccata-like figures alternate between the hands and are
passed back and forth between the instruments; Lento mid-section.
Mutatio feminea: Andante beginning, lyric, fragile and dolce character, free cadenzalike section leads to fast material of opening movement; concludes with free improvisation based on proportional
notation. Expressionistic with neo-Classical rhythmic elasticity and
an almost Romantic warmth and continuity of sound. Character-
metamorphosis of figures. D.

Michael Merlet (1939–   ) France

Musique pour Deux Pianos (Leduc 1965) 12 min. Prelude (Adagio-
Allegro): chromatic, expressionistic, large chords, large dynamic
range, octotonic, tremolo, *pp* closing. Andante: ostinato-like figure,
sometimes a single repeated note, sometimes repeated changing
chords; flexible meters; large span required. Scherzo: thin textures,
glissandi, four eights with three eighths, buoyant writing, strong
dance rhythms. M-D to D.

Anny Mesritz-van Velthuysen (1887–1965) The Netherlands

Kleuren 1938 (Donemus) 12 min. Rood; Pastel-blauw; Geel; Paars;
Groen; Oranje. Suite of strongly contrasting movements, a mixture
of styles including neo-Classicism and Impressionism. Traditional
pianistic treatment; requires large span. M-D.

Olivier Messiaen (1908–   ) France

Messiaen, the great man of French music today, commands unforget-
table, equilibrium-upsetting tonal and rhythmic palettes in his exultant
music. As one writer put it, "The music cannot be made to sound 'spiritual,' it IS spiritual." Rhythm in its many varieties is his chief concern. A
large number of important contemporary composers (including Boulez,
Stockhausen, Xenakis) have been his pupils at the Paris Conservatory.

Visions de l'amen 1943 (Durand) 45 min. Amen de la Création: celebrates
the text, "God said, 'Let there be light!' And there was light!"; Piano
II expresses the theme of light's creation in large, solemn chords
while Piano I sets ringing a clamor of bells; entire piece is a crescendo
that begins "in absolute quiet, in the mystery of primitive nebu-
lousness which contains the power of light." Amen des étoiles, de la
planète à l'anneau: an exciting barbaric dance. Amen de l'Agonie de
Jésus. Amen du Désir. Amen des Anges, des Saints, du chant des
oiseaux: denotes angels and saints chanting as they prostrate themselves before the throne of God; gradually birds begin to sing—actual
songs of the nightingale, blackbird, finch, and warbler notated precisely but in speeds slower than they are produced by the birds—

surrounding the stately chant with a joyous tumult of chirping. Amen du Jugement. Amen de la Consommation. Impressionistic harmonies, symbolic leitmotifs, and row-like ideas. "I have allotted to the first piano the rhythmic difficulties, chord clusters and all problems in velocity, charm and quality of sound; to the second piano I have allotted the principal melody, thematic elements and everything that demands emotion and power" (from the score). Some of the numbers could be performed singly or in groups of two or three. Messiaen had in mind to "demand from these instruments the maximum of force and of multifarious sonorities." Virtuoso technique demanded, and much ensemble experience required. D.

Leopold de Meyer (1816–1883) Austria
De Meyer studied with Czerny.
Grand Duo sur le Désert de Fel. David Op.44 (Schott). Written in nineteenth-century salon style. M-D.

Helmut Meyer-Bremen (–   ) Germany
Theme and Variations Op.5 (C.M.F. Rothe)

Jan Meyerowitz (1913–   ) USA, born Germany
Homage to Hieronymus Bosch 1944 (Rongwen 2032) 23½ min. Saint John of Patmos: passacaglia-like idea unifies the movement, textures thicken, *pppp* conclusion. Prodigal Son: theme evolves through various voices only to be located finally in the bass. Ecco homo: dynamic extremes, syncopation, unusual scale passages. Moderately dissonant; thick textures; dramatic style; dark tone color for much of the work penetrated alternately by suffering and ecstasy; many contrapuntal rhythms; reminiscent of Bartók and Hindemith; percussive treatment. D.

Donal Michalsky (1928–1976) USA
Sonata 1956–7 (AMC) MS, 24pp. Three contrasting, untitled movements. I: freely tonal, strong rhythms, octotonic, wide dynamic range, cantabile contrasting section, tremolo chords. II: *pp* espressivo, 6/8, fast repeated notes, large scalar gestures, sinister tensions. III: con forza, glissandi, trills, four 16ths with triplets, exploits extreme ranges of keyboards, stretto crescendo molto coda, brilliant conclusion; contains elements of nobility and bombast. M-D.

Paul-Baudouin Michel (1930–   ) Belgium
Musicoide 1971 (CeBeDeM) 19½ min. For prepared pianos.

Francisco Mignone (1897–   ) Brazil
Most of these works display Mignone's orchestral thinking, especially in the thick textures, which require the performers to underline the more important ideas and subdue the accompanimental material.

Congada 1921 (OMB) 4 min. Arranged from the opera *O Contratador de Diamantes*. The congada is a dance type which deals with the coronation and royalty theme among African tribes, particularly those of Angola. ABA; main theme is strongly Lydian and appears over an open fifth ostinato, which retains its rhythmic character throughout. A show piece, exotic and effective. M-D.

Cucumbizinho 1931 (OMB) 2½ min. The Cucumbi was a Negro dance popular in both Bahia and Rio de Janeiro. The indication for the left hand to "imitate the cavaquinho" gives a clue to the style of the piece. Fast-moving harmonic progression is repeated several times with varied melodic material; brilliant; mild bitonality. M-D.

Valsa de esquina No. 2 (Waltz of the Street Corner) 1938 (OMB) 3 min. ABA, improvisatory. Embodies the rhythms and melodic figures of the various types of waltzes found in traditional Brazilian music. Int. to M-D.

Valsas-Choro Nos. 8, 10, 11, 12 (OMB) 12 min. Slightly more developed pianistically than the *Valsa de esquina*. Nos. 8 and 10 ABA; Nos. 10 and 11 five-section rondo form. M-D.

No Fundo do Meu Quintal (In the Depth of My Garden) 1945 (Ric BA 1976) 1 min. Originally for solo piano; transcribed by the composer for two pianos. Introduction, interlude, coda. Delicate; plaintive square tune appears twice. Int. to M-D.

Samba-Ritmico 1953 (MS available from composer: Rua Pompeu Loueiro 148 20.000 Rio de Janeiro, R. J. Brazil) 5 min. Strong rhythms; Mixolydian; built on a dominant-seventh chord, which it constantly reinforces; shifts up half step at two places; added tones; bitonal; parallel seventh chords; more of a harmonic elaboration than a melodically developed structure. M-D.

Sai-Sai (Go Away, Go Away!) 1956 (MS available from composer) 2½ min. Two sections, both repeated. Charming, fluffy scherzo with enough gentle and sophisticated dissonance to raise it above the level of just another samba. Wistful; contrary-moving glissandos. M-D.

Paulistana I 1968 (MS available from composer) 8 min. Based on several themes from near São Paulo, developed in sections. Diatonic with seventh chords, added tones, bitonal, some Impressionistic influence. M-D.

Marcel Mihalovici (1898–   ) France, born Rumania

Cantus Firmus Op.97 1970 (Heugel) 9pp., 4 min. An eight-bar bass evolves into an expressive work of large and involved proportions; thick textures; varied meters. D.

Louis Milde (–   ) France

Duo Op.11 (Lienau). Andante and Rondo.

Robin Milford (1903–1957) Great Britain
Fishing by Moonlight (Hin 303 1955) 14pp., 6½ min. "This work was suggested by van der Neer's picture 'Fishing by Moonlight,' which gives a sense of great activity within an enveloping calm, and the whole is lit by the radiant glow of moonlight" (from the score). Andante espressivo: gently rocking barcarolle style, Doppio movimento mid-section, descriptive writing. M-D.

Darius Milhaud (1892–1974) France
Milhaud used a variety of techniques, both old and new. Polytonality, contrapuntal textures, folk song, and jazz are all utilized in generous measure. In addition, contrasting moods of tenderness and gaiety were popular with this prolific composer. The deep impression made on him by Latin America inspired a number of his works.

La Boeuf sur le Toit 1919 (The Nothing Doing Bar) (ESC 855 1976). This ballet of Jean Cocteau was originally cast in two-piano form and then orchestrated. This score, reduced for piano, four hands by the composer is effective on two pianos. Based on South American (mainly Brazilian) folk tunes. Titled sections immediately follow each other. Much variety in the distribution of melody and accompaniment. Rondo-like tango theme recurs between each two sections. Players are able to imagine what is taking place on stage since all the parts of the Cocteau scenario are included in the score, M-D.

Le Carnaval d'Aix 1926 (Huegel; Millikin University) 40pp. Originally for piano and orchestra, orchestral reduction for second piano by the composer. 15½ min. Suite of twelve short pieces, the first six and one or two others are excellent on two pianos. Le Corso. Tartaglia. Isabelle. Rosetta. Le bon et le mauvais tuteur. Coviello. Le Capitaine. Polichinelle. Polka. Cinzio. Souvenir de Rio (Tango). Final. Contains some of the flavor of *Scaramouche*. Fairly dissonant and somewhat humorous. M-D.

Scaramouche (Clown) Op.165b (Sal 1937) 27pp., 9 min. Probably the most famous two-piano work; it was culled from two sets of stage music, one of which had been associated with a production of Moliere's play *Le Médecin Volant*. Milhaud reshaped this music during the 1937 International Exposition in Paris. This clown shows us three moods: Vif: rambunctious, polytonal, theme characterized by its strong pulse and offbeat accompaniment, witty, "white music" (played mainly on white keys); should be loud but not rude; requires good octave technique. Modéré: expressive cradle song, pastoral, polyphonic texture in mid-section. Brazileira: in the style of a lively samba, a stunning "knock-out." The whole suite is a delight, spontaneously lyrical, rhythmically vigorous, gaily discordant, and poignantly nostalgic in its Brazilian evocation. M-D.

Fantaisie Pastorale Op.188   1938 (Sal) 22pp. 10 min. Originally for piano and orchestra, reduction for two pianos by the composer. Lacks key signature but freely tonal around F, mainly homophonic. Flowing, double glissando in thirds, octotonic. M-D.

La Libertadora Op.236   1943 (Ahn & Simrock 1960) 20pp., 7 min. Five original dances. Each movement reflects some Latin American style. Vif: folk-like tunes give this an exuberant character; 2/4 is used occasionally with the mainly 3/4 meter. Animé: opening reminiscent of Debussy's *Gardens in the Rain;* glissando opens the door for a new tune in the upper register; first theme returns with parts reversed. Modéré: a tango with one idea is developed in different keys with a constantly recurring accompaniment figure of sixteenth note, eighth note, sixteenth note. Vif: a lively dance in varied rhythms; frequent interaction between instruments; Spanish rhythm; hemiola treatment; concludes *pp.* Animé: uses Samba rhythm; tunes are Latin American inspired; excitement builds at the conclusion, where a syncopated fragment of the Samba rhythm is repeated in octaves three times (the last in canon). Both pianos have accented octaves to conclude this truly exciting work. Written at the same time Milhaud was writing his opera *Bolivar,* about the great South American liberator, and that seems to be the relationship with this work. Good high school pianists could play and would enjoy this piece. Arranged rather conservatively and resembles duet style. Piano I often has strict melody while Piano II has accompaniment exclusively in the bass clef. Sometimes this procedure is reversed. Can be played at one piano if players are careful to switch parts when necessary. Solo arrangement available from same publisher. M-D.

Les Songes (Daydreams) Op.237   1943 (Sal) 19pp. Scherzo: facile writing, mainly pentatonic, many tempo changes. Valse: short, nostalgic, moderate tempo, recalls Saties's *Gymnopedie.* Polka: animated and brilliant, more contrapuntally complicated. This suite, derived from a ballet of the same name composed in 1933, can serve as a refreshing substitute for the overworked *Scaramouche.* M-D.

Le Bal Martiniquais Op.249   1944 (MCA) 24pp. Chanson Créole: chordal, short and lyrical, in calypso style, pandiatonic. Beguine: rhythmic, brilliant. The orchestral version of this visit to Martinique is more effective. Based on several folk tunes from the French West Indies. Would serve well as a dessert piece to end a program. M-D.

Carnaval à Nouvelle Orléans Op. 275   1945 (MCA) 28pp., 9 min. Mardi gras! chic à la paille [Creole expression of joy]: vigorous. Domino noir de Cajan [the domino is a carnival costume]: lyrical and fast, unusual meter. On danse chez Monsieur Degas [they are dancing at Monsieur Degas's home]: dancelike rhythms. Les mille cents coups [a Creole exaggeration of the French "400 blows," an expression of excitement]: catchy syncopations. Cross-rhythms; coloration and dynamic contrasts are cleverly divided between the two instruments. The whole work displays strong South American influence but is based on French tunes from Louisiana. More effective in the orchestral version. M-D.

Kentuckiana Op.287 1948 (EV) 22pp., 6½ min. Built on twenty Kentucky mountain tunes. Quodlibet effect, shifting meters, predominantly contrapuntal. The resulting complex texture creates rhythmic problems, seems unable to control the thematic profusion. Milhaud's ways with American folk tunes are so similar to his ways with French airs that this suite might be called a "Suite Française." Began as an orchestral work for the Louisville Orchestra. M-D.

Paris Op.284 1948 (ESC 1959) 36pp. Suite for four pianos. Montmartre. L'île Saint-Louis. Montparnasse. Bateaux-Mouches. Longchamps. La Tour Eiffel. Colorful, freely tonal, instruments treated individually, imitation, chordal, octotonic, some superimposed tonalities. Skillfully written programmatic suite that depicts different aspects of Parisian life in a very imaginative way. Piano I is slightly more difficult than the others. M-D.

Suite Op.300 1951 (Heugel) 74pp., 18 min. Originally for two pianos and orchestra, arranged for three pianos by the composer. Entrée. Nocturne. Java fuguée. Mouvement perpétuel. Final. Uses polytonality for dramatic tension; strong contrapuntal and rhythmic usage with some rhythmic patterns piled up in a manner comparable to the stacking of polytonalities. The *Java* is a popular French dance in an alternating 3/4 and 2/4 time. Extended, appealing, but not Milhaud's strongest writing. M-D.

Six Danses en Trois Mouvements Op.433 1970 (ESC) 21pp. For two pianos simultaneously playing two different dances per movement; or for one piano, in two suites of three dances or one suite of six dances. Tarantelle–Bourrée; Sarabande–Pavane; Rumba–Gigue. Milhaud has cleverly put together this suite in which one piano plays a Tarantelle while the other piano plays a Bourrée, etc. Light writing that employs some bitonality, cross-rhythms between instruments, and folk-like tunes. The two-piano version is preferred, although the writing is not terribly pianistic and at times seems forced. The complex texture creates rhythmic problems. M-D.

See: Forrest Robinson, "The Two-Piano Music of Darius Milhaud," AMT 16, April-May 1967, 27, 42–43.

Jacques Miller (1900–   ) USA, born Russia
South of the Rio Grande (JF 1933; LC) 12pp. Lento maestoso introduction leads to a Presto con spirito section followed by a Moderato, Allegro con spirito, Lento sostenuto, and Con Spirito conclusion.

Latin American rhythms, octotonic, glissandi, fast alternating octaves. M-D.

John L. Mills-Cockrell (1943–   ) Canada
Fragments 1966 (BMI 1967). For two pianos and stereomagnetic tape. Extensive performance directions. Four sections, players may begin playing anywhere they wish. Aleatory, improvisatory, pointillistic, strings plucked and struck, avant-garde. M-D.

Leopold Mittmann (–   ) Germany
Blues (Zimmermann).
Study (Zimmermann).
Jazz (Zimmermann 1929; LC) 9pp. Virtuoso treatment. M-D.

Robert Moevs (1920–   ) USA
Moevs studied at Harvard University and for ten years in France and Italy. He has taught at Rutgers University since 1964.
Ludi Praeteriti 1976 (Games of the Past) (EBM; AMC) 20pp., 8 min. Twelve-tone, long trills, clusters, subtle sonorities, Boulez influence. The compositional procedure used is systematic chromaticism, "a modification of serial techniques in which a pitch collection is systematically exhausted but not in a rigidly ordered way" (DCM, 493). Opens with a Largo, soft, sparse, and spacious. As the tempo quickens it becomes more impatient and agitated. Textures thicken and sonorities increase as the piece reaches its final climax. Parts of equal difficulty; refined pedaling required. D.

Herman Mohr (1830–1896) Germany
Rondo Brillante A♭ Op.31 (Carl Simon). Andante introduction leads to Allegro. Strong Brahms influence. M-D.

Stephen Montague (1943–   ) USA
Montague received his bachelor's and master's degrees from Florida State University and his doctorate from Ohio State University. He now lives in London.
Paramell V 1981 (Edition Modern) 12pp. Many fast figurations repeated at various dynamics, interspersed with some large chords, strings muted with fingers, clusters, harmonics. Amplification of both pianos may be gradually introduced beginning on p. 11 and increased to the end. Vibrant, sonic colors, wide range of effects. Avant-garde. M-D.
Inundations I 1975 (Edition Modern 1784) 21 min. For three pianos, 12 hands, and tape.
Quiet Washes 1974 (Edition Modern 1776b). For three pianos and three trombones. Time length is variable.

Timothy Moore (1922–   ) Great Britain
Reciprocal Rumbas (Galliard 1966) 11pp., 3½ min. Modal, one instru-

ment carries melody while other provides the rumba rhythm, contrasting mid-section in major, *pp* ending "senza rall." Int. to M-D.

Donald N. Morrison (1917–   ) USA

Suite for Two Pianos 1981 (MS available from composer: 4023 Sarasota Ave., Sarasota, FL 33580) 33pp. Passacaglia: seven contrasted statements of the tonal (d) subject, varied meters. Intermezzo: Adagio, quartal harmony, freely tonal, full of melancholy, eerie restlessness and uneasiness behind its charm. Rondo: Allegro, thin textures, contrasting sections, cheerful, strong conclusion, neo-Classic. Morrison writes well for the medium; gentle and engaging chromaticisms are intermingled with straightforward diatonic harmonies. The drama and dramatic progress of the work are brought about by many subtleties indicated in the phrasing and the tempi. A worthy composition full of fresh and individual sonorities. M-D.

Finn Mortensen (1922–   ) Norway

"Bach, Bruckner, and Stockhausen have been the most important composers in Mortensen's development" (DCM, 498).

Sonata Op.26 1964 "Wheel-of-Fortune" (Norsk Komponistforening) 16½ min. Twelve fragments on one large page, form is variable. "Each of the two pianos has six fields. The first piano is to be played from the top towards the bottom, and the second piano in the opposite direction. Between the two groups of fields there is a time-line which designates the duration of the various fields" (from the score). Clusters, avant-garde. Improvisation required. M-D to D.

Impressions Op.32 1971 (NMO) 10 min.

Jan W. Morthenson (1940–   ) Sweden

Stereos (Reimers 1981). A formidable work from the Swedish avant-garde. D.

Ignaz Moscheles (1794–1870) Germany

Moscheles was a close friend and frequent two-piano partner of Felix Mendelssohn.

Duo Concertante Op.87b. See entry under Mendelssohn.

Hommage à Handel Op.92 (Ruthardt—CFP 8677; Steingraber; Augener; K&S; LC) 34pp. Broad opening then fast and energetic. Historical interest, with all the elegant Romantic attributes of the period. Moscheles and Johann Cramer played this piece in London in 1822 and created quite a stir. Moscheles described the circumstances surrounding this work as follows: "I found J. B. Cramer on the point of giving his yearly concert. He showed me two movements of a Sonata which he wished to play with me, and expressed a desire that I should compose a third movement as a finale; only I was not to put any of my octave passages into his part, which he pretended he could not play. I can refuse him nothing. I shall therefore be obliged to strive and write something analogous for him, the disciple of Mozart and Handel" (*Recent Music and Musicians as Described in the Diaries and Correspondence of Ignaz Moscheles*, pp. 43–44). The finale that Moscheles quickly composed is this work. M-D.

Grand Duo Concertant Les Contrastes Op.115 (K&S; Artia; LC) 27pp. Andante con moto leads to Allegro maestoso fuga; Andante religioso; Allegretto Siciliano. Plenty of display for all. M-D.

Melodic Contrapuntal Studies Op.137b (K&S). Based on ten preludes from J. S. Bach, *Well-Tempered Clavier,* with second-piano added by Moscheles. M-D.

Lawrence Moss (1927–   ) USA
Omaggio II (Seesaw) for two pianos and tape.

Moritz Moszkowski (1854–1925) Poland
Caprice G 1905 (R&E).
Deux Morceaux 1906 (R&E). Poem de mai. Melodie G.
Etude (R&E 1904; LC) 12pp. Rhythmic theme, repeated notes exploited. M-D.
Five Spanish Dances Op.12 (GS L1777). Still retains a certain charm. M-D.
Mazurka D (R&E 1905).
Minuet Op.56/6 (R&E 1902; LC) 7pp. Attractive melodies, salon style. Int. to M-D.
See: Frederick Kitchener, "The Piano Music of Moszkowski," *The Monthly Musical Record,* 57, no. 675 (March 1, 1927): 72–73.

Wolfgang Amadeus Mozart (1756–1791) Austria
Mozart played many duets with his sister, Maria Anna, but he also played on two keyboards with Clementi, Josephine von Aurnhammer, Barbara Ployer, and Constance von Weber, who became his wife.
Concerto F K 242 1776 (Badura-Skoda—Eulenburg; K; Br&H). Allegro; Andante; Rondeau. For three pianos and orchestra. Originally composed to be performed with orchestra; can be effective unaccompanied with all pianos playing tutti passages. Related in chamber music style to concertos of J. C. Bach. Three levels of difficulty, with Piano I the most involved. Piano II features some interesting solo lines, while Piano III must be alert to counting rests. The Br&H edition contains an alternate arrangement for two pianos. Cadenzas in all movements. Amiable and pleasing but reaches no great heights of inspiration. M-D.
Concerto E♭ K 365 1779 (CFP; GS; IMC; K; cadenza by R. Casadesus—Sal) For two pianos and orchestra. The orchestra is dispensible if all tuttis are played by both pianists. Allegro; Andante; Rondo. Some-

what similar to Mozart's *Sonata* for two pianos D K 448, with the same smiling euphony and a wealth of short, pretty tunes. Technical demands comparable to those of two-piano sonata K 448; parts evenly balanced. M-D.

Sonata D K 448 1781 (Br; Br&H; CFP; Hughes—GS 1504; IMC; Zen On). Allegro con spirito: flowing and facile. Andante: charming, ingratiating melodies over Alberti bass. Allegro molto: exuberant concluding rondo, contrasts a simple theme with dramatic arpeggio, scale, and sequence patterns. This work was written in November 1781 for performance by Mozart and Josephine von Aurnhammer. Antiphonal presentation of all material. It was composed in Mozart's best musical spirits, gay and *galant*. "The art with which the two parts are made completely equal, the play of the dialogue, the delicacy and refinement of the figuration, the feeling for sonority in the combination and exploitation of the different registers of the two instruments—all these things exhibit such mastery that this apparently superficial and entertaining work is at the same time one of the most profound and most mature of all Mozart's compositions" (Alfred Einstein, *Mozart—His Character—His Work* [London: Cassell, 1946], p. 273).

Andante and Variations G K 501   1786 (Henle; Ferguson—OUP in collection, *Style and Interpretation*, vol. 5; Br; CFP; VU; Ric; K; GS). Another work that seems to have been intended for performance on two pianos rather than for duet performance on one keyboard. On the MS the inscriptions "cembalo I mo" and "cembalo II do" have been scratched out and replaced with the directions "mano dritta" and "mano sinistra." But it does seem that Mozart originally had in mind another work for two pianos. The variations are engaging and charming as the simple theme develops between performers. M-D.

Sonata C K 521 1787 (Br). Allegro: bold. Andante: lyrical with contrasting middle section. Allegretto: amiable rondo. There is good evidence that this work was intended for two instruments. The two parts are treated equally, with no partiality shown to the primo or secundo. The parts were originally marked "Cembalo I mo" and "Cembalo II do." The work gains by being performed on two instruments. M-D.

Fantasia for Musical Clock Work K 608 (Busoni—IMC 585; Busoni—Br&H 5220; LC) 16pp. The two-piano idiom lends itself admirably to a mechanical subject, for the effort of synchronizing the two instruments tends in itself to produce a mechanical style. The contrapuntal texture here manifests such clarity and independence of parts that it anticipates the neo-Classic style of Stravinsky. M-D.

Sonatas C K 545; F K 533; F K 494; G K 189h (GS 1921). Published separately with a second-piano part by Edvard Grieg. Stylistically inconsistent. M-D.

Magic Flute Overture (Busoni—IMC 449 1949) 19pp. Stylistically sound, no extra padding. M-D.

Larghetto and Allegro E♭ without K. number. Based on a theme of Maximilian Stadler (G. Croll—Br 4754 1964; P. Badura-Skoda—GS) 16pp. A 35-bar Larghetto leads to the 190-bar Allegro. Mozart completed the Larghetto and the exposition of the Allegro. Equal interest in both parts. Both editors have completed the work but Badura-Skoda's reconstruction is the most successful. M-D.

Adagio and Fugue c K 546, K 426 (Badura-Skoda—GS; Krause—Br&H). Fugue was originally composed for two pianos in 1783. When Mozart arranged it for string orchestra he added the Adagio, K 546 as a prelude. Badura-Skoda has arranged the Adagio for two pianos. Some surprising harmony in the Fugue, perhaps the greatest fugue that has been written since Bach. In an elaborate foreword Badura-Skoda explains the musical thoughts that governed this presentation. M-D.

Klaviermusik. Works for two pianos and for piano four hands. Part I: Works for two pianos, vol. I in Series IX for the *New Complete Edition* (E. Fritz-Schmid—Br 4501 1955) 51pp. Preface in German. Facsimile. Contains Sonata D K 488 (375a); Fuge c K 426; Grave (8 bars) and Presto (44 bars) K Anh. 42 (375b); Sonatensatz B♭ K Anh. 43 (375c) 16 bars; Fuge G K Anh.45 (375d) 23 bars; Allegro c K Anh. 44 (426a) 22 bars. Urtext. M-D.

Jan Mul (1911–   ) The Netherlands

Suite 1944 (Donemus) 7½ min. Arietta; Fuga; Intermezzo (Fuga II); Pastorale. Requires emotional intensity (especially in the Fuga and Intermezzo) and freedom in the Pastorale; some neo-Classic influence. M-D.

Sonate 1953 (Donemus) 22pp. Allegro; Poco allegretto; Allegro. Thin textures, traditional forms and pianistic treatment, MC. M-D.

Sigfrid Walther Müller (1905–1946) Germany

Müller died in a Russian prison camp. He studied with Karg-Elert, Martienssen, and Straube.

Variationen und Fuge über ein lustiges Thema, Op.4 (Br&H 5410 1927; LC) 55pp. Written in a style similar to Reger's. D.

Hugh E. Mullins (1922-   ) USA

Mullins is a member of the music faculty of California State University, 5151 State University Drive, Los Angeles, CA 90032.

Statistics 1977 (MS available from composer). For three pianos. 6 min. Adagio: some parts play in strict time, others are independent but with same underlying quarter note tempo; harmonics; many pedal effects. Allegro: the parts in the score are not visually coordinated though they are directly under one another; can use any combination of three indicated sections; some sections repeated a number of times. Traditional and avant-garde notation, traditional pianistic figures mixed with MC harmonic treatment. Instruments are out of syncronization so it is difficult to recognize traditional writing. D.

Herbert Murrill (1909–1952) Great Britain

Dance on Portuguese Folk Tunes (J. Williams) 4 min. A series of variations on a pleasant tune bound together in a kind of rumba tempo. Mid-section is like a Furiant in major mode. An unpretentious set that might fit well into the second half of a program but is not a concert closer. M-D.

Johann Müthel (1729–ca.1790) Germany

Sonata E♭ (A. Kreutz—Nag 176) 47pp. First movement (untitled): SA, flowing figuration, cadenza-like passages. Adagio mesto e sostenuto, con affetto: c, octotonic scalar passages, embellished melody. Allegretto: SA, dancelike, sweeping figurations, cadenza-like passages. M-D.

N

Yoshinao Nakada (1923–) Japan
Songs in Praise of Beauty (Zen-On 168220).
Theme and Variations based on a Japanese Melody 1966 (Ongaku-no-Tomo). For two pianos, eight hands.

Conlon Nancarrow (1912–) USA
Nancarrow presently lives in Mexico City.
Study No. 40 for Two Player Pianos (*Soundings*, Fall 1977).
Study No. 41 for Two Player Pianos (*Soundings*, Fall 1980).

Emilio A. Napolitano (1887–) Italy
Huella (Ric BA 10898 1953) 18pp. Strong Latin American rhythms juxtaposed with melodic sections. M-D.

Barrozo Netto (1881–1941) Brazil
Minha Terra (R. Britain—Ric BR 2142 1957) 9pp., 2½ min. Britain has made a highly effective arrangement. Colorful Latin American rhythms, lush harmonies, *ppp* closing. Int. to M-D.

Frederick C. Nicholls (1871– ?) Great Britain
Sonata. In Homage to Brahms (OUP 1934; BrM).

Leonid Nicolaiew (–   ) USSR
Suite b Op.13 (Jurgenson).
Variations on a Theme of Four Notes Op.14 (Jurgenson).

Riccardo Nielson (1908–) Italy
Musica a due pianoforti (SZ 1940) 35pp., 18 min. Vibrant first movement opens with a short (one-page) Molto lento. Passacaglia: concludes with a Fugato. Dissonant, atonal. M-D to D.
Sonata (Bongiovanni 2376 1954) 28pp. Allegretto pastorale: contrapuntal and complex. Theme and three variations in cancricans, inversus, and inversus cancricans. Giga: fast and bouncy. Twelve-tone. M-D to D.

Lazar Nikolav (1922–) Bulgaria
Sone 1952 (CFP 1978).

Sonata 1952 (CFP 9572 1978) 36pp. Preface in English and German. Three contrasting movements that show solid craftsmanship; Bartók and Shostakovitch influences; Romantic overtones throughout. Requires technical dexterity of both players but well worth the effort of learning the work. M-D to D.

John Jacob Niles (1892–1980) USA
These three arrangements are based on American folk tunes.
My Little Mohee (GS 1934; LC) 7 pp. Charming, simple treatment with the mid-section "in the manner of a hymn." Int.
Green Beds (GS 1947; LC) 6pp. Int.
The Story of the Bee (GS 1947; LC) 6pp. Based on "Do Take Care of the Bee Boys." Int.

Lionel Nowak (1911–   ) USA
Arabesque on Two Folk Tunes 1944 (ACA) 13pp. Melody is generally treated in one instrument with the accompaniment in the other. Octotonic, rolled chords, chromatic flowing lines, feathery syncopations, evolves cleverly, big conclusion. M-D.

Emmanuel Nunes (1941–   ) Portugal
Nunes studied with Stockhausen and attended the New Music Darmstadt courses from 1963 to 1965.
Litanies du Feu et de la Mer 1969 (Sal). For one, two, three, four, or five pianos, 25 to 60 min.

O

Roh Ogura (1916–   ) Japan
Dance Suite 1953 (Ongaku No Tomo Sha 1980) 44pp. Neo-Classic, French influence, melodic, freely tonal. M-D.

Maurice Ohana (1914–   ) France
Ohana is one of France's most respected composers, a musician of Spanish extraction who has created a highly personal style rooted in the mysteries of folk music and bathed by the Mediterranean sun. He is fond of African and Andalusian folk music.
Sorôn-ngô (Sal 1969) 12½ to 14 min. Reproduction of MS, very legible, 24pp. Explanations and annotations in French. Avant-garde, some conventional notation, aleatory sections, clusters, tone rows, highly complex. D.

Silvio Omizzolo (–   ) Italy
Fantasia-Ouverture da Concerto 1946 (Ric 128696; LAP) 24pp. Allegro marcato introduction leads directly to a striding Sostenuto, un poco maestoso, developed mid-section, Presto coda. Preference for harmonic seconds. M-D.

Norman O'Neill (1875–1934) Great Britain
Variations and Fugue on an Irish Theme Op.17 (Schott 1905; BrM; LC) 27pp. Nine carefully contrasted variations and fugue. M-D.

Henry Orland (1918–   ) USA, born Germany
Morphine Metamorphoses 1978 (MS available from composer: 21 Bon Price Terrace, St. Louis, MO 63132) 5 min. One movement. M-D.

Hans Osieck (1910–   ) The Netherlands
Berceuse Sentimentale et Marche Joyeuse sur quatre notes 1960 (Donemus) 12pp. The four notes are B-E-E-D. An expressive Andantino leads to Allegro con spirito in a Tempo di marcia. Clever, MC sonorities, ostinato-like figuration, exciting conclusion. Large span required. M-D.
Chant Anglais 1967 (Donemus) 6pp. Andante cantabile: lovely melody is

set with quartal harmony, equal interest in the two instruments, tonal, *pp* with an E added sixth chord. Int. to M-D.

Le Petit Rêve 1956 (Donemus). For three pianos. 3pp. Andantino semplice con moto: flowing lines, freely tonal, chorale-like tune heard in one instrument or another at all times. Based on a theme from the third piece (Always Dreaming) of Osieck's *Eight Short Character Sketches* 1950 for piano duet. Int.

Rondo sur une danse Russe 1948 (Donemus) 12 min. Presto: bitonal, flexible meters, rhythmic, quartal harmony, fast parallel full chords. Large span required. M-D.

Hisatada Otaka (1911–1951) Japan

Midare—Capriccio für zwei Klaviere Op.11 1939 (Ongaku No Tomo 1968) 38pp., 10 min. "The title 'Midare' has no direct bearing on the Japanese harp music with the same name. The first stanza starts out abruptly with various rhythms interwoven and thus the title was derived" (from the score). Lento introduction, followed by sections marked Vivace capriccioso, Tranquillo o cantabile, Tempo wie zu Anfang, Andante-tranquillo, Vivace, Meno mosso, con moto quasi andante. Strong rhythms, pseudo-oriental sonorities, double glissandos, fast alternating octaves. D.

Joseph Ott (1929–   ) USA

Events 1969 (AMC) 4 min. For two pianos with audience participation. Contains instructions for performers and audience. Score is two pages of figures and numbers. Avante-garde. Requires pianists with much experience in this medium to bring it off successfully. M-D.

Matrix 2 1968 (AMC) 10pp., 4 min. Harmonic clusters used for echo effect, serial, pointillistic, builds to large climax and ends with "echo effect a morendo." M-D.

P

Luis de Pablo (1930–   ) Spain

Comme d'Habitude 1971 (Sal) 20 min. For one pianist on two pianos and a synthesizer.

Ignace Jan Paderewski (1860–1941) Poland

Fantaisie Polonaise Op.19 (Bo&Bo 1895). Originally for piano and orchestra; arranged for two pianos by the composer. 21 min. One movement divided into three large sections. Based on Polish folk songs. Includes double glissandos, complex textures, and brilliant figuration. D.

Carmine Pagliuca (–   ) Italy

Variazioni su tema di Domenico Scarlatti (EC 1974) 73pp. Andante theme in d is followed by nine contrasting variations; the final one is by far the most difficult. Variation 4 is a fugue with effective use of stretto. Neo-Classic, freely tonal. Exceedingly pianistic throughout. M-D.

Roman Palester (1907–   ) Poland

Variati 1963 (SZ 6643 1967) 11 min. Theme. Interlude. Coda, followed by four variations. Twelve-tone, complex rhythms. D.

Robert Palmer (1915–   ) USA

Sonata 1944 (PIC 1959; AMC) 32pp., 15 min. Allegro energico: bold pesante rhythms contrast with graceful and cantabile sections. Andante sostenuto: serious, quiet octotonic opening works up to a marziale mid-section before settling down to a variation of the opening material. Allegro giusto: fugal, different time signatures in the two players' parts but easy to follow. Flexible meters in all three movements. An impressive work that deserves more hearings. D.

Selim Palmgren (1878–1951) Finland

Maskenball Op.36 (Lienau 1914) Vol. 1: Extempore. Dancing-girl. Vol. 2: The Black Mask. Funny Suite: uses two interior ostinati in contrary motion between the bass and soprano parts, which state the main melody in unison. Requires well-developed technique coupled with a dramatic sense. M-D.

Leopold van der Gilse Pals (1884–   ) Switzerland, born Russia
Sonata e (Br&H).

Howard Pancoast (1943–   ) USA
Pancoast is a Denver composer-pianist who has studied at the Eastman
School of Music and the University of Colorado.
Variations for Two Pianos (Myklas 1981) 6 min. This set of six variations
and coda is based on a theme that lends itself well to the crafting of
"pattern" writing, which makes the variations sound more difficult
than they are. Uses a few MC chords such as major sevenths and
thirteenths in rather traditional chord progressions. Large span required. M-D.
Two Piano Rondo Op.7 (Myklas 1981) 12pp. Rhythmical and accented,
clever syncopation, octotonic, repeated octaves, short slower section before return to opening idea and closing, bright and cheerful.
M-D.
Duo (Myklas). M-D.

Héctor Panizza (1875–1967) Argentina
Tema con Variaciones (Ric).

Gen Parchman (1929–   ) USA
Elegy 1963 (Seesaw 1971) 5pp., 3½ min. Works to climax, subsides, coda,
pp conclusion. Warm colors, effective. M-D.

Edmund Parlow (1855–   )
Three Pieces Op.84 (K&S). Bolero. Notturno. Waltz.

Robert Parris (1924–   ) USA
Toccata (ACA).

Carl Parrish (1904–1965) USA
Valse Viennoise (JF 1928; LC) 15pp. Charming, colorful, not easy. Int. to
M-D.

Ian Parrott (1916–   ) Great Britain
Fantasy and Allegro 1946 (Lengnick) 27pp., 11 min. Much imitation between instruments, thin textures, MC. M-D.

Michael Parsons (1938–   ) Great Britain
Parsons studied at Oxford and the Royal College of Music and also
studied experimental music with Cornelius Cardew at Morley College,
London. He teaches in the Fine Arts Department of Portsmouth Poly-
technic.
Rhythm Studies I and II (in *Score—An Anthology of New Music—GS*
1981) 1p. "Each figure is repeated over and over. Pianist one begins
playing figure one, and Pianist two enters soon after, beginning figure
one on a different beat. After a number of repetitions Pianist one

changes to figure two while Pianist two continues playing figure one. Then Pianist two moves on to figure two (beginning it on a different beat from Pianist one) . . . etc. Do not pause between figures. Move through the piece in this way, playing alternately the same figure and adjacent figures and when on the same figure avoid unisons" (from the score). Varied tonal rhythmic figures are fully composed, jazz influence. Avant-garde. M-D.

Bernardo Pasquini (1637–1710) Italy
Pasquini composed fifteen sonatas for two keyboards. Many of them use the three movements Allemande, Courante, and Gigue, and although they are titled sonatas, they are actually forerunners of the suite. The individual movements, especially those in quick time, are short and concise, but despite their conciseness, skeletal notation, and schematic arrangement, the sonatas display considerable variety.
Sonata d (W. Danckert—Nag 231; Shedlock—Novello). Given in its original form (bass line only) and arranged for performance. Allegro: vigorous bass part, intricate counterpoint. Adagio: dialogue between instruments. Vivace: tosses imitation between the players. Shedlock gives his own realization of parts for all three movements. Int. to M-D.
Sonata 10 e (Bèrben 1312). Bass lines are filled with rhythmic vitality and contain within themselves the germ of perfect musical structure. Requires sensitivity and fantasy on the part of the performers. M-D.
Sonatas g, F (F. Boghen—Durand). Must be realized from the bass line, as that is the only part given.

Corrado Pasquotti (1954–   ) Italy
Racconti 1974 (SZ) For two pianos, three performers. 9 leaves, photostat. 14½ min.

Émile Passani (1905–   ) France
Rapsodie Provençale (Jobert).

Lee Pattison (1890–1966) USA
The Arkansas Traveler (GS 1925) 11pp. Fine arrangement of this old fiddlers' tune, clever counterthemes, excellent encore. M-D.

I. L. Pavia (–   )
Polka Viennoise on a Theme by Johann Strauss (OUP).

Willem Pelemans (1901–   ) Belgium
Pelemans writes in a late-Romantic style.
Sonata I 1947 (CeBeDeM) 20 min.
Sonata II 1954 (CeBeDeM) 13 min.

Leonard Pennario (1924–   ) USA
Fireflies Op.3/1 (Summy-Birchard 1942; LC) 6pp. Light, fanciful, effective. Int. to M-D.
March of the Lunatics (Leeds).

Barbara Pentland (1912–   ) Canada
Two-Piano Sonata 1953 (CMC) 11 min. Allegro con moto; Andante; Allegro giocoso. Well-crafted serial writing. M-D.

Clermont Pépin (1926–   ) Canada
Ronde Villageoise 1956; arranged 1961 (CMC) 4 min. Int.

Ronald Perera (1941–   ) USA
Perera graduated from Harvard University and studied composition with Leon Kirchner. He is presently a member of the music faculty of Smith College.
Tolling 1979 (MS and tape available from composer, c/o Music Department, Smith College, Northampton, MA 01063) 31pp. For two pianos and tape. Contains performance directions. Five large sections with smaller subsections. A fundamental tension is generated by the pervasive A's and the more or less successful forays in between these repeating A's to establish alternative pitch centers. Strong tritone influence, "quasi mandolina" tune often serves to fill in melodically the outlined tritone; glissandi on and plucked strings, harmonics, clusters, "inside" and "on keys" playing, tolling effects on tape, pointillistic, wide dynamic range, avant-garde. D.

Vincent Persichetti (1915–   ) USA
Persichetti is one of the most distinguished voices from what might be termed the muscular-conservative school of American music.
Sonata Op.13 1940 (EV 1955; AMC) 28pp., 14 min. Photostat of MS. Lento: stately theme builds to a climax that leads to a quicker-paced section with cadenza-like figures, declamatory, rhapsodic, brilliant closing. Allegretto: waltzlike, Ravel inspiration, delicate and graceful at the beginning; builds to a grand, lusty ending. Largo: short, serious, delicate, and poignant. Vivace: robust and rhythmic, changing meters. Consistent in its dissonant style, freely tonal. All movements based on same thematic material but developed along different lines, constantly shifting key centers, changing meters and tempos, thick textures, some foggy sonorities, polytonal. A splendid work, thoroughly traditional in its neo-Romantic virtuoso deployment of instrument against instrument; full of expertly crafted effects that really sound. D.

Émile Pessard (1843–1917) France
Suite Pittoresque (Lemoine).

Rudolf Peters (1902–   ) Germany
15 Variations on an original Theme Op.10 (Simrock).

Pierre Petit (1922–   ) France
Le diable à deux (ESC 1972) 12pp. Opening and closing Presto sections in 12/8, 3/2 enclose a tuneful mid-section Valse lente. Some knocking on the piano lid is required. Freely tonal around C, octotonic, fleeting two with three *pp* closing. M-D.

Felix Petyrek (1892–1951) Czechoslovakia
Six Concert Etudes 1934 (UE; Bèrben) 48pp. Short studies in fast 16th notes, double notes (thirds and sixths), arpeggios, and interlocking chords. Traditional harmony. M-D.
Toccata and Fugue in the Mixolydian Mode 1934 (UE) 24pp. Toccata: broad, expansive, uses a short chorale theme later used in Fugue I. Fugue II: spirited, a mirror fugue. Organlike texture. D.

Isidor Philipp (1863–1958) France
Caprice en doubles notes (GS 1941; Hamelle) 1½ min. An elfin-like study with most of the writing in thirds between the instruments, chromatic, wisps away to nothing. M-D.
Choral de Bach (Sal).
Concertino sans orchestra (Sal). For three pianos. Prélude: features a pensive and tranquil development of the opening three-bar theme. Barcarolle: presents a diatonic melody accompanied by gently rocking rhythms, floating arpeggios, and shimmering glissandos. Scherzo et intermezzo: vivacissimo; polyrhythmic; bustling Scherzo is followed by a slower, whimsical intermezzo which in turn is abruptly interrupted by the recapitulation of the vigorous Scherzo. Toccata: after a vigorous introduction to the perpetuum mobile, brilliant Toccata, a sonorous, lyrical theme (passed among all three pianos) is contrasted with scalar passages in thirds, octaves, and *pp* broken chords. Gigantic closing section uses theme from the first movement stated in rhythmic augmentation. M-D.
Feux-Follets (Jack o'Lanterns) Op.24/3 (GS 1953). Brilliant; fine encore. Requires fleet fingers. Int. to M-D.
Menuet de Haendel (Sal).
Menuet de Mozart (Sal).
Variations de Beethoven (Sal).

Robert Phillips (–   ) USA
Chaconne and Toccata 1964 (Seesaw 1976) 24pp. Chaconne is generally on the quiet and flowing side while the Toccata is fast and contains strong rhythms. Freely tonal, trills, subito effects, figures in alternating hands. M-D.
Sonatina 1970 (Seesaw 1973) 21pp. Allegro; Interlude; Vivace. Expanded

tonal idiom, octotonic themes, tremolo chords in both hands of one pianist while other moves through various figurations, neo-Classic. M-D.

Riccardo Pick-Mangiagalli (1882–1949) Italy

Humoresque Op.35 (Carisch) 66pp., 14 min. Somewhat on the order of the Richard Strauss *Burleska* but without as many varied moods. M-D.

Gabriel Pierné (1863–1937) France

Fantaisie-Ballet Op.6 (Leduc; BrM) 17pp. Originally for piano and or-chestra; arranged for two pianos by the composer. Sectionalized, strong dance influence. M-D.

Scherzo-Caprice Op.25 (Leduc).

Poème symphonique Op.37 (Leduc).

La Samaritaine, 2e prélude (Lemoine).

Tarantelle (Leduc) from Second Suite.

Willem Pijper (1894–1947) The Netherlands

Sonata 1935 (Donemus 1948) 33pp., 12½ min. Facsimile of MS. Allegro aperto, ma pesante: waltz rhythm in one piano juxtaposed against 5/4 in other piano, gliding parallel chords. Grave: disjunct melody. Mod-erato assai: many pianistic busy figurations, dramatic gestures, chromatic, ends without fanfare. The work is characteristic of Pij-per's polytonal, polyrhythmic, and rather unemphatic style. Loosely hinged to tonality by sprinkling of Impressionistic ostinato chords. D.

Daniel Pinkham (1923–   ) USA

Four Short Pieces (ACA).

Octavio Pinto (1890–1950) Brazil

Scenas Infantis (GS 1934) 25pp. Run, Run! Ring Around the Rosy. March, Little Soldier. Sleeping Time. Hobby Horse. This delightful programmatic work, originally for solo piano, takes on a new and almost too showy character in this arrangement by the composer. Although its original simplicity is lost, this set is especially enjoyable for young teenagers. Int. to M-D.

Eugenio Pirani (1852–1939) Italy

Gavotte Op.34 (CF).

Etude de Concert Op.51 (Schlesinger 1893; LC) 15pp. Arpeggio figuration and many chords. M-D.

Fantasia d Op.87 (Lienau).

Paul A. Pisk (1893–   ) USA, born Austria

My Pretty Little Pink (MCA 1945; LPA; LC) 7pp. Clever imitative writ-ing, a merry fugue based on a Southern folk tune. Int.

Johann Peter Pixis (1788–1874) Germany
Rondeau Hongroise Op.33 (Richault; NYPL).
Variations brillantes sur un thème original Op.112 (Hofmeister; NYPL).
Variations on "The Huguenots" Op.137 (Ric).

Raoul Pleskow (1931–   ) USA
Music for Two Pianos 1965 (Seesaw) 29pp., 9 min. Facsimile score. A
    strong, blocky work in three untitled movements. Set in big dissonant
    overlapping cycles; contains remarkable rhythmic display. Beautiful
    division of duties between the two instruments, arm clusters, plucked
    strings. A quotation from *Trio* by Stefan Wolpe (Pleskow's teacher)
    appears in the second movement. A solid and impressive piece. D.
Suite 1977 (ACA). Six short untitled movements. Tightly organized, ex-
    pressionistic, contrapuntal textures, asymmetrical meters, concen-
    trated variation technique, atonal. D.

Simon Pluister (1913–   ) The Netherlands
Divertimento 1977 (Donemus) 17 min. Entrata; Rondo; Scène de Ballet;
    Farmer's Hornpipe; Intermezzo; Hornpipe II. Chromatic, strong
    rhythms. Hornpipes appear to be based on folk tune material. Color-
    ful, effective. M-D.

Edouard Poldini (1869–1957) Hungary
Study on the Impromptu Op.90/2 by Schubert (Hainauer: BrM).
Au Château de Cartes (House of Cards Suite) (CF). Le Roi (The King).
    Sérénade à la Dame de Coeur (Serenade to the Queen of Hearts).
    Danse des Valets (Dance of the Jacks).

Robert Pollock (1946–   ) USA
Introduction and Dance 1967 (APNM) 21pp., 6 min. Facsimile score.
    Serial, pointillistic, flexible meters, harmonics, glissandi, economy of
    material. Pianistic in conception yet makes few concessions to the
    nature of the instrument. No surface gloss or virtuosity of the more
    blustering type; clean-limbed ideas unfold within ornate surround-
    ings. Schoenberg influence. M-D to D.

Manuel Ponce (1882–1948) Mexico
Mexican Idyll (PIC 1952) 8pp. Flowing scale passages, 6/8 tune, effective
    native charm, excellent encore. M-D.

Luctor Ponse (1914–   ) The Netherlands
Feestgericht Op.26 1957 (Donemus) 77pp. Allegro molto ritmico; An-
    dante; Vivace tumultuoso; Allegro molto. Thin textures, flexible
    meters, neo-Classic orientation, equal distribution between players.
    M-D.
Musique pour ballet, No. 2 Op.28 1959 (Donemus) 36pp. Allegro mod-

erato; Andante misterioso. Similar to Op.26 but makes greater use of octaves and pointillistic technique. M-D to D.

Marcel Poot (1901–   ) Belgium
Rhapsodie 1947 (CeBeDeM) 20pp., 9 min. Facsimile score. A one-movement work, freely tonal, contrasting tempi. M-D.
Legende Epique (ESC).

Archibald James Potter (1918–   ) Ireland
Phantasmagoria 1960 (Association of Irish Composers) 20 min.
Finnegans Wake 1961 (Association of Irish Composers) 10 min.

Francis Poulenc (1899–1963) France
With Poulenc, color was as important an element of composition as linear drawing is to the painter. He possessed a unique inventive gift and a rich imagination.
Sonata for Piano, Four Hands or Two Pianos 1918, rev. 1939 (JWC) 18pp. Prélude: c, ABA with coda, B section based on second idea of the A section, no real development; only a few foreign key areas presented with some dramatic and dynamic tension. Rustique: C, ABA, coda based on B, gently hypnotic. Final: C; divided by tempos—Tempo 1, presto, Tempo 1, coda; rhythmic ostinato from Prélude returns at bar 49; mid-section is cyclic and developmental. A compact, integrated work written with dry astringency and "wrong-note" harmonies. Reflects subtlety of Ravel and joviality of Satie. More effective on two pianos. M-D.
Aubade 1929 (Sal). Originally for piano and 18 instruments; reduced by Poulenc for two pianos. This hybrid between a concerto and a ballet is a multi-section work. Numerous short motives; sharp contrast between wit and brilliance in some sections and the Gallic melancholy of others; some sections reminiscent of the music hall. Improvisatory style. M-D.
L'Embarquement pour Cythère 1951 (ESC) 11pp., 2½ min. A Valse-Musette. Simple tune is wistful and catching; a little dissonance is cleverly sprinkled in. Inspired by Watteau's painting, Poulenc's work was originally written for his film score *Le Voyage en Amérique*. This amusing little rondo must not be taken seriously—it only tips its hat and winks over its shoulder at Watteau's canvas. Themes alternate from one piano to the other. Int.
Capriccio (d'après *Le Bal Masqué*) (Sal) 5 min. Varies from the earlier *Caprice,* based on same work, by an eight-bar introduction and a brief quasi-cadenza inserted at rehearsal number 14. This ready-made and accessible work deserves more playing. Thick polytonal chords mixed with scalar figuration and lyric melodies. A witty and

delightful lampooning of French musichall ditties and the cancan. Requires an infectious rhythmic bounce and a proper saucy flair. M-D.

Sonata 1953 (JWC; ESC) 19 min. Prologue: C♯, slow, ends slower, large dynamic range (*fff* to *ppp*), colorful octave use. Allegro molto: a, scherzo-trio-scherzo, obvious pianistic devices cleverly used. Andante lyrico: C♯, key signature holds it in tow, mood of contemplation and serenity; Poulenc thought this the center and most important movement. Epilogue: quotes from the Prologue and Andante movements; idiomatic Poulenc at a fast tempo. The work displays a rich, gleaming instrumental texture based on Poulenc's choral style, a masterpiece. D.

Elégie (en accords alternés) [in alternating chords] 1959 (ESC) 11pp., 6 min. ABA, coda. Quiet, slow, melancholy, lovely melody, syncopated full chords effective between the two pianos, Impressionistic. A note in the score from Poulenc indicates the work should be played in an improvisatory manner with much pedal. M-D.

Henri Pousseur (1929–   ) Belgium

Mobile 1956–58 (SZ 1961). Three "mobiles" appear on inserted sheets, cues in French, ten pages of interpretive notes in four languages. One of these inserted sheets, chosen at random, provides material to be played during the performance of the principal score. Movement of the hand during changes of position is part of the composition. "Three speeds for changing position of the hand are defined, for each piano, in the course of Section I" (from the score). Provides insight into the type of game that a composer plays with performers. Aleatory, pointillistic. The work never seems to achieve an effective conclusion. D.

Jan Pouwels (1898–1974) The Netherlands

Tango 1935 (Donemus) 4 min. Octotonic, tango rhythm, contrary double thirds, polytonal, big climax then subito *p* closing. M-D.

Lorna, proloog en 3 balletten 1948 (Donemus) 22 min. Proloog; Vlinderballet; Ballet der revelusouwer; Herfstballetten I en II. Contrasted movements, spread-out arpeggiation, octotonic, dance directions, colorful. M-D.

John Powell (1882–1963) USA

In the Hammock (Scene Sentimentale) Op.19 1920 (GS; LC) 9pp. For two pianos, eight hands. Features a flowing theme over undulating figuration. M-D.

Dirge—Natches-on-the-Hill: Three Virginia Country Dances Op.26 1932 (GS; LC; John Powell Foundation, Box 37711 Richmond, VA 23211)

7 min. American folk tunes combined with a colorful pianistic style.
M-D.

Etore Pozzoli (1873–1957) Italy
Allegro di Concerto (Colombo 129804).
Tarantella (Colombo 120087 1926) 17pp. Contains some brilliant, scintil-
lating, and highly effective writing. M-D.

Almeida Prado (1943–   ) Brazil
Aurora 1975 (Tonos) 21 min. Originally for piano and orchestra; reduction
for two pianos by the composer.

Sergei Prokofiev (1891–1953) USSR
Waltzes (in vol. 11 of Collected Works of Sergei Prokofiev—K) A suite of
Schubert waltzes transcribed and arranged by Prokofiev. See more-
complete entry under Schubert.

Hugo Puetter (1913–   ) Germany
Duo Concertante c♯ (Müller).

Q

Pascual Quaratino (1904–   ) Argentina

Malambo (Ric BA 11859 1960; LC) 11pp. Allegro animato, strong Latin American rhythms, freely moving and repeated chords interspersed with lyric lines, driving closing section. M-D.

Canto de la Llanura (Ric BA 11858 1960; LC) 7pp. Andantino espressivo; lilting rhythms accompany sensuous melodies. This piece and *Malambo* would make a good contrasting group. M-D.

Marcel Quinet (1915–   ) Belgium

Novelettes 1973 (CeBeDeM) 41pp., 8 min. Two large pieces that exploit the instruments thoroughly. Pianistic treatment reminiscent of Rachmaninoff but more contemporary sounding. Neo-Classic and atonal. D.

Dialogues 1975 (CeBeDeM) 43pp. 9 min. Originally for two pianos and orchestra; reduction for third piano by the composer. Two large sections, atonal. Much dialogue between the instruments. M-D.

R

Niels Otto Raasted (1888–1966) Denmark
Five Variations and Fugue on a Theme of Dietrick Buxtehude Op.14
(Leuckart).

Henri Rabaud (1873–1949) France
Divertissement sur des Chansons Russes Op.2 (Enoch 1899; LC) 18pp.
Sectionalized; effective finale. Slavic "sounds," a few haunting
tunes. M-D.

Sergei Rachmaninoff (1873–1943) USA, born Russia
Rachmaninoff's two-piano writing is of the highest order. Its sonorous
harmonies and florid decoration result in unusually effective music for the
medium. A breathless motion permeates most of his two-piano works,
and their technical resourcefulness is unexcelled since Liszt.
Russian Rhapsody 1891 (Leeds 1955; USSR) 35pp., 8½ min. This is not a
sequence of folk tunes but a set of variations on a theme that may or
may not be of folk derivation. More Slavic and simpler than the
Symphonic Dances Op.45; features a number of lovely filigrees. Although a vivid virtuoso piece, it lacks the degree of textural contrast
and thematic invention that Rachmaninoff achieved in his later works
for two pianos. Brilliant, along the lines of Liszt's *Hungarian Fantasia*. M-D.
Prelude c♯ Op.3/2 1892 (Foley 1938; LC) 9pp. Arranged by the composer.
An outstanding example of an arrangement of an effective solo work
that is just as effective for two pianos. Int.
Suite I Op.5 "Fantasy" 1893 (Bo&H; IMC) dedicated to Tchaikowsky.
Barcarolle: lyric and florid, much repetition of same melody. O Night
of Love: colorful and passionate. Tears: agonizing and despairing,
pianistic decorations around a four-note motif. Easter: large climax
with imitation of bells and Russian liturgical chant. Thick textures,
rich sonorities, long movements (Easter is the shortest). Movements
are prefaced by poems—musical images of four poetic texts. Explores a greater variety of sonorities obtainable from the two instru-

ments than in the *Russian Rhapsody*. This is one of the very few works that sound as if two pianos were the only possible medium for the music. Sumptuous melodies, sonorous chordal structures, pyrotechnical figuration, and even some unabashed musical imitation (bird calls in the second movement, chimes à la Mussorgsky in the fourth). D.

Suite II Op.17 1901 (Bo&H) 24 min. Introduction: a march in a chordal setting, rich in harmonic structure and strongly rhythmic, ABA plus coda. Waltz: a virtuoso essay in controlled momentum; middle section reveals the melodic Rachmaninoff encountered in the smaller pieces of Op.16 *(Moments Musicaux)*. Romance: emphasizes emotional qualities; closely related to the second and third movements of the Second Piano Concerto. Tarantella: principal theme is an Italian folk song; the two pianos reach almost orchestral stature. Written with a full knowledge of the possibilities of the idiom. D.

Symphonic Dances Op.45 1940 (Foley; Schott) 102pp., 26 min. Arranged by the composer for two pianos. Non Allegro; Andante con moto (Tempo di valse); Lento assai—Allegro vivace. A strong work in its own right and not an outline or study for the orchestral version. It is approached in the same manner as the piano works of Ravel that he transformed into orchestral masterpieces. Displays adventurous, pungent harmonies (notably the shifting, ambiguous harmonization and sinister, unsettling chromatic figures in the lilting central waltz), contrasts of texture, and rhythmic subtleties, often suggesting jazz influence. D.

Italian Polka (Belwin Mills 1938). Arranged for two pianos by the composer.

Album for Two Pianos (Schott BM3500). Includes Prelude c♯, Op.3/2; Waltz and Romance, from *Suite* II Op.17; Piano Concerto II, Op.18, complete.

Josef Joachim Raff (1822–1882) Switzerland
Raff attained a prominent place in German musical life and exerted a powerful influence.

Ode au Printemps Op.76 (Schott) 23pp. Contrasting moods and sections, a glittering "morceau de concert" in every possible way. M-D to D.

Chaconne a Op.150 1870 (CFP; Costallat; LC) 16pp. Allegro introduction (tristamente e maestoso) leads directly to the Chaconne (Quasi Andante). Each variation exploits a different figuration. M-D.

Fantaisie g Op.207a (K&S; LC) 55pp. Four large contrasting sections, straightforward Romantic writing. The Larghetto is especially attractive. M-D.

Valse Impromptu (Schott).

Nikolai P. Rakov (1908–   ) USSR

Humoresque, Waltz and Polka (USSR 1948; LC) 48pp. Grateful writing throughout. The syncopation in the Polka has strong appeal. M-D.

Bernard Rands (1935–   ) Great Britain

Espressione IV 1964 (UE 14156) 19pp., 9 min. Aleatory, traditional and proportional notation, harmonics, much use of damper pedal, strings plucked, clusters, tones sounded by tapping with fingernails or knuckles on the keyboard but without depressing the keys, five different types of pause, similar in style to Boulez *Structures,* avantgarde. Requires split-second ensemble. M-D.

Espressione V-B (UE) 5–15 min.

György Ranki (1907–   ) Hungary

"1514" Fantasy 1962 (EMB 4095) 21 min. For two pianos and percussion. After woodcut series by Gyula Derkovits, 1514. Five contrasting movements; expanded tonality. Virtuoso pianism required. D.

Gunter Raphael (1903–1960) Germany

Toccata Op.45 1937 (Süddeutscher Musikverlag 1613).

Jabonah Op.66 1948 (Br&H 1951) 21pp., 10 min. Originally a ballet suite for orchestra; arranged for two pianos by the composer. Allegro molto; Lento; Allegro moderato; Allegro feroce. Colorful, driving rhythms, glissandi. Requires large span. M-D to D.

Sam Raphling (1910–   ) USA

Bagatelle Cubana (PIC).

Israel Rhapsody (PIC).

Square Dance (Edition Musicus 1946) 7pp. From "American Album." Original tunes and rhythms, syncopated chords and repeated figures, changing meters, glissando ending, clever. M-D.

Eda Rapoport (1900–   ) USA

Suite for Two Pianos 1941 (AMC) 18pp., 12 min. Out for a Stroll. By the Sea. Sunset. Dance of the Fireflies. Contrasting movements in a slightly expanded Romantic idiom. M-D.

Karl Aage Rasmussen (1947–   ) Finland

Genklang 1972 ("Echo" or "Resonance") (WH 4310 1977) 33pp., 20 min. For grand piano (four hands), prepared piano, honky-tonk (mistuned) piano, and celesta. Explanations in English. Provides a variety of sonorities in tonal and rhythmic patterns. Requires five keyboard players at four instruments. One grand piano is played by two performers, one piano is prepared with screws and rubber, and a third is mistuned and set apart from the others. The fifth performer plays a celesta. Threads of Mozart (K.311) and Czerny are interlaced with a collage of sounds that also includes Mahler. Will make the listener play guessing games! M-D.

Maurice Ravel (1875–1937) France

Ravel's synthesizing genius produced a uniquely personal style that exploits the use of modal melodies and the intervals of the seventh and ninth. Ravel extended the pianistic traditions of Franz Liszt but expressed himself in a quintessentially French way.

Sites auriculaires 1895–97 (Sal) 12pp. Habanera; Entre cloches (Among Bells). "This bizarre title, easily the strangest in Ravel's catalogue, indicates the spiritual influence of the enigmatic Erik Satie, whom the composer visited during his student days. Ravel apparently envisioned two places (sites), which were to be visited, or comprehended, as it were, by means of the ear. The first piece, Habanera, suggests a Hispanic landscape, and is the first of many compositions in Ravel's oeuvre. An epigraph, taken from Baudelaire's 'A une Dame créole,' from the collection *Les Fleurs du Mal,* focuses upon the sensuous exoticism found in the music. The Habanera was later orchestrated and is well known as the third movement of the *Rapsodie Espagnole.* Entre Cloches evokes an unspecified site engulfed in bells. The spiritual influence of Edgar Allan Poe is apparent in this composition, which is an important forerunner of 'La Vallée des cloches' (The Valley of the Bells) from the piano suite *Miroirs.* The premiere of *Sites Auriculaires* took place in Paris on March 5, 1898, and marked Ravel's formal debut as a composer" (from the introduction by Arbie Orenstein). M-D.

Sheherazade 1898 (Sal 1975). From the *Ouverture de Féerie* for orchestra, reduced for piano, four hands or two pianos by Ravel. 40pp. This version was written first, and an orchestrated version is dated November 1898. This picturesque overture was written as an introduction to a fairy tale opera inspired by the *Thousand and One Nights* that was never even sketched out by Ravel. The formal structure is: introduction (bars 1–24), exposition (24–88), development (89-179), modified restatement (180–217), and return of introduction (218-34), which serves as the coda. Extensive use of whole-tone scale, suggestions of misty oriental exoticism (Persian-like melody). Has a spiritual kinship with Ravel's song cycle *Sheherazade* and is strongly influenced by Rimsky-Korsakov's orchestral suite *Sheherazade.* M-D.

Introduction and Allegro 1906 (Durand) 25pp., 13 min. Originally for harp, string quartet, flute, and clarinet; arranged for two pianos by Ravel. This work sounds especially congenial on two pianos—the solo harp after all, is not that dissimilar. M-D.

Rapsodie Espagnole 1907 (Durand) 16½ min. Arranged for two pianos by the composer. Prélude à la nuit. Malaguena. Habanera. Feria. Requires a brilliant, symphonic approach. All the specifics of the orchestral version are as graphic as they are with the symphonic counterpoint. Achieves the same stunning brilliance in this arrangement as in the originals. M-D.

Ma mere l'oye (Mother Goose Suite) 1908 (Durand). Pavane de la Belle au bois dormant: cool, clear, quiet counterpoint. Petit Poucet: wandering figures, descriptive bird calls. Laideronnette, Impératrice des Pagodes: pentatonic, gamelan imitations, exotic bell-like sonorities. Les Entretiens de la Belle et de la Bête: moderate waltz characterizing the conversation between Beauty and the Beast. La Jardin Féerique: slow sarabande with pealing bells as conclusion. The original score was for two pianos, according to Michael Field in "Piano Music for Four-Hands," *Musical America,* 69, October 1949, 27. A lucid score that draws its inspiration from folk art. The third movement includes a brisk theme that resembles the nursery tune "Peter, Peter, Pumpkin Eater." An unusual feature of this suite is the fact that it is almost entirely pianissimo. At one place in the third movement the directions are *ppp sans nuances* (without shadings). M-D.

Frontispiece 1918 (Sal 1975) 4pp. (15 measures). For two pianos, five hands. This work was first printed in *Les Feuillets d'Art* (1919, No.1). "It was composed at the request of the Italian poet Ricciotto Canundo, whose *S.P. 503 Le Poème de Vadar* is a collection of philosophically oriented reflections based upon the author's combat experiences in World War I. Ravel's composition captures some of the exoticism, water images, and evocations of nature found in the poetry" (from the introduction by Arbie Orenstein). Constant triplet figuration, ornamented melody, grace-note punctuation, unusual ostinato usage, parallel chords at conclusion. Experimental. M-D.

La Valse 1919–20 (Durand) 42pp., 17 min. Arranged for two pianos by Ravel. Mouvement de Valse Viennoise. A sinister re-creation of Johann Strauss's nineteenth-century Vienna. Requires tight control and a fiendish, measured quality. D.

Bolero 1928 (Durand). Arranged for two pianos by Ravel in 1930. 30pp. The second pianist may "stop" (press on the strings) the opening ostinato with his left hand and simulate the timbre of the snare drum if the constant repetition becomes monotonous. Colors and hypnotic spell must be uncannily evoked. M-D to D.

Jean Henri Ravina (1818–1906) France
Ravina wrote elegant and attractive salon piano pieces, which enjoyed considerable vogue. He published four-hand arrangements of all of Beethoven's symphonies.

Grand Duo sur l'Opéra Euryanthe de C.M. von Weber Op.9 (Schott).
Souvenirs de Russie, Fantasie, Grand Duo Op.64 (Schott).

Gardner Read (1913–   ) USA
Sonata da Chiesa Op.61a (Seesaw 1971) 20pp. Transcribed for two pianos by the composer. Intrada; Canzona; Ricercare. Eclectic style, chordal, contrapuntal, modal, driving rhythms in the Ricercare. M-D.

Vladimir Rebikoff (1866–1920) Russia
Cauchemar Op.26 (Jurgenson; LC) 21pp. Quatrième Tableau Musical-Psychologique. Chromatic, fast octaves, cantabile melodies, varied moods, fluent writing. M-D.

Louis Rée (1861–1939) Great Britain
Rée was a pupil of Leschetizky; gave two-piano concerts with his wife, Susanne Pilz-Rée; and published transcriptions for two pianos.
Variations and Fugue on an Original Theme Op.14 (Forberg).
Suite Champêtre Op.21 (Robitschek).
Scherzo Op.32 (Forberg 1909; LC) 14pp. Chromatic lines, fleeting, big climax. M-D.

Max Reger (1873–1916) Germany
Variations and Fugue on a Theme by Beethoven Op.86 1904 (Bo&Bo) 63pp., 28 min. Twelve massive variations of highly complex counterpoint and full late-Romantic instrumental sonorities. Fugue provides comic relief. Marches steadily toward a grandiose summing-up of previous thoughts and ideas. Reger later orchestrated this score. D.
Introduction, Passacaglia and Fugue Op.96 1906 (Bo&Bo) 25 min. Gigantic, broad and powerful, thick textures. Much harmonic and contrapuntal interest, especially in the clockwork fugue. Combines majesty of style with haunting Romantic melancholy and restless chromaticism. D.
Variations and Fugue on a Theme by Mozart Op.132a ((Simrock; CFP 1915) 57pp., 27 min. Transcription from orchestral work by Reger. Theme is from the Sonata A, K.331. D.
Complete Edition, Vol.14 (Br&H). Contains all the four-hand, two-piano works, including Piano Concerto f Op.114.

Steve Reich (1936–   ) USA
"The music of Steve Reich tends to be absolutely spellbinding. Reich's music is so original in impulse and form that it challenges all past assumptions about the goals of the art" (Alan M. Kriegsman, *The Washington Post*, February 24, 1972).
Piano Phase 1967 (UE 16156) 2pp., 15–20 min. For two pianos or two

marimbas. His earliest acknowledged instrumental composition, the work in which Reich discovered that the technique of "phasing" (i.e., staggered repetition) could be applied in live as well as in tape music. One pianist repeats over and over again a pentatonic motif of twelve 16th notes (later condensed to eight and then four 16ths), with the second pianist moving ahead in small gradual tempo adjustments. It is carefully—almost obsessively—structured, but sounds spontaneous or even improvised. Time-space notation. Sustains a soothingly hypnotic or trancelike effect through repetition of the basic music materials; intellectually involving and sensuously appealing at the same time. M-D.

Carl Reinecke (1824–1910) Germany
Reinecke was a close friend of Mendelssohn and Schumann in his youth. All the following works have interest and are well written in a classic nineteenth-century style. Emotional impact is slight but themes are unusually persuasive. Most are in the M-D category.

Andante and Variations Op.6 (Hofmeister 1843; BrM). Modeled on Robert Schumann's Op.46.

Variations on a Sarabande by Bach Op.24b (J.Schuberth 1874).

Impromptu on a Motif from Schumann's "Manfred" A Op.66 (Br&H 1860).

Pictures from the South Op.86 (CF). Originally for solo piano.

Improvisations on a French Folk Song "La Belle Grisélidis" Op.94 (Br&H 1870).

Improvisations on a Gavotte by Gluck Op.125 (CFP 1879).

Festival Overture Op.148 (Br&H). Originally for orchestra.

Variations on "A Mighty Fortress is Our God" Op.191 (Forberg). Originally for orchestra.

Overture to Klein's drama Zenobia Op.193 (Br&H). Originally for orchestra.

Prologus solemnis in Form einer Ouverture für grosse orchester Op.223 (Br&H 1893; LC) 27pp.

Three Sonatas (CFP; Hofmeister; LC) Op.240 1898: F, 12pp. Op.275/1 1906: G, 29pp. Op.275/2: C, 47pp.

Four Pieces Op.241 (CFP). Etude (LC). Minuet (LC). Scherzo in canon form (LC). Allegretto Giojoso (LC).

Karel Reiner (1910–   ) Czechoslovakia
Předehra a Tanec (Overture and Dance) (CHF) 28pp. Předehra: a broad Maestoso with spread-out sonorities leads to an Allegretto; other contrasting sections follow; Allegro assai coda. Tanec: 5/4, rhythmic, two-note ideas, expressive throughout, thin textures, final three pages use melodic octaves to reinforce the main melodic ideas. The

Tanec requires rhythmic incisiveness and thrusting shapes to create its dramatic ambiguities and expressive sections. Neo-Classic, MC. M-D.

August Reinhard (1831–1912) Germany
Waltz Suite Op.94 (Br&H; Simon; LC) 13pp. Four contrasting waltzes. M-D.

Alfonso Rendano (1853–1931) Italy
Allegro in A Minor (EC 10103 1978) 30pp. Preface in Italian

Armando Renzi (1915–   ) Italy
Adagio e Rondo variato (Zanibon 4238) 18 min.
Viaggio d'Orfeo, nomos citaredico (Zanibon 4264) 22 min.

Franco Renzulli (–   ) USA
Two Conversations (Seesaw).

August Reuss (1871–1935) Czechoslovakia
Fantasie Op.42 (Tischer & Jangenberg).

Roger Reynolds (1934–   ) USA
Less Than Two 1979 (CFP). For two pianos, two percussionists, and four-channel computer-generated sound. For a quartet of skilled chamber music musicians. M-D to D.

Josef Rheinberger (1839–1901) Liechtenstein
Duo a Op.15 (Hamelle; K&S; Fritzsch 1868; BrM; LC) 30pp. Allegro alla breve; Canon a due; Finale-Molto vivo e brusco. Pleasant and effective, somewhat similar in style to Brahms. M-D.
Duo Op.149a (K&S). After the Suite for organ, violin, cello, and string orchestra. Transcribed for two pianos by the composer.

Rhené-Baton (1879–1940) France
Menuet pour Monsieur, frère du Roy Op.5 1901 (Durand 1909; LC). 12pp. Originally for orchestra, arranged for two pianos by the composer. Colorful, flowing, tuneful. M-D.

Marga Richter (1926–   ) USA
Melodrama—Suite for Two Pianos 1958 (CF) 49pp., 16 min. Andante–Allegro. Allegretto. Theme and [9] Variations. Andantino. Presto. Contains a number of styles including lyric, boogie-woogie, neo-Classic, post-Romantic. Strong pianistic understanding on the part of the composer. Theme and Variations movement seems the most successful. M-D to D.

August Riedel (–   ) Germany
Variations über R. Schumann's "Fröhlicher Landmann" Op.13 (Rieter-

Biedermann 1887; BrM) 11pp. For two pianos, eight hands. Charming, clever, and worth reviving. Int. to M-D.

Tom Riedstra (1957–   ) The Netherlands
Kapstok 1978 (Donemus) 14 min. For two pianos and six percussionists.

Wallingford Riegger (1885–1961) USA
Dance Suite 1933–35 (PIC) 46pp., 11 min. Written for modern dance groups. Evocation: expresses "the spirit of tragedy" (from the score), trills, tremolos, tonal and atonal material. The Cry: brooding and somber, slight touch of jazz, thin textures. New Dance: twelve-tone influence, motoric, ostinato rhythm, Latin American style, expresses joyous affirmation, much rhythmic variety. M-D.
Scherzo Op.13a 1932 (PIC 1954; AMC) 22pp., 7 min. Twelve-tone; row is treated in various ways and finally appears in an exciting toccata texture; contrasted sections. A large concert piece. D.
Canon and Fugue Op.33 1954 (SP; AMC; UCLA) 7pp. Originally for strings. Canon: d, Allegro non troppo. Fugue: makes a fine climax. M-D.
Variations Op.54a 1954 (AMP) 18 min. Handsome materials. Their development in short, concise variations is imbued with a piquancy and a sure sense of purpose and determination. Contains two cadenzas. D.

Ferdinand Ries (1775–1846) Germany
Ries also wrote a Trio for two pianos and harp.
Sonata B♭ Op.32 1816 (Brockhaus). Ries probably showed this work to his teacher, Beethoven, for inspiration. M-D.
Sextet Op.142 (Schott) For two pianos (or harp), clarinet, horn, bassoon, and double bass.

Vittorio Rieti (1898–   ) Italy, born Egypt
Rieti embraced the neo-Classic cause and has consistently remained faithful to it.
Second Avenue Waltzes 1942 (AMP 1950) 49pp. Six contrasted concert waltzes full of delicious Viennese lilt and clichés, laced with some polytonal chord textures. Graceful, melodious, not banal, even when they quote (knowingly) Verdi's *La Traviata* and Ravel's *Valse*. Popular on programs. M-D.
Suite Champêtre 1948 (AMP) 39pp. Bourrée: energico e spiccato; a few "wrong notes" add spice. Aria et Ecossaise: forced dissonance in the Aria while the Ecossaise is a fluffy delight. Gigue: fuguelike, clever,

contrasted legato and staccato sections, strong B♭ closing. A sharply etched, rather acid piece; its neo-Classicism is Franco-Russian after the Boulanger-Stravinsky persuasion. Full of pseudo-archaic tunes, most of them charming. Aims to entertain. M-D.

Chess Serenade 1945 (AMP) 48pp. Prelude: ingeniously interwoven keyboard figures. Gavotte: rather commonplace. Serenade: interesting harmony and color effects. Valse: deliberately banal, in Rieti's familiar (by now!) style of banter. Clown March. An entertaining balletic suite. Delightful, effective, spontaneous, clever, tongue-in-cheek musical commentary. Requires two experienced pianists to do it justice. M-D.

New Waltzes for Two Pianos 1956–57 (AMP) 73pp. Belinda Waltz. Valse Caprice. Valse Champêtre. Valse Légère. Valse Lente. Rondo Waltz. Tonal, delightful, lean textures, strong lyric melodies. M-D.

Chorale Variations and Finale 1961 (Gen 1971) 32pp. Adagio religioso chorale, nine variations, and coda. Strong chromatic vocabulary, crawling with vivacious pianistic figurations, lengthy. M-D.

Three Vaudeville Marches 1969 (Gen) 20pp. Early twentieth-century salon style. M-D.

Valse Fugitive 1970 (Gen) 7pp. Same vintage as the *Three Vaudeville Marches*. M-D.

Scherzo-March 1976 (Gen) 11pp. Rhythmic, much use of triplets. M-D.

Gossip 1979 (Gen). The publisher suggests that the lonely duo-pianist tape the "other" part and play along. Slight material, many sequences, monotonous accompanying figures. I can find no spicy conversation involved, even between the instruments. Int. to M-D.

Two Pieces for Two Pianos (Gen 1980) 4 min. Introduction and Bagatelle. Moonlight Dance. Romantic sonorities, rubato, graceful, pleasing. M-D.

Heinrich Rietsch (1860–1927) Germany
Fantasy f (Forberg).

Jean Rivier (1896–   ) France
Quatre sequences dialoguées pour deux pianos (Billaudot 1973) 45pp., 19 min. Allegretto piacevole. Presto jocando. Quasi notturno: uses a twelve-tone row handled freely. Allegro ruvido: a mixture of styles and moods. Full of percussive effects, many accents, tempo changes, and a pulsating abrasive directness that occasionally gives way to moments of great tenderness. MC, polytonal. Requires first-rate pianism and ensemble experience. D.

Mervyn Roberts (1906–   ) Great Britain
Two Chorales (Novello 1947; LC). Andante sostenuto. Allegro tranquillo. Tonal, flowing. Int. to M-D.

Variations on an Original Theme (Novello).

Edwin Robertson (1938–   ) USA
Robertson is a product of the University of Richmond, the SBTS, and Florida State University. He is presently a member of the music faculty of the University of Montevallo, Montevallo, AL 35115.

Three Movements for Two Pianos 1978 (MS available from composer) 34pp. Allegro: flowing 6/8, freely tonal, works to a big climax. Adagio: twelve-tone influence, a few new notations, recitative-like, long pedal effect closes movement. Allegro energico: rhythmically active sections contrast with chorale and invention-like sections, drives to impressive closing. M-D.

George Rochberg (1918–   ) USA
Prelude on "Happy Birthday" 1969 (TP) For almost two pianos. 4pp. Tune begins quietly and builds to *fff*, bell sonorities, decrescendo of tune to the end. A radio may be turned on loud to heighten the effect. M-D.

Marguerite Roesgen-Champion (1894–   ) France, born Switzerland
Trois Valses (Senart 1937; LC) 23pp. Valse Romantique. Valse Triste. Valse 1930. In Poulenc style. Int. to M-D.

Richard Roessler (–   ) Germany
Sonata Op.22 (Simrock 1912; LC) 58pp. Allegro con fuoco; Moderato e grazioso; Molto vivace; Molto sostenuto—Presto. Style sounds like a combination of Reger and Saint-Säens. M-D to D.

Jean Roger-Ducasse (1873–1954) France
Au jardin de Marguerite (Durand 1912). Originally a symphonic poem for double chorus and orchestra; transcribed for two pianos by the composer. Choeur de la dispute des fleurs. Interlude. Prélude et choeurs.
Le joli Jeu de furet (Durand 1911) 19pp. Originally for children's choir and orchestra; transcribed for two pianos by the composer.
Suite française 1907 (Durand 7740; LC) 41pp. Originally for orchestra; transcribed for two pianos by the composer. Ouverture. Bourrée. Récitatif et Air. Menuet vif. M-D to D.
Variations plaisantes sur un thème grave 1907 (Durand 7875) 29pp. Originally for harp and orchestra; transcribed for two pianos by the composer. Well laid out between the instruments. M-D to D.

Bernard Rogers (1893–1968) USA
Music for Two Pianos and Percussion 1937 (Margun BP6034) 6 min.

Julius Röntgen (1855–1932) The Netherlands
Scherzo Op.33 (Alsbach; LC) 11pp. M-D.
Ballade Op.36b (Carl Simon). Based on a Norwegian folk melody.

Guy Ropartz (1864–1955) France
Fantaisie D (Sal).
Piece b (Durand 1899) 24pp. Franck influence, moderately effective florid
melodic writing. M-D.
Symphony II (Sal). Arranged for two pianos by the composer.

Ned Rorem (1923–   ) USA
Sicilienne 1950 (PIC 1955; AMC) 8pp. In three sections (each repeated),
flowing, more tonal than some of his solo piano works, delightful and
refreshing counterpoint, Ravel influence, has delicacy and charm. M-
D.
Four Dialogues 1953–54 (Bo&H) 20 min. For two solo voices and two
pianos. Texts by Frank O'Hara. "The form is strict sonata whose
four sections relate the old comedy of boy meets girl. . . . As for the
pianists, they may consider themselves of equal importance to the
singers: the music was created as a Quartet of Dialogues" (Ned
Rorem). M-D.

Sydney Rosenbloom (1889–1967) Great Britain
Variations and Fugue Op. 16, on an original theme (Augener 1915; Ashdown; BrM; LC) 29pp. Six variations and a fugue in late nineteenth-
century Romantic style. M-D.

David Rosenboom (1947–   ) USA
Movement for Two Pianos 1965 (AMC) 23pp. Contrasting sections, expressionistic and neo-Classic influences, flexible meters, wide arpeggio figuration, expanded tonality. Opening material (varied) returns
at conclusion. M-D.

Jacques Rosenhain (1813–1894) Germany
Fantasia Appassionata Op. 40 (Hofmeister). Grand Duo. Also for piano
and harp.

Leonard Rosenman (1924–   ) USA
Duo (PIC).

Manuel Rosenthal (1904–   ) France
La Belle Zélie Suite Romantique 1948 (Jobert 1959) 64pp. Pastorale en
rondeau. Le valet malicieux et la soubrette mélancoliques. Minuet
burlesque. Ballabile. L'Escarpolette. Final (Can-Can). Sonorities too
thick for entertainment music. M-D to D.

Gioacchino A. Rossini (1792–1868) Italy
La Danza—Tarantella a (Schott 04877; LC) 8pp. Transcribed by Franz
Liszt. From *Soirées Musicales*. Brilliant, short, and effective. An
opening cadenza by Liszt adds considerable interest. M-D.

Albert Roussel (1869–1937) France

Evocations Op.15 1910–11 (Durand 8143; LC) 21pp., 42 min. Originally for orchestra; transcribed for two pianos by the composer. Les Dieux dans l'ombre des Cavernes: a musical depiction of the impact that viewing images of Hindu deities has on Europeans. La Ville rose: a scherzo inspired by the ancient town of Jaipur. Aux bords du fleuve sacré: deals with the attractions of nature in the holy city. Shows a fondness for acidulous harmonies and rather dense textures. Influence of Indian music seen in the flat second, raised fourth, and flat sixth degrees of the scale. Throughout his life, Roussel, a well-practiced traveler, was fascinated with the Near and Far East, and *Evocations* is but one of many compositions reflecting this fascination. D.

Pour une fête de printemps Op.22 1920 (Durand 9939; LC) 23pp., 12 min. Transcribed for two pianos by the composer. This atmospheric symphonic poem contains a pleasing freshness of sonorities that arise naturally from the melodic and contrapuntal thought. Displays more sense than sensibility, more integrity than imagination. Bitonal usage creates an impression of tension and heightens the poignancy of the emotional situation. M-D. to D.

Francis Routh (1927–   ) Great Britain

Routh writes in an accessible contemporary style that has much logic and conviction.

Concerto for Two Pianos Op.32a 1976 (Redcliffe) 67pp., 23 min. Quick: SA, contrasts lie in the tonalities of the different sections, starting from an identifying chord spelled out in the opening. Slow: Impressionistic style used to a greater extent than in the outer movements; based on a two-chord sequence; inward, contemplative, suggestive of a private world, for each individual listener to enter as he wills; rate of harmonic change is slow; constructed around a central point or pivot (Piano I C in bar 36) to which the first part descends, and from which the second part (Piano II) immediately starts to grow. Lively: SA, correspondingly uncomplicated in mood and style, full of gaiety, no pedal in this entire movement. Sparkling writing in the two outer movements. M-D.

Gaspard le Roux (ca.1660–1707) France

Le Roux may be considered a summing up of the French keyboard traditions and the springboard for the final brilliant and consummate splash of François Couperin.

Pieces for Harpsichord 1705 (A. Fuller—Alpeg 1959). Contains arrangements of five pieces for two harpsichords *(Pièces pour deux clavecins):* Allemande La Vaunert; Gavotte en rondeau; Menuet; Second

Menuet; Courante; and a Gigue that does not appear anywhere else in the collection. Int. to M-D.

Howard Rovics (1936–   ) USA
Ives Surprise (ACA).

David Rowland (1939–   ) Great Britain
Kaleidoscope 1976 (Donemus). For two pianos and two percussion players, 104pp. Seven movements, each requiring different percussion instruments. 1.: large *ff* chords including some in tremolo between the hands; eight Balinese gongs, eight flat gongs, and eight mounted cow bells provide rhythmic interest; large span required. 2.: two xylophones, more full chords, marcato. 3.: two vibraphones (without motor), irregular unsynchronized sections, dynamic extremes, thin textures. 4.: two large Balinese nipple gongs, three timpani, six tam tams, four large cymbals, three flat gongs, one large bass drum; clusterlike sonorities contrasted with single notes; percussion has melody. 5.: vibraphone (without motor), xylophone; pointillistic, long pedals. 6.: eight tom toms, two large tam tams; duplets in percussion against many fast changing triplet chords in both pianos; chromatic. 7.: two sets of tubular bells, two sets of lower octave crotales; Impressionistic, *mp* conclusion. The entire work is a kaleidoscope of varied textures, sonorities, and rhythms. D.
Kaleidoscope II 1980 (Donemus) 33pp. Reproduced from holograph, photostat.

Alec Rowley (1892–1958) Great Britain
Figurines (J. Williams; BrM) 4 min. Pleasing, slick, and extremely well written for the instruments. Int. to M-D.
Pastorale (Bo&H). M-D.
Prelude and Toccata (JWC 1943; LC) 16pp., 5 min. Flowing, 3-page Prelude followed by a motoric Toccata. M-D.
Suite (Lengnick 3729) 27pp., 9 min. Allegro risoluto; Moderato; Allegretto; Allegro moderato. Freely tonal, thin textures, parallel chords, strong lyric line. M-D.

Anton Rubinstein (1829–1894) Russia
Fantasia f Op.73 1865 (C. Simon; Hamelle; LC) 79pp. Dedicated to Rubinstein's brother Nicolas. Lento–Allegro con fuoco; Moderato assai; Andante con moto (theme and 11 variations). This work is a catalogue of nineteenth-century style and pianistic gestures. With the Rubinstein brothers performing it, a success was surely assured! M-D to D.
Polka (R&E 1906; LC) 11pp. Sectionalized; one part is a fugue. M-D.

Beryl Rubinstein (1898–1952) USA
Suite for Two Pianos 1939 (GS). Prelude: rondo, light and cheerful. Canzonetta: melodic, big climax. Irish Jig: an animated Celtic dance. Masks: varied meters, barbaric, exciting. Well dispersed between the instruments, Impressionistic, thoroughly pianistic. A gaily rhythmed and amusing piece. M-D.

Ernst Rudorff (1840–1916) Germany
Variations E Op.1 (Br&H)

Zbigniew Rudzinski (1935–   ) Poland
Three Songs for Tenor and Two Pianos (AA) 7 min. To lyrics by Ezra Pound, James Joyce, and William Rose Benét. English text.

Wim de Ruiter (1943–   ) The Netherlands
Relations 1978 (Donemus) 35pp., 10 min., photostat. Explanations in Dutch and English. Serial, sectionalized, extensive pedal usage, presto 16th-note passages to be played without metric accents, pointillistic, extreme dynamic range, avant-garde. Large span required. D.

Adolf Ruthardt (1849–1934) Germany
Sonata quasi Fantasia Op.31 (K&S). In one movement.

S

Camille Saint-Saëns (1835–1921) France
In economy of means, clarity of texture, and balance of parts, Saint-Saëns
is one of the foremost composers of two-piano music. He was especially
fond of two-piano playing and valued it very highly.

Tarantelle Op.6 1851 (Durand 3482; LC) 29pp. Originally for flute,
clarinet, and orchestra; two-piano reduction by the composer.

Duo Op. 8 1859 (d'après les Duos pour piano et orgue) (Durand).

Introduction et Rondo Capriccioso Op.28 1870 (Durand; IMC) Originally
for violin and orchestra; transcribed by Debussy.

Le Rouet d'Omphale, Poème Symphonique Op.31 1871 (Durand 2033;
LC) 33pp. Originally for orchestra; two-piano reduction by the composer.

Marche Héroique Op.34 1871 (Durand 1304; UCLA) 18pp. Originally for
orchestra; transcribed by the composer for two pianos, four hands
and also for two pianos, eight hands (Durand 2907).

Variations on a Theme of Beethoven Op.35 1874 (Durand; GS) 49pp., 16
min. Based on the Trio of the Minuet to *Sonata* E♭ Op.31/3. The
eight ingenious variations, fugue, presto, and coda constitute brilliant
two-piano writing and overflow with Gallic charm. They maintain
throughout a fair semblance of Beethoven's manner and matter. Fast
alternating chords between the instruments pose a special problem.
"The famous Parisian understood composing for two pianos as no
one since his time has really understood it. So well does his music fit
the medium, that he has been called the Chopin of Two-Piano Literature. Grounded in the classics (Saint-Saëns edited many works of the
ancients), wise in his selection of material, talented and indefatigable,
his products were bound to be worthy. To this background may be
added his love of Oriental music. There are but a few of his compositions which are not tinged with the freshness of an Eastern flavor. In
the *Variations* the Oriental cast is to be noted particularly in the
section known as the *Funeral March* and the bars immediately following" (from the program annotations of a Luboshutz and Nemenoff
recital). M-D to D.

Phaëton Op.39 1873 (Durand 1958; LC) 15pp. Originally for orchestra; reduced for two pianos by the composer. M-D

Danse Macabre Op.40 1874 (Durand 2099) 13pp. Originally for orchestra; transcribed for two pianos by the composer. This descriptive transcription is almost as effective as the original version. M-D.

La Jeunesse d'Hercule, Poème Symphonique Op.50 1877 (Durand 2330; LC) 17pp. Originally for orchestra; two-piano transcription by the composer. M-D.

Symphonie II a Op.55 1878 (C. Debussy—Durand 1908; UCLA) 31pp. The transcriptions by Debussy are outstanding and show the high regard he had for his fellow countryman. M-D.

Minuet and Gavotte Op.65 1881 (IMC 1729) 12pp. From the *Septet;* transcribed for two pianos by the composer. Charming and graceful writing. M-D.

Polonaise Op.77 1890 (Durand) 19pp, 10½ min. Overly long for its limited inspiration; much pianistic embellishment compensates for invention. M-D.

Scherzo Op. 87 1890 (Durand; IMC) 30pp. Light but brilliant. One of the thrilling virtuoso numbers of the two-piano repertoire. Exemplifies the composer's transparent and scintillating technique applied to canon. Requires facile pianism. M-D.

Caprice Arabe Op.96 1894 (Durand) 17pp. One movement. A virtuoso display piece with large skips, broken octaves, and fast figuration. D.

Caprice Héroïque Op.106 1897 (Durand) 22pp. Varied sections, an arsenal of pianistic gestures. M-D.

Cyprès et Lauiers Op.156 1919 (Durand; LC) 31pp. Originally for organ and orchestra; two-piano transcription by the composer. Requires fine octave and tremolo technique. M-D.

Etienne Marcel Airs de Ballet 1883 (C. Debussy—Durand 4155) 35pp. Originally an opera. Introduction. Entrée des Ecoliers et des Ribaudes. Musette guerrière. Pavane. Valse. Entrée des Bohémiens et des Bohémiennes. Final. An outstanding transcription. M-D.

Carnival of the Animals 1886 (Berkowitz—Durand) 40 min. Effective transcription for two pianos by Ralph Berkowitz. Fourteen numbers make up this "Grande Fantaisie Zoölogique," one of Saint-Saëns's most effective works. Originally scored for two pianos and orchestra; also highly effective when performed using just the piano parts from that version, without the orchestra. M-D.

Karel Salmon (1897–1974) Israel, born Germany

Salmon studied at the universities of Heidelberg and Berlin, as well as at the Academy of Arts, Berlin, where Richard Strauss was his teacher. He settled in Jerusalem in 1933.

Suite on Greek Themes 1943 (IMI 1966) 68pp., 18 min. Based on a collection of Greek folk songs and dances. Syrtos thrakikos: a slow dragging dance. Theme and Variations. Intermezzo—The Lemon Tree: constant repetition of theme in various textures. Finale—Horra Hellenica: two sections, Greek and Jewish elements intermingle; at the end the themes appear simultaneously. Salmon's most popular piece. D.

Lionel Salter (1914–   ) Great Britain
Scottish Reel (Lengnick 1947; LC) 16pp. Uses the following tunes: Green Grow the Rashes, Loch Rynach, Sweet Molly, Perth Assembly, Colonel McBain, Wind that Shakes the Barley, Countess of Sutherland, Pease Strae. "The nature of this piece demands that the tempo remain absolutely constant throughout" (from the score). Int.

Leo Samama (1951–   ) The Netherlands
Variations and Fantasies on a Passacaglia Theme 1977–78 (Donemus) 30pp., 15 min. Photostat of MS. A Molto lento section exploiting repeated octaves in one instrument and major seventh chords in the other leads to a Festivo section, where main ideas are displayed in full chords. Other contrasting sections explore unusual sonorities in an expressionistic style. Unusual but easy-to-read notation; textures range from very thin to very thick; highly dissonant. D.

Swend David Sandström (1942–   ) Sweden
Concentration 1972 (NMS 1975) 17pp.

Claudio Santoro (1919–   ) Brazil
Duo für 2 Klaviere 1972 (Tonos) 5pp., 6 min. Directions in German. Harmonics, clusters, pointillistic gestures, improvisation, glissandi on strings, avant-garde. M-D.

Ramón Santos (1941–   ) Philippines
Five Pieces for Two Pianos 1970 (Sundry Music Publishing House 1975). Includes performance directions. Prelude. Game. Intermezzo. Dialogue. Elegia. Aleatory, dynamic extremes, harmonics, pointillistic, tremolos, clusters, avant-garde. D.

László Sáry (1940–   ) Hungary
Catacoustics 1967 (EMB 6203) 15 min. Serial, traditional, and proportional notation, with the third movement using no barlines. Arm and hand clusters, unusual meter signatures: $4+1/8$, $10+1/8$, etc. Avant-garde. D.

Gustav Satter (1832–1879) Austria
Satter became famous through his concert tours of the Americas. His compositions were praised by Berlioz.
L'Union, Morceau de Salon Op. 73 (Schott).

In der freien Natur Op. 77 (Ludwig Hoffarth). Wald-, Wasser-und
   Bluemengeister.
Trois Morceaux Lyriques Op.81 (Schott). Marche. Chanson. Dance.
Trois Romances sans Paroles Op.82 (Schott).
Poème Op.87 (Schott).
Tarantelle de concert (J. André).

Emil von Sauer (1862–1942) Germany
Die Spieluhr (Boite à musique) (Schott 1932; LC) 11pp. Originally for solo
   piano; transcribed for two pianos by the composer. Colorful musical
   representation of a music box. One of Sauer's most popular works.
   M-D.

Henri Sauguet (1901–   ) France
Much of Sauguet's work contains some of the refined popular elements
found in Satie.
Les jeux de l'amour et du hasard 1932 (ESC). Although rather flimsy in
   musical character and content, this suite does possess wit and a
   certain charm. M-D.
Valse brève 1949 (ESC) 12pp. Written for Gold and Fizdale. Ideas are
   well spread between the two instruments. Graceful, flowing and effective. M-D.

Alice Sauvrezis (–   ) France
Dialogues (Leduc 1913; LC). Suite of nine contrasting pieces. Int.
Duo (Durand).

Carl Maria von Savenau (–   ) Germany
Two Preludes e♭, b Op.22 (Cranz).
Phantasiestück Op.41 (Khant).

Robert Saxton (1953–   ) Great Britain
Sonatas 1977 (JWC) 21pp., 10 min. Sectionalized, long trills, expressionistic, decorative elements, pointillistic, serial influence, proportional rhythmic relationships, much percussive use of the
   instruments, little use of pedal, evaporates to a secco *pp* final chord.
   Shows sensitive appreciation of instrumental sound. Ornamental textures are built from the superposition of delicately detailed lines that
   blur the distinction between melody and harmony by containing one
   within the other, while the rhythms tend to evolve from this linear
   development and to contribute to the pulse of the surrounding textures rather than to underline their metrical background. The basic
   material is quite simple, often taking the form of undulating, irregu-
   larly divided figurations, but complex in the ways in which these
   figures are made to interrelate and to yield a developing continuity
   from recurrences of the same material in different contexts. The

gentle rise and fall of the musical landscapes seldom include sharp contours, so that their contrasts are those of muted colors and subtle shading, and their charm lies less in definition than in suggestion of what their surface textures may reveal. D.

Boguslaw Schaeffer (1929–   ) Poland
Schaeffer is an active experimentalist. He teaches at the Cracow Academy of Music, and his *Introduction to Composition* is considered a very important textbook.
Blues No. 1 for two pianos and tape (AA 1972) 15 min. The tape contains excerpts (short and in some cases unrecognizable) from recordings by outstanding jazz musicians, while the pianists, improvising and— as the composer wishes—"freely passing from one jazz style to another," create a specific kind of mosaic, influenced by the tape- recorded excerpts they hear. The work is homogeneous and has a rather suspensive atmosphere. D.
15 Elements (AA 1971).
Quartet 2 + 2 1965 (Edition Modern 1695) 4 min.

Philipp Scharwenka (1847–1917) Poland
March Op.42/1 (GS 1881; LC).
Hungarian Intermezzo Op.42/2 (GS 1881; LC).
Wedding Festival Op.42/3 (GS 1881; LC). Three books. All are colorful but dated. M-D.
Frühlingswogen Op.87 (C.Simon 1892; LC) 42pp. This symphonic poem was originally for orchestra; transcribed for two pianos by the com- poser.

Xaver Scharwenka (1850–1924) Poland
A Polish Dance (TP).

Harold Schiffman (1928–   ) USA
Variations 1966 (MS available from composer: c/o School of Music, Florida State University, Tallahassee, FL 32306) 9 min. Chromatic theme, twelve contrasting variations, theme returns at end. Thin tex- tures, flexible meters, variations evolve naturally, expanded tonality, neo-Classic. An expertly developed showpiece. M-D.

Josy Schlageter (–   ) Switzerland
Suite im alten Stil (Hug).

Heinrich Kaspar Schmid (1874–1953) Germany
Schmid continued the Romantic tradition of the Bavarian School.
Paraphrases on a Theme of Liszt Op.30 (Schott 1920; LC) 28pp.

Theodor Karl Schmidt (1869–1948) Germany
Prelude and Fugue (Br).

Yves R. Schmidt (1933–   ) Brazil

As aulas do Visconde de Sabugosa 1964 (da série "Miniaturas Lobateanas"). For two pianos, eight hands. (Vitale 1976). 2 min.

Überfall, Norder Strasse n.° 46 1959 (série "Impressões Européias) (Ric BA 3176 1972) 4pp., 2 min. Thin textures, expressionistic, misterioso, atmospheric. M-D.

Aloys Schmitt (1788–1866) Germany

Konzertstück Op.23 (Schlesinger 1893; LC) 30pp. Seemingly inspired by the Carl Maria von Weber piece of the same title. M-D.

Florent Schmitt (1870–1958) France

Schmitt wrote over 120 compositions. Most are difficult to perform, full of massive sonorities and bold dissonances, and epic in style. Only a few have been played in the United States.

Etude pour le Palais Hanté (Haunted Palace), d'Edgar Allan Poe Op.49 (Durand 1904) 15 min. Originally for orchestra; reduction for two pianos by the composer.

La Tragédie de Salomé Op.50 (Durand) 26 min. Originally a ballet based on a poem by Robert d'Humières; reduction for two pianos by the composer.

Trois Rapsodies Op.53 1904 (Durand) 50pp., 18 min. Française: expresses Schmitt's admiration for Chabrier. Polonaise: evokes Chopin. Viennoise: inspired by Johann Strauss. These rhapsodic tone poems succeeded so well after their premiere that they later were flamboyantly orchestrated, and in that guise are still popular in France today. Highly pianistic and effective. M-D.

J'entends dans le lointain Op.64 1917 (Durand) 6 min. Originally for solo piano; arranged for two pianos by the composer.

Symphonie concertante Op.82 1932 (Durand) 30 min. Originally for piano and orchestra; arranged for two pianos by the composer. This three-movement work shows strong Fauré influence, considerable structural power, rich color, and impressive eloquence. M-D.

Maurice Schoemaker (1890–1964) Belgium

Tombeau de Chopin—Variations sur le Prelude No. 20 1949 (CeBeDeM) 13½ min.

Arnold Schoenberg (1874–1951) Austria

Schoenberg developed German post-Romantic music. At the beginning of the twentieth-century he went over to atonality, and in the 1920s he developed the twelve-tone system. To this day most of his music remains musician's music, yet it positively drips with emotion. But still his approach is academic. Emotions are examined rather than declared.

Complete Works (Schmidt—Schott/UE 1973). Abteilung II: Klavier- und Orgelmusik. Reihe A, Band 5, 192pp. Contains works for organ; two

pianos; and piano duet; plus an appendix of four twelve-tone fragments, one of which is for two pianos (1941). Contains a two-piano
version of *Zweite Kammersymphonie* Op.38b (1941–42), which frequently differs from the orchestral version in dynamics and phrase
marks as well as some radical changes of pitch. Op.38b is the final
autograph source of this Chamber Symphony. Material is well distributed between performers. D.

Five Orchestra Pieces Op.16 1909 (CFP 3378) 34pp., 17½ min. Arranged
for two pianos by Anton Webern. Vorgefühle. Vergangenes. Farben.
Peripetie. Das obligate Rezitativ. Atonal, effective distribution of
material between pianists. In the last piece Schoenberg arrived at a
musical style that eliminated thematic repetition almost completely.
Development of intervallic material is fragmented in all five of these
works. Subtly expressive and rhythmically complex. They are not
twelve-tone. D.

Hermann Scholtz (1845–1918) Germany
Scholtz edited Chopin's works for C. F. Peters publishing company.
Variations on an Original Theme Op.77 (Leuckart 1898; LC) 23pp.
Theme and eight variations, inspired by Robert Schumann. M-D.

Bernhard Scholz (1835–1916) Germany
Contrapuntal Variations on a Gavotte by Handel Op.54 (Hainauer 1882;
LC; BrM) 12pp. Nine variations treated in a somewhat "olden style"
approach. Last variation is more extensive and difficult than the rest
of the work. M-D.

Hermann Schroeder (1904–   ) Germany
Duplum (Schott 6233 1970). For harpsichord and organ, or two positive
organs, or two pianos. Allegro moderato; Larghetto; Vivace. Thin
textures, imitation, quartal harmony, octotonic, neo-Classic, flexible
meters. M-D.

Heinz Schroeter (1907–   ) Germany
Bagatellen Op.9 1951 (Schott 4290; BrM) 24pp. Toccatina. Walzer. Invention. Pastorale. Ostinato. Perpetuum mobile.

Franz Schubert (1797–1828) Austria
Waltzes (in vol. 11 of Collected Works of Sergei Prokofiev—K) 7½ min.
This suite was written by Prokofiev during his travels abroad in 1920
and published in 1923. He selected his examples from various sets of
Schubert's waltzes. The suite is constructed on the principle of con-
trasts, with the opening theme recurring often as a unifying factor.
The result is a rondo-like form, which reminds one of the opening
piece of Schumann's *Faschingsschwank aus Wien* Op.26. Prokofiev

and the noted Soviet pianist Samuel Feinberg played this suite as an encore in Moscow on February 4, 1927. Int. to M-D.

Edwin Schultz (1827–1907) Germany
Introduction and Gavotte Op.60 (C. Simon).
Polonaise C Op.64 (C. Simon; BrM) 7pp. Square-cut phrases but contains some interest. M-D.
Rondino Op.84/1 (BrM 1883). For two pianos, eight hands.
Rondo à la Polacca Op.130 (Cranz).
Three Rondinos Op.162 (CF; GS) F; G; a.
Ballet-Scene B♭ Op.203/1 (C. Simon 1896; LC) 3pp.
Reiterstückschen d Op.203/2 (C. Simon 1896; LC) 3pp.
Duo Op.248 (O. Wernthal 1902; LC) 7pp.

Paul Schumacher (–   ) Germany
Easy Variations on "Muss i denn, muss i denn zum Städtle hinaus" Op.25 (K&S 1826; BrM) 5pp. Theme, four variations, coda Langsam—Schnell. Attractive. Int.
Prelude and Fugue b Op.52 (C. Ruehle).
Prelude and Fugue B♭ (Praeger & Meier).

Georg Alfred Schumann (1866–1952) Germany
Variations and Fugue on a theme by Beethoven (Op.77) Op.32 (Simroch 1903; LC) 39pp. This work takes the Saint-Säens *Variations* Op.35 as its model. M-D.

Robert Schumann (1810–1856) Germany
Andante and Variations Op.46 1843 (CFP; GS; Durand; Heugel; Augener) 33pp., 12½ min. This is one of the great works for two pianos, although it is even more effective in its original version for two pianos, two cellos, and horn. The variations are not numbered and are to be played without interruption, yet they are well defined and easily distinguished. They frequently go far afield from the theme. Especially lovely is the quiet coda, which conveys the impression of an evaporating cloud of sound. This work established a prototype for Romantic feeling and could well serve, beyond the purely musical realm, as a striking example of the artistic ideals of its period. Ernest Hutcheson calls it "beautiful, pianistically grateful, and universally popular." The premiere was given by Clara Schumann and Felix Mendelssohn in the Leipzig Gewandhaus on August 19, 1843. M-D.
Six Etudes en forme de canon Op.56 (C. Debussy—Durand; IMC 1783) 23pp. In C, C, E, A♭, b, B. Excellent examples of Debussy's art of transcription.
Original Compositions for two pianos, Books I and II (K).

Giora Schuster (1915–   ) Israel, born Germany
Schuster teaches acoustics and orchestration at the Tel Aviv Music
Teacher's Training College and at the Oranium Seminary Music Institute.
Accents for Two Pianos and Percussion (IMP). Free use of all twelve
   tones, disjunct melody, constant dynamic changes and sudden ac-
   cents. M-D.

Eduard Schütt (1856–1933) Russia
Variations on an Original Theme Op.9 (Cranz).
Valse-Paraphrase d'après Chopin Op.58/1 (Simrock) 7 min.
Impromptu-rococco Op.58/2 (Simrock 1899; LC) 15pp. Late nineteenth-
   century style, octaves, large chords, flashy conclusion. M-D.
Andante and Scherzino d Op.79/1,2 1907 (Simrock; Wright State Univer-
   sity Library, Dayton, Ohio 45435). Two contrasting movements, ef-
   fective Romantic writing. M-D.

Nico Schuyt (1922–   ) The Netherlands
Ouverture "De varkenshoeder" 1954 (Donemus) 6 min. Allegro giocoso:
   bitonal, octotonic, resembles Stravinsky style of the 1920s. M-D.
Van verre 1979 (Donemus) 2 min. 5/8, ostinato-like figures, thin textures,
   final C chord. Int. to M-D.

Elliott Schwartz (1936–   ) USA
Pentagonal Mobile (ACA) 13 min. For five grand pianos; also available
   for piano and tape. Extreme stylistic contrasts—melodic lyricism or
   simple triads often juxtaposed against complex, noisy, quasi-
   improvisatory textures, which may shift as foreground or background to each other. Players have substantial freedom within
   complex textures, deciding when or how often to play specified passages. Avant-garde. M-D.

Paul Schwartz (1907–   ) USA
Chamber Concerto for Two Pianos Op.18 1944 (AMC) 38pp., 12 min.
   Allegro agitato; Andantino con moto; Allegro molto. Outer movements are written in a motoric neo-Baroque style. The middle movement is bitonal, chordal with changing meters, builds to *fff* climax
   and finally concludes *ppp*. MC and attractive. M-D.

Ludwig Schytte (1848–1909) Denmark
Schytte studied with Louis Rée, a pioneer in the two-piano field.
Two Concert Pieces Op.115 (K&S). Carnival. Festival March.
In the Ball Room Op.139/2 (Schott; A. P. Schmidt).

James S. Sclater (1943–   ) USA
Sclater did his doctoral work at the University of Texas in Austin.
Suite for Two Pianos 1976 (Mt. Salus Music, 709 E. Leake, Clinton, MS
   39056) 23pp. Prologue: tempos vary between instruments. Quick-

step. The Devil's Waltz. Reflections: long pedals. Finale: similar to a Hoe-Down. Epilogue: resembles Prologue. Freely tonal, lean textures, folk influence, string glissando. Highly attractive, MC. Has much audience appeal through use of strong rhythms. M-D.

Cyril Scott (1879–1971) Great Britain

Two Pieces from Impressions from the Jungle Book (Rudyard Kipling) (Schott 2647 1938; LC) 16pp., 6 min. The Jungle: Adagio. Dance of the Elephants: Allegro. Clever and effective. M-D.

Theme and Variations 1947 (Elkin) 15 min. Theme is announced in dissonant block chords. Eleven variations, quartal, modal and Impressionistic harmonies, thick textures, animated Quasi Fuga climax. Displays a resourceful ingenuity and variety of variation treatment. M-D.

Russian Fair 1957 (Elkin).

Danse Nègre Op.58/5 (Elkin 1935; LC) 13pp. Transcribed for two pianos by the composer. Molto vivace, rhythmic, and flowing. M-D.

Lotus Land (Elkin 1948; LC) 8pp. Arranged for two pianos by the composer. Int.

Alexander Scriabin (1872–1915) Russia

Fantasy Op. Posth. a 1893 (Bartlett and Robertson—OUP 1940). Also in collection *Alexander and Julian Scriabin—Youthful and Early Works* (Garvelman—Music Treasure Publications) 6 min. The following editorial notes are from the OUP edition: "The Editors obtained the MS. of this work, now published for the first time, from Dr. Jacob Weinberg, of New York, who has supplied the following note: 'Alexander Nikolayevitch Scriabin composed his two-piano Fantasy in December 1892 and January 1893, according to the MS. He was then twenty-one and just graduated from the Moscow Conservatory. The Fantasy belongs to the period of the composer's Mazurkas, Op.3, and Allegro Appassionato, Op.4, and shows the same Chopinian influence. The original MS. is possessed by Professor Emil K. Rosenoff (of whose daughter Scriabin was godfather). First public performance by Dr. Weinberg and Professor Rosenoff in Moscow, January 16, 1916.' (J. W., New York, August 1938.)

"A little more than the usual 'editing' has been necessary in presenting this piece, and it should perhaps be recorded what has been done. (1) The first piano in the original had by far the greater share of musical interest, while the second piano was for the most part an accompaniment. In order to make it more interesting for the second player, we have changed over the parts from time to time, without any alteration of the actual notes. (2) In some places one of the pianos had passages of great technical difficulty, especially for small hands, and here we have 'rescored' the passages, dividing the notes between the two parts, again without alteration of the actual notes. (3) The final page (in this edition) appeared to us to be so thin in the original, just where a big climax seemed necessary, that we concluded that it had not been fully written out, and have (we hope discreetly) filled in the harmonies and doubled the octave passage.

"Practically all the expression marks are the editors'. The piece should be played throughout in a freely romantic and highly coloured style, very 'rubato' in the expressive parts and highly rhythmical in the more strenuous sections." M-D.

Gisella Selden-Goth (1884–   ) Austria
Praeludium und Fuge (UE 1957; BrM) 29pp.

Randolph Shackelford (1944–   ) USA
For Two Pianos (Zanibon 5246) 12 min.

Ralph Shapey (1921–   ) USA
Deux for Two Pianos 1967 (TP). Two movements of most intricate, complex writing. Ensemble problems are staggering. Piece is well organized, and some amazing sonorities await those performers who can successfully unravel its intricacies. Second movement: Piano I = 66, Piano II = 44. The composer says: "Piano I is 2/3rds of piano II triplet. However, the element of disparity is built in and desired through the obvious difficulty of each performer playing at strict tempo." D.

Herbert F. Sharpe (1861–1925) Great Britain
Variations on a Hungarian Air Op.46 (C. Woolhouse 1889; BrM).

Dmitri Shostakovich (1906–1975) USSR
Concertino Op.94 1954 (MCA; IMC 2373) 32pp., 10 min. This energetic and virtuosic, one-movement work was written for the composer's son, Maxim. *Ff* Adagio introduction to the Allegretto section, which is interrupted by an Adagio in the center of the composition. Note the long crescendo. Octotonic, C major scales with added notes, rhythmic emphasis assigned to Piano II. Lightly scored, with Piano I somewhat more difficult. Accessible both musically and technically. Not music for the ages but very engaging for the moment. M-D.
Festive Overture Op.96 1954 (K) 32pp. Full of sarcasm, pastiche, and grotesque naturalism. Octotonic, tremolos, wide dynamic range. Int. to M-D.
Prelude and Fugue Db Op.87/15 (USSR) 10pp. Arranged for two pianos by the composer. Allegretto. Highly effective. M-D.
Tarantella (Sikorski 1964; USSR) 11pp. From the film *The Gadfly* of 1955. Presto, a few changing keys but tonal, brilliant, and effective. M-D.

Arsene Siegel (1897–   ) USA, born France
The Windy City—Four Snapshots of Metropolitan Chicago 1946 (AMC)
44pp. Evening Silhouettes on the Near North Side. Lights and
Shadows on the Buckingham Fountain. Way Down South at 47th and
Parkway. The Municipal Airport. Colorful, could be choreographed.
MC idiom with strong nineteenth-century influence. M-D.

Paul J. Sifler (1911–   ) USA, born Yugoslavia
Concertino B♭ for Two Pianos 1975 (Fredonia) 13pp. Moderato; Andante;
Allegretto. "For the second year piano student. The solo may be
played independently of the second piano part" (from the score).
Tuneful, octotonic, optional cadenza in Allegretto, effective and attractive. "This work was designed to give impetus to the young pianist—a first taste of ensemble music with his teacher or other
advanced pianist" (letter to the author dated August 27, 1981). Int.

Tomasz Sikorski (1939–   ) Poland
Two Pieces for Two Pianos (AA 1973) 2 leaves. Listening Music (1973).
Diaphony (1969). Published separately. Explanations in Polish and
English. Duration ad libitum. A few short fragments are given for
each piece with directions. They are to be used as the basis for
improvised pieces. Includes such directions as "Start simulta-
neously. Second piano plays first piano part Poco meno mosso";
"Optionally delayed entrance after first piano"; "Stop simultaneously
at any moment"; "Optional number of repetitions"; "Pass to B after
A with rest, or A¹ with rest." Avant-garde. M-D.

Edward Silas (1827–1909) The Netherlands
Bourrée Op.79 (R&E).

Ann Silsbee (1930–   ) USA
Letter from a Field Biologist 1979 (ACA) 17 min.

Homer Simmons (1900–   ) USA
Alice in Wonderland (JF 1941; LC). The Gryphon and the Mock Turtle;
The Cheshire Cat; The Queen of Hearts; The Duchess; The Dor-
mouse; The Lobster Quadrille. Attractive suite. Pieces published
separately. M-D.
Deep River (Axelrod 601 1942; LC) 5pp. A colorful and elegant setting of
this moving American spiritual. M-D.
The Old Dutch Clock (EV 1948; LC) 8pp.
Scherzino (JF).
Tango at Midnight (JF 1940; LC) 8pp. From Suite *Partita Americana*.
Phantasmania (GS 1929; LC) 43pp. Transcribed from original orchestral
version.

Anton Simon (1851–1918) France
Deux Morceaux Op.60 (Jurgenson 1900; LC) 14pp. Mélodie. Danse. M-D.
Petite Suite Op.63 (Jurgenson 1902) 20pp. Elégie; Fugue; Petite Valse;
   Barcarolle; Ronde fantastique. M-D.
Both Op.60 and Op.63 are written in a late nineteenth-century salon style.

Jean-Marie Simonis (1931–   ) Belgium
Mouvements Op.22 (CeBeDeM 1971) 48pp., 12 min.

Netty Simons (1913–   ) USA
Illuminations 1970 (ACA) 40 min. Snow Water (7pp.): no barlines, dynamics generally remain around *ppp,* harmonics, pointillistic; all note
   durations are indeterminate with each pianist playing at will unless
   otherwise instructed; plucked and struck strings. Drops of Laughter
   (30pp.): uses techniques similar to those in Snow Water, plus clusters, faster repeated notes, long pedals. One Flower—Two Gardeners
   (11pp.): very fast, much use of una corda pedal. Five Sprays of the
   Snow Fountain (31pp.): as fast as possible with each pianist playing
   at his own speed, independent of one another to section B; string
   glissandi, clusters silently pressed on keys for harmonics, mallet used
   on string, "sprinkling sound," fast dynamic extremes. Expressionistic; contains some exotic sonorities. D.
Two Dot (ACA) 14 min. Graphic score.

Christian Sinding (1856–1941) Norway
Variations e♭ Op.2 1889 (WH) 33pp. Nineteenth-century Lisztian style,
   serious theme, virtuosic. M-D to D.
Two Duets Op.41 (WH). Andante. Deciso ma non troppo allegro.

André Singer (1907–   ) USA
Sonata 1952 (AMC) 23pp., 13½ min. Allegro; Andantino; Allegro. Transparent textures, neo-Classic, freely tonal. Finale contains some skit-
   tering subtleties. All in all a well-groomed work. M-D.

Otto Singer (1833–1893) Germany
Singer studied with Moscheles and Liszt and taught at the Cincinnati
College of Music.
Andante with Variations Op.1 (Br&H).

Larry Sitsky (1934–   ) Australia
Sitsky "describes his style as 'expressionistic (i.e., dealing with extreme
emotional states)' and influenced by the music of Bartók, Berg, and Bloch
and by the esthetics of Busoni, on whom he has done extensive research"
(DCM, 684). He is head of composition studies at the Canberra School of
Music.
Concerto for Two Solo Pianos 1967 (Bo&H 19953) 45pp. Contains per-
   formance notes including definitions of notational signs. Clusters,

strong rhythms, dynamic extremes, long pedals, aleatory sections, cadenza passages, contrasting sections, glissandi, crushing conclusion. Directions like "start together, approximately—it does not matter much here," add to flexibility of the work. Requires big octave technique. D.

Nikos Skalkottas (1904–1949) Greece
Return of Ulysses (Margun BP7104) 27 min.

Lucijan Marija Skerjanc (1900–1973) Yugoslavia
Fantazija (JWC 1949).

Nicolas Slonimsky (1894–   ) USA, born Russia
My Toy Balloon (SP 1950; AMC; UCLA; LC) 12pp. (6) Variations on a Brazilian Tune. The theme is a popular carnival song in Brazil. Includes original words and translation. "The song is connected with the carnival custom of Brazilian youngsters of sending up paper balloons with a piece of burning wax suspended underneath to generate hot air and propel the balloon upwards. It was the playful belief that if the balloon landed within reach of the sender, he or she would be married before the next carnival" (from the score). MC. M-D.

Roger Smalley (1943–   ) Great Britain
Accord 1974–75 (Faber 0285 1978) 54 pp., 45 min. Facsimile edition. The basic material of this work is a single chord out of which the horizontal, melodic aspects of the music grow and proliferate. *Accord* means harmonious agreement, and examples of it occur in this complex, major work designed with five symmetrically planned related sections. Tonal and atonal materials are blended together to produce a rich variety of harmony and texture. Much of the work is concerned with the composing-out of complex vertical aggregates of chords. Busoni's shadow hovers over the entire work. "*Accord* brings together many of the preoccupations of my preceding works, from *Pulses* (1967) onwards; it is also perhaps a turning point in that the pieces I have been working on since it was completed represent a radical depature. To say that they are tonal may appear surprising; this article indicates why and how that is possible" (Smally, "Accord," MT, 116, December 1975, 1054–56). An engulfing experience for the audience, bold and direct, deeply moving in places. Altogether an exuberant and powerfully constructed piece. After the two-piano works of Busoni, Messiaen, Boulez, and Stockhausen, the medium seems to be best reserved for the most carefully considered yet technically complex statements. Few composers have made contributions to this medium that would permit them to join this distinguished quartet, but perhaps *Accord* would qualify Smalley for membership. D.

Bedrich Smetana (1824–1888) Czechoslovakia

Rondo C (CFP 4479; Br) 11pp. For two pianos, eight hands. Shorter than the Sonata, polka influence. Int. to M-D.

Sonata e (Hin 19; Artia) 27pp. For two pianos, eight hands. In one movement. Modeled on the Liszt Sonata b, clever if not distinguished themes, plenty of zest. M-D.

Leo Smit (1921–   ) USA

Duet—Unlike Olympian Jove from *The Alchemy of Love* 1963 (CF) 3 min. Modal, flowing 9/8, lyric. Requires large span. Int.

Virginia Sampler 1959 (CF) 19 min. A ballet arranged for two pianos by the composer. The Town. The Townspeople. The Frontiersman. Gigue. The Gentleman's Ecossaise. Waltz for the Pristine Lovers. The Unidentified Lady (on Horseback). March for a Beloved General: includes use of a snare drum. Freely tonal contrasting movements, colorful and effective, brilliant conclusion. Requires large span. M-D.

Julia Smith (1911–   ) USA

American Dance Suite 1938–57 (TP 1968) 21pp., 9½ min. One Morning in May. Lost My Partner. Negro Lullaby. Chicken Reel. Four Americana pieces inspired by cowboy, old-fiddler, Afro-American lullaby, and square-dance tunes. Traditional style; neo-Classic influence interlaced with a few clusters. Reminiscent of the Copland *Appalachian Suite* period. Int. to M-D.

Stuart Smith (1948–   ) USA

Smith teaches at the University of Maryland Baltimore County.

A Fine Old Tradition 1971 (Media Press). For two pianos, alto sax and percussion. 8 min. Contains performance directions. Section A: some notes are free in duration; dynamics and articulation to be determined by the performer and should be varied; uses non-pitched percussion instruments. Section B: each note should have a different dynamic; notes should be played with a sporadic rhythmic motion; uses standard vibraphone. Mixture of traditional and new notation. Mildly avant-garde. M-D.

William O. Smith (1926–   ) USA

Four Studies 1962 (AMC) 13pp. Energetic; Freely; Spirited; Intimate. Expressionistic; harmonics; flick, pluck, strike, stop, sweep length of string; fingertips and fingernails are used as well as rubber erasers, wood pencil and lead pencil, metal (key or pencil). A cleverly contrasted set. M-D.

Padre Antonio Soler (1729–1783) Spain

Soler was one of the most striking personalities in eighteenth-century

Spanish music. Perhaps these concertos amused the Infante of Spain during dull evenings at the palace. They are some of the earliest *galant* and most extensive works for two keyboards. Originally written for two obbligato organs, they are effective on two pianos and various keyboards (fortepiano, harpsichord, clavichord). They point up the versatility of Soler's sunny creations. All have two movements except No. 2
Six Concertos for Two Keyboards (UME, published separately; Kastner—Schott 6230 and 6231).
Concerto I C (Marchi—Bèrben) 5½ min. Andante: binary form. Minué: ornamental variations. M-D.
Concerto II a 11½ min. Andante: chaconne character. Allegro: gigue-like. Tempo de Minué. Empfindsamkeit style. M-D.
Concerto III G. Andantino: lively rhythms. Minué: imitative effects, flamboyant variations, versatile trio. Best known of the six. M-D.
Concerto IV F. Afettuoso—Andante non Largo: majestic. Minué: set of four unfolding variations. M-D.
Concerto V A 8½ min. Cantabile; Minué. Similar to but longer than *Concerto IV*. Unusual registration. M-D.
Concerto VI D 8 min. Allegro; Minué. Ingenious and attractive. M-D.

Arthur Somervell (1863–1937) Great Britain
Variations on an Original Theme (Augener 1902; BrM).

Alberto Soresina (1911–   ) Italy
Short Sonata on Military Bugle Calls (Ric). A light, clever, facile work. Parallel chords using fourths and fifths add the main contemporary quality. Int. to M-D.

Tim Souster (1943–   ) Great Britain
Souster studied composition with Richard Rodney Bennett and also worked with Stockhausen, Berio, Henze, Cardew, and Barraque.
Afghan Amplitudes 1976 (OdB) 8½ min. For three players of electronic keyboards and percussion, one of whom must double on rock drum-kit as well as conventional percussion. Characterized by weighty kicking bass ostinati, rich variety of timbre, and vigorous rhythmic polyphony. The musicians extemporize on many levels over the framework material, combining a discipline and caprice that is direct, energetic, and sometimes exhilarating. D.

João de Souza Lima (1898–   ) Brazil
Introduccion y Toccata (Vitale).

Charles Spinks (1915–   ) USA
Variations on a Greek Folk Song Op.6 (Hinrichsen 1951). A simple folk theme is richly ornamented and surrounded with highly colored harmony. Theme goes through seven contrasting transformations in a

scherzo, a fast dance, as a solo for Middle Eastern dulcimer, one showing bell and harp influence, a 5/8 ostinato, a majestic song, and a busy finale. Definitely influenced by Brahms's variation technique. M-D.

Michal Spisak (1914–1965) Poland
Koncert (Concerto) *for Two Solo Pianos* 1949 (PWM; LC) 56pp.

Alexander Spitzmueller (1896–1962) Austria
Concerto II Op.39 (UE 1953). For two solo pianos. 25 min.
Praeludium und Fuge (UE 12151).

Karel Srom (1904–   ) Czechoslovakia
Merrily 1951 (CHF) 10 min. Allegretto moderato (Guten Morgen); Valse Lente (Vogelscheuche); Presto (Fangenspiel). Neo-Classic, whimsical, fairy-tale inspiration, clever, effective musically and pianistically, MC. M-D.

Patric Standford (1939–   ) Great Britain
Taikyoku Op.35 Symphony for two pianos and percussion (Redcliffe 1976) 15pp. Standford says this "piece is, in fact, my fourth Symphony, despite its possibly unconventional instrumentation" (letter to the author, November 20, 1981). *Taikyoku* is Japanese for "a great or large work." Requires blocks, temple blocks, castanets, claves, cowbells, marimba, two xylophones, vibraphone, drums, glockenspiel, and triangle. Allegro moderato e agitato, con moto: strong rhythms, octotonic, many repeated octaves and full chords; leads directly to movement II, eighth note = 156: fleeting chromatic figuration; Vivace section alternates with Un poco meno mosso section; glissandos lead to pesante section with punctuated full chords increasing the tension; stringendo conclusion. III, quarter note = 63: dolce repeated syncopated seventh chords unfold into triplets and duplets, thin texture evolve into *pp* haunting conclusion. An altogether effective piece of contemporary writing. M-D.

Robert Starer (1924–   ) USA, born Austria
Starer teaches at Brooklyn College. His Central European heritage of expressionism provides the basis for dramatic tension.
The Fringes of a Ball (TP 1962) "Waltz variations on a theme by William Schuman." 15pp., 4 min. A tone-row is taken from the dance piece *Performance*. Both it and Schuman's theme are printed in the score. Starer's treatment is in a mildly humorous, uncomplicated tonal style with some blue notes and changing meters. Both pianists variously have a "go" with the theme after a fourteen-bar introduction. The non-theme part consists of nostalgic blurring, counterthemes, and tremolo chords, all leading to a grand *fff* closing. M-D.

Jacques Stehman (1912–1975) Belgium

Colloque 1943 (CeBeDeM 1960) 21pp., 5 min. Facsimile of MS. One movement, freely tonal, virtuoso conclusion. M-D to D.

Montmartre 1974 (CeBeDeM) 8pp., 2 min. First part: Vivio—Giocoso—Ritmico. Second part: delicious waltz, à la Poulenc. M-D.

Tres Rhythmes 1955 (CeBeDeM) 10 min.

Daniel Steibelt (1765–1823) Germany

Steibelt was a colorful figure who entered into a contest of pianistic skill with Beethoven.

Duos (Br&H).

Robert Stewart (1918–   ) USA

Rondeau for Two Pianos (ASUC Journal of Music Scores, vol. VII. Available through EAM).

Milan Stibilj (1929–   ) Yugoslavia

Condensation 1967 (Br 6101) 25pp., parts. For two pianos, trombone, and percussion. Requires two bongos, three tom toms, bass drum, two cymbals, and tam tam. "Considered from a formal point of view, the composition is constructed on the principles of simple harmonic motion, which are represented in the note-values. Because the precisely determined rhythmic elements pass from one instrument to another, the underlying structure of the form remains fixed, despite the simultaneous use of improvised passages, which allow each interpreter to maintain his independence" (from the score). Pointillistic, serial, avant-garde. Extreme ensemble problems in precision. D.

Ernstalbrecht Stiebler (1934–   ) Germany

Klangmoment 1961 (Edition Modern 1708) 8 min.

Karlheinz Stockhausen (1928–   ) Germany

Stockhausen has developed serial composition beyond where Webern left off. He has composed both important electronic music and major instrumental works.

Plus Minus, 2 X 7 Seiten für Ausarbeitungen (Pages for realization) 1963 (UE 13993) 35 min. A blue-print work. Consists of 7 pages of "forms" symbolically notated, which may be realized by up to 7 players simultaneously (instruments not specified), and 7 pages of notes. These notes are simply more "form" of a different sort, and the realizer must then, according to 35 rules, make a great many decisions as to the "content" he wishes to insert into these forms. Avant-garde. M-D to D.

Aus den sieben Tagen 1968 (UE 14790) 40 min. Consists of fifteen brief sets of instructions in suggestive evocative language that is almost meaningless; it is everything and nothing. Here is a translation of one of the "pieces": "Treffpunkt" (Meeting Point). Everyone plays the same tone—lead the tone wherever your thoughts lead you—do not leave it, stay with it—always return to the same place." Avant-garde. D.

Mantra 1970 (Stockhausen-Verlag 1975) 65 min. Totally serial, reminiscent of late 1950s and 60s style, offers a new perspective on tonality and tonal construction. Fully notated, systematically complex, similar to certain works by Stefan Wolpe and Charles Wuorinen. Each pianist also plays a woodblock and a set of crotales. In addition there are two sine-wave producing oscillators, for which parts appear in the score. Their pitches are sent to a ring-modulator with the piano's sounds and ring-modulated with them, the result being sent out via loudspeakers. The "mantra" is a thirteen-note cell treated in twelve transformations, each transformation focusing on one of the original thirteen notes. The composer says of this work: "The unified construction of *Mantra* is a musical miniature of the unified macrostructure of the cosmos, just as it is a magnification into the acoustic time-field of the unified microstructure of the harmonic vibrations in notes themselves" (*Stereo Review*, August 1972, p.82). The work seems the apotheosis of inexorable linear evolution. Avant-garde. D. See: Jonathan Harvey, *The Music of Stockhausen*, pp.126–31, for further analysis of this piece.

Wolfgang Stockmeier (1931–   ) Germany
Suite nach alter Manier 1958 (Möseler 1977) 27pp. Praeludium; Tempo di Valse; Courante; Aria; Menuett; Gigue; Epilog. Neo-Classic, free repetition of certain indicated figures, unmeasured sections. Some parts are atonal but the style is basically freely tonal. M-D.

Richard Stoker (1938–   ) Great Britain
Duologue Op.47 (Ric).
Portrait of a Town Op.52 (Ric). For two pianos and narrator.

Joop Stokkermans (1937–   ) The Netherlands
Balletmuziek 1962 (Donemus) 42pp. Contrasting sections, i.e., Moderato, Allegro vivace, Andantino, Moderato tempo primo, Tempo di valse, etc. Unfolds in colorful and effective MC writing, involving both instruments equally, dramatic gestures at conclusion. M-D.

Gregory Stone (1900–   ) USA
Burlesque Tzigane (EBM 1936) 22pp. A musical caricature on a celebrated gypsy theme, in the style of Liszt, Chopin, Sarasate, Tchaikowsky, and Wagner. Weaves together some well-known tunes. M-D.
Boogie Woogie Etude (Chappell 1947) 15pp. Left hand of Piano II projects

the boogie-woogie figuration while other hands add elaborate chords and runs. M-D.

Alan Stout (1932–   ) USA
Fantasy Op.62/4 (ACA). For two harpsichords or pianos, and percussion.

Igor Stravinsky (1882–1971) USA, born Russia
Stravinsky's two-piano idiom depends heavily on rhythmic and percussive writing.
Le Sacre du Printemps 1911–12 (Bo&H) 83pp. This boiled-down reduction was made by the composer for piano, four hands when the work was being composed and before the orchestration was completed. Stravinsky recommended that it be played on "two separate pianos." On June 9, 1912 Stravinsky played it with Debussy, who took the secondo part. On the following November 5, Debussy wrote to Stravinsky: "Our reading at the piano of *Le Sacre du Printemps* is always in my mind. It haunts me like a beautiful dream, and I try in vain to reinvoke the terrific impression. That is why I wait for the stage performance like a greedy child impatient for promised sweets." The simpler the musical substance, the less well it comes off in this reduction. The more complex, rhythmically varied, richly colored passages come off brilliantly. Stravinsky knew exactly what he was doing in this piano(s) version, and most of it is thrillingly and surprisingly idiomatic. D.
Concerto for Two Solo Pianos 1935 (Schott 2520) 21 min. Con moto: lengthy, stormy, and heavy. Notturno: atmospheric, an air with coloratura ornaments. Quattro variazioni: a set of extended variations, similarities with opening movement. Preludio e fuga: chorale-like Preludio leads to a virtuoso Fuga. Piano II provides a supporting role to Piano I. Polyphonic complexities, angular and strong melodic material, violent emotional content. This work was undoubtedly motivated by Stravinsky's desire to introduce his son Soulima as co-performer. They played its world premiere. D.
Concerto E♭ ("Dumbarton Oaks") 1937–38 (Schott 2791) 12 min. Reduced from original chamber orchestra instrumentation for two pianos by the composer. Tempo giusto; Allegretto; Con moto. Highly effective but this reduction never quite approximates the colorfulness of the original orchestration. Requires a dazzling account of the score with each melodic fragment carefully delineated. M-D to D.
See: Herbert Eimert, "Stravinsky's Dumbarton Oaks," *Melos,* July 1947, p.247.
Sonata 1943–44 (Schott 4015) 10 min. Moderato: flowing with emphasis on fourth and seventh scale tones. Theme with (4) Variations:

chorale, dancelike, fugue, fast toccata, big ending. Allegretto: ABA, flowing folk-like theme in mid-section. Piano II is more of an accompaniment; treated like chamber music, with no contest between the players. Gentle mood prevails throughout. M-D.

Scherzo à la russe 1944 (Schott 10646) 17pp. 4 min. Transcribed by the composer from the orchestral version originally created for Paul Whiteman's orchestra. Vigorous rhythms and nationalistic melodies, reminiscent of the dances in the ballet *Petrouchka*. Jazz ensemble, a *tour de force* in this two-piano version. M-D to D.

Septet 1953 (Bo&H) 24pp., 11 min. Reduction for two pianos by the composer (Untitled.) Quarter note = 88; Passacaglia; Gigue. Makes use of the technique of preconceived tone-rows but is not strictly dodecaphonic. Contains an amazing degree of thematic integration. This reduction is remarkably pianistic. M-D.

See: Erwin Stein, "Stravinsky's Septet," *Tempo* 31, Spring 1954.

Agon 1957 (Bo&H) 20 min. Transcribed for two pianos by the composer. A difficuilt score in which seventeenth-century dance forms are passed through the Stravinsky filter and emerge purposely distorted and dissonant. *Agon* is also a pivotal work, being one of the first Stravinsky scores to contain elements of serial technique. The pianists are required to be more like traffic cops than emotionally responsive interpreters. D.

See: C. Burkhart, "Stravinsky's Revolving Canon," MR, 29/3, 1968, 161–64.

Donald C. Johns, "An Early Serial Idea of Stravinsky," MR, 23, November 1962, 305–13.

Robert Tangeman, "Stravinsky's Two-Piano Music," MM, 22, January–February 1945, 93–98.

Karel Stromenger (1885–   ) Poland

Rondo (PWM 1962; LC) 12pp. Based on Polish folk tunes, tonal around D, bright and cheerful, attractive. Would make an excellent program opener. Int. to M-D.

George Templeton Strong (1856–1948) USA

Choral sur un thème de Leo Hassler (1601) "Wenn ich einmal scheiden soll" 1929 (Henn 1933; LC) 6pp. Originally for string orchestra; reduction for two pianos by the composer. The "O Sacred Head" tune is carefully presented in canon between the instruments. Beautifully worked out. M-D.

Le Roi Arthur 1916 (Henn 1921) 57pp. Poème symphonique. Originally for orchestra; two-piano reduction by the composer.

Hubert Stuppner (1944–   ) Great Britain

To Dance a Sound Up and Down (Zanibon 5472) 12 min.

Dana Suesse (1911–   ) USA
Danza a Media Noche (Dance at Midnight) (JF 1933; LC) 16pp. A seductive rumba with a few intricate spots. M-D.

Fernando Sulpiza (1936–   ) Italy
Glad (Bèrben 1975) 9pp. Balletto for two pianos. Twelve-tone, expressionistic, low pedal point A, pointillistic, changing meters, extensive use of grace notes. Last two pages are motoric in rhythmic drive to the end. M-D to D.

Carlos Surinach (1915–   ) USA, born Spain
Flamenquerias 1951 (AMP) 27pp., 10 min. Soleares: biting, bright, tasty, light, fast Moorish dance. Romance: a rather sour but colorful Oriental tal "song without words." Sevillanas: a brilliant, tingling, and animated dance with ingenious rhythmic and harmonic clashes. This colorful suite in mainly diatonic idiom uses dissonance lightly. Generally effective but has some awkward pianistic spots. Uses an 18-note scale. M-D to D.

Margaret Sutherland (1897–   ) Australia
Burlesque and Movement 1958 (J. Albert).
Canonical Piece 1957 (J. Albert).
Pavan 1957 (J. Albert).

Giles Swayne (1946–   ) Great Britain
Synthesis for Two Pianos 1974 (Novello 10 023510) 13 min. Highly organized, proportional rhythmic relationships, pointillistic, long pedals, dynamic extremes, clusters, harmonics, exact synchronization between instruments not required at all times, an orchestral slapstick used, glissandi, long trills. Engagingly free of presumption and fresh in its counterpoint of brilliant swirls, single sustained notes, chordal motifs, and stark lines. For adventurous pianists; large span required. D.

Józef Swider (1930–   ) Poland
Swider teaches in the Department of Composition at the State College of Music, Katowice, Poland.
Allegro, Moderato per due pianoforti 1953 (PWM 1970) 25pp. Allegro: freely tonal, octotonic, thematic motifs developed, glissandi, agitato section has brilliant conclusion. Moderato: marchlike in 5/4, strong rhythmic gestures, neo-Classic. M-D.

Jadwiga Szajna-Lewandowska (1912–   ) Poland
Szajna-Lewandowska is mainly concerned with work for the ballet (connected with the Wroclaw Pantomime Theater) and teaching.
Funerailles 1970 (PWM) 15pp., 7½ min. Adagietto; Andante con moto; Allegro drammatico; Andante quasi marcia. Tremolo, trills, disso-

nant chordal treatment; conclusion at *ppp* level for Piano I, *ffff* for Piano II. MC. M-D.

Sándor Szokolay (1931–   ) Hungary

Bagatelles 1978 (UE 17110) 16pp. For harpsichord and harp, or two pianos. Each of the four short movements uses a particular technique (inversion, ostinato, etc.), combines fantasy and wit with a rhythmic flexibility to make these pieces fun to play. M-D.

T

Germaine Tailleferre (1892–1982) France
Tailleferre composed primarily to entertain. Her lively but fragile tunes careen across the keyboards supported by gong sounds that are captivatingly apparitional (especially in the *Jeux de plein air*). A member of the French "Les Six," she has been somewhat of a musical curiosity the past half century. She tasted musical fame in the 1920s but composed comparatively little music after that.
Jeux de plein air ("Outdoor Games") 1919 (Durand) 19pp., 7 min. La Tirelitentaine. Cache-cache mitoula. Based on French folk tunes. Lilting; parallel sevenths. Thin textures produce some rich sonorities. Deserves more hearings. M-D.
Deux Valses 1928 (Lemoine 1962). Valse lente E; Valse brillante g. Delightful, many parallel fifths, ninth and eleventh chords, long trills. Int. to M-D.

Toru Takemitsu (1930–   ) Japan
Corona for Pianist(s) 1962 (Sal) 15 min. The number of pianists is variable.

Louise Talma (1906–   ) USA
Four Handed Fun for Two Pianos 1939 (CF 2649;AMC; LC) 3½ min. A sprightly one-movement scherzo full of scale passages and bouncing staccato ideas tossed between the players, ABA, clever counterpoint. An excellent encore. M-D.

Elias Tanenbaum (1924–   ) USA
Music for Two Pianos 1968 (AMC) 27pp. One movement, pointillistic, black and white key clusters, harmonics, string glissandos and plucked strings. Repeat figures at will, improvise figures on strings with soft vibe mallets, execute some notes as they appear proportionally within the beat, hit strings with palm of hand. Some uncoordinated sections between the two instruments (free flight). Avantgarde. M-D.

Alexandre Tansman (1897–   ) Poland
Carnival Suite (MCA 1948) 39pp. Mardi Gras; Streets; Cakewalk. Taken

195

from the composer's score for the motion picture *Flesh and Fantasy.* Despite its characteristic piquant Latin rhythm and harmony, the work is too long for the musical material. M-D.

Fantaisie sur les valses de Johann Strauss (ESC 1964). Concert waltz, Impressionistic, Strauss melodies heard in rapid succession. M-D.

Sonatine Transatlantique (Leduc). Arranged by the composer from the solo-piano version. Fox-trot; Spiritual and Blues; Charleston. Attractive jazz improvisation style. Large span required. M-D.

Mario Tarenghi (1870–1938) Italy

Nine Variations on Prelude XX by F. Chopin Op.68 (Ric 1907; LC) 54pp. M-D.

Eight Variations on the Minuet Theme of Op.99 of Robert Schumann Op.40 (Carish 1906; LC) 55pp. Nineteenth-century style and pianistic usage throughout. M-D.

Prelude and Fugue g (Ric).

Bruce Taub (1948–   ) USA

Passacaglia-Variations (ACA).

Colin Taylor (1880–1973) Great Britain

Three Impromptus (Lengnick 1938; LC) 11pp. Popinjay. Lyric. Sumer is a-cumin in. Pleasant. Int.

Alexander Tcherepnin (1899–1977) USA, born Russia

Rondo Op.87a 1957 (CFP 6074; AMC) 12pp. Russian folk-song mood, brilliant, tonal, flexible meters in mid-section, pianistic throughout. M-D.

Ivan Tcherepnin (1943–   ) USA

Son of Alexander.

Drei Stucke (Belaieff 406 1976) 8 min. Explanations in German and English. Silent Night Mix: thin sonorities mixed between instruments at a quiet dynamic level. Pièce sans titre: Allegro, briskly, well articulated, changing meters, careful pedal instructions. Alleluia: based on a Gregorian chant, Allegro, steady, calm and flowing, notes within brackets should be brought out, though discreetly. Much of the success of this piece relies on the placement of the instruments: "If there is an audience the two pianos should be placed as to surround it as much as possible with their sound. . ." (from the score). Expanded tonalities. M-D.

Thomas Dyke Tellefsen (1823–1874) Norway

Tellefsen was a pupil of Chopin and Kalkbrenner.

Sonata Op.41 (Costallat; BrM). Imitative of Chopin with some Norwegian folk-song influence. M-D.

Simeon Ten Holt (1923–   ) The Netherlands
Sekwensen 1965 (Donemus). For one or two pianos. 7 min. Performance
directions in Dutch and French. Six short sections. Graphic notation,
clusters, pointillistic, avant-garde. D.

Nicholas C. Tgettis (1933–   ) USA
Night Freight 1976 (MS available from composer: 14 Abern St., Salem,
MA 01970) 9 min. One movement. Int. to M-D.

Sigismond Thalberg (1812–1871) Germany
*Grosse Fantaisie und Variationen für zwei Pianoforte üben Themas aus
Oper Norma von Bellini* Op.12 (André 7178; NYPL; LC) 12pp.
Themes presented in opening section, two variations, fanciful clos-
ing. M-D.
Grand Variations de Concert sur un thème des Puritains (Bellini)
(Schuberth). "Hexameron" variations written in conjunction with
Liszt and Herz. See fuller entry under Liszt.

Karl Thern (1817–1886) Hungary
Thern was the father of Louis and Willi Thern, pioneers of two-piano art
and probably the first professional two-piano team.
Romance Op.48 (R&E).
Scherzo Op.58 (R&E).
Nocturne D♭ Op.66 (R&E; BrM) 11pp. Varied sections, many notes,
colorful trill conclusion. M-D.
Theme and Variations in the Italian Manner Op.67 (R&E 1883; BrM).
Andantino Op.72 (R&E).
Tarantella Op.73 (R&E).

Ferdinand Thiériot (1838–1919) Germany
Two Pieces Op.36 (C. Ruehle). Intermezzo. Humoreske.
Two Pieces Op.40 (W. Gebauer).
Two Pieces (Military Characters) Op.82 (J. Rieter 1904; LC) 7pp. Auszug.
Reiterstück. M-D.

Eric H. Thiman (1900–1975) Great Britain
Thiman's style is melodic, harmonically traditional, and pleasing to the
ear.
Suite E 1947 (Cramer; BrM) 33pp. Alla menuetto: lush harmonies.
Fughetta: Baroque influence. Sarabande: Romantic harmony. Riga-
don: sparkling and witty, sea-chantey influence. M-D.
The Sussex Milkmaids (W. Rogers 1940; LC) 7pp. Attractive. Int.

Andrew Thomas (1939–   ) USA
Thomas is a product of Cornell University and of The Juilliard School,
where he is a member of the pre-school division composition department.

Music for Two Pianos 1977 (ACA) 10 min. Skillfully written in a fresh-sounding style that is thoroughly contemporary; mixes numerous contrasting textures (linear, chordal, octaves, chromatic figuration), freely tonal around d. Intense, energetic, and effective throughout. The poem "Upon Westminster Bridge" by William Wordsworth "functions as a kind of oblique program note" (letter to the author, June 19, 1981). M-D.

An Wasserfluessen Babylon 1973 (ACA) 17 min.

François Thomé (1850–1909) France
Les Noces d'Arlequin (Lemoine 1886; BrM). Salon style.
Simple aveu (Durand).

Virgil Thomson (1896–   ) USA
Thomson is the Peter Pan among American composers. As debunker of artistic pomposity, he is the transatlantic counterpart of Erik Satie.
Synthetic Waltzes 1925 (EV 1948; AMC) 18pp., 6 min. Originally composed for piano duet, revised in an edition for two pianos by the composer. One of Thomson's most successful spoofs. A chain of waltzes in one continuous movement, in different keys, in a quirkish diatonic and eclectic Romantic style, kind of a Strauss pot-pourri. The waltzes are synthetic (exactly as the title says), funny, and good. They would add spice to a program. M-D.
Walking Song 1952 (GS; LC) 7pp. Arranged for two pianos by Gold and Fizdale. From music for the film *Tuesday in September*. Folk-song influence, "walking tempo," jaunty and casual, glissando, highly effective, quiet. Int.

Francis Thorne (1922–   ) USA
Broadway and 52nd 1955–56 (Suite for Two Pianos) (Forlivesi 1959; AMC) 25pp. Opening Number; Blues; Strip-tease; Mambo. Ballet-like, MC, Gershwin influence. Large span required. M-D.
Rhapsodic Variations 1964 (EBM; AMC) 13 min. Jazz influence, properly unrestrained at spots. M-D.

Michael Tippett (1905–   ) Great Britain
Fantasia on a Theme by Handel 1942 (Schott 10122) 16 min. Originally for piano and orchestra; transcribed for two pianos by the composer. Theme is from Handel's *Suites de pièces pour le clavecin* of 1733. Short, five clever variations, luxuriant tonal style, effective concluding fugue. M-D.

Loris Tjeknavorian (1937–   ) Iran
Tanz der Jugen (from *Ballet fantastique* Op.2) (Dob 14.947 1975) 4pp. Allegretto grazioso, freely tonal around b♭, pastoral quality, octotonic. M-D.

Louis Toebosch (1916–   ) The Netherlands
Suite Polyphonica Op.30b (Donemus 1962) 33pp. Facsimile. Intrada: short, leads to a Passacaglia: linear. Ricercare: broad tempo, contrapuntal. Fuga: fast, much use of light staccato touch. Quartal and quintal harmonies, freely tonal. M-D.

Hans Tornieporth (–   ) Germany
Duo zu zwei Klavieren über den Frühlingsstimmen—Walzer von Johann Strauss (Schott 3711 1940; LC) 24pp. A virtuoso concert transcription. M-D to D.

Vlastimir Trajkovic (1947–   ) Yugoslavia
Duo (ESC 1979). Originally for piano and orchestra; arranged for two pianos by the composer. A study in sudden contrasts, much use of pedal, plenty of atonal histrionics, ends on an octotonic F spread over three octaves. Given the proper performers this could produce a powerful effect. Moderately avant-garde. D.

Harold Triggs (1900–   ) USA
Triggs and Vera Brodsky were a well-known two-piano team for a number of years.
Autumn Legend (JF 1936; LC) 7pp. An expressive little character piece. Large span required. Int. to M-D.
Danza Brasiliana (CF 1947; LC) 13pp., 3 min. Similar in Giubiloso style to Arthur Benjamin's *Jamaica Rhumba*. Excellent encore. Int. to M-D.
Negro Spiritual: "Death, Ain't yuh got no Shame?" (GS 1937; LC) 11pp. Chromatic. M-D.
Six Surrealist Afterludes 1940 (AMC) No. 6 only, 10pp. Driving martellato effects interspersed with fugal textures, rapido conclusion, neo-Classic. M-D.
Tyrollienne (JF 1936; LC) 11pp. A bouyant waltz. Int.
Valse (GS 1937; LC) 11pp. To Josef and Rosina Lhevinne. M-D.

Joan Trimble (1905–   ) Great Britain
Bard of Lisgoole 1938 (Bo&H) 3 min. Irish Air. Modal, embellished melody, mainly in c. M-D.
The Green Bough 1942 (Bo&H) 10pp., 4½ min. Modal, lyric, "slow—with feeling and freedom." Int. to M-D.
Sonatina 1940 (Bo&H) 22pp., 8½ min. Moderato, con moto; Minuet; Rondo. M-D.

Romuald Twardowski (1930–   ) Poland
Improvvisazione e toccata 1974 (PWM) 5½ min. Improvvisazione: freely rubato, chromatic, major seventh chords. Toccata: motoric, bitonal, clusterlike sonorities plus clusters, harmonics. Stunning. M-D.

U

Hermann Unger (1886–1958) Germany
Chamber Variations (Kammervariationen) on an original Theme Op.8
   (Tischer & Jangenberg).

Anton Urspruch (1850–1907) Germany
Variations and Fugue on a Theme by Bach Op.13 (Cranz).

V

Renier Van der Valden (1910–   ) Belgium

Beweging (Movement for two pianos) 1965 (CeBeDeM) 23pp., 8 min. Poor facsimile MS. Opens with a twelve-tone row built over ostinato; row is later treated canonically between the instruments. Mainly atonal, serial influence, many trills and running figuration in upper register, octotonic, thick textures. D.

Concertino 1965 (CeBeDeM) 44pp., parts. 12 min. For two pianos, two trumpets, horn, trombone, and tuba. One movement with varied moods and tempi. Serial, octotonic, chordal, scalar, atonal, trills. Pulls freely toward b. Piano parts are of equal interest. Effective combination. M-D.

Nicholas Van Slyck (1922–   ) USA

Piano Partners with Two Keyboards 1980 (MS available from composer: 700 Huron Ave., Cambridge, MA 02138) 44pp. 20 short pieces with such titles as: Joining Hands; Lydia's Song; Greek Courage; Old Russia; Walzette; Mountain Climbing; Count Your Change. Attractive MC settings; a group or the entire set could be performed. Int.

Six Textures 1973 (MS available from composer) 16pp. Contrasting pieces, neo-Classic, harmonics. Well written for the medium. M-D.

Ralph Vaughan Williams (1872–1958) Great Britain

Introduction and Fugue 1946 (OUP) 44pp., 14 min. This piece is almost improvisatory fantasia, with material from the introduction interspersed throughout and fugal sections—some brief, some extended—coming and going. Powerful; contrapuntally complex. Harmonically stark at times but with passages of broad melodic material to offset the starkness and pungency. An extended work of large architectural design developed with craftsmanship. Contains some thrilling moments. D.

Ary Verhaar (1900–   ) The Netherlands

Concertino Op.1 1931 (Donemus) 10 min. Con (5) Variazioni; Intermezzo; Caprice. Freely tonal, traditional pianistic treatment, neo-Classic tendencies. M-D.

Intonazione, Canzone e Fuga Op.34 1948 (Donemus) 13 min. Intonazione: dramatic. Canzone: flowing. Fuga: robust; *pp* ending. MC.
M-D.

John Verrall (1908–   ) USA
Prelude, Intermezzo and Fugue 1964 (CFE; LC) 17pp. Prelude: freely
tonal, cantando, dolce grazioso, octotonic. Intermezzo: adagio e
mesto, expressive, melodic; five-bar Allegro section leads to Fugue:
bold, some dynamic contrasts, Allargando closing. M-D.
Suite 1966 (AMC) 18pp. This work seems to have evolved from the one
above. Lento (Pastorale Prelude): a six-bar Lento leads to an
Amabile cantando section; a brief Allegro section climaxes at bar 18
with, "Don't try to fit together"; returns to the Amabile character
followed by Andante (Canons); short closing with full singing tone.
Nocturne (Andante moderato): many starts and stops with a faster,
violent mid-section. Finale (Allegro): much imitation between instruments. Freely tonal. M-D.

László Vidovszky (–   ) Hungary
Double 1972 (EMB z8323). For two differently prepared pianos that present contrasting versions of the same musical material (chordal—
linear, rubato—giusto, synchronous—asynchronous). D.

Aleksandr A. Vinkler (1865–1935) Russia
Variations et Fugue sur un thème de J.S. Bach Op.12 (Belaieff 1906;
BrM: LC) 39pp. Seven variations and fugue. Reger influence. M-D.

Giulio Viozzo (1912–   ) Italy
Trenodia (Ric 129137).

Jan Van Vlijmen (1935–   ) The Netherlands
Construzione 1960 (Donemus) 8 min. Vivo, ma non troppo: characterized
by a symmetrical design, the second half being a rhythmical mirror of
the first. Lento: divided into three parts—a slow, concentrated introduction; introvert (a rhythmical inversion of the introduction),
with the accent on tone color; and a contrasting Vivo con fuoco with
a canon in retrograde. Fast changing meters, pointillistic, clusters,
expressionistic, wide dynamic range. Pays great attention to tone
color and rhythmical movement. M-D to D.

Adolf Bernhard Vogel (1873–1961) Germany
Andante and Variations Op.14 (Khant).

Jean Vogt (1823–1888) Germany
Prelude and Fugue Op.18 (Br&H).
Prelude and Finale Fugato Op.82 (C.A. Challier).

Robert Volkmann (1815–1883) Germany
Variations on a Theme by Handel Op.26 (Schott).

Jan V. Voříšek (1791–1825) Bohemia
Grand Ouverture c Op.16 (O. Zuckerova—Br 19113 1971) 32pp. A sonata-
rondo preceded by a slow introduction (Maestoso). The rondo (Allegro) consists of two contrasting areas: the first, dramatic, develops
the principal subject recurring in various forms; while the second,
lyrical, grows out of cantabile subjects. Voříšek's only piece for two
pianos differs from the rest of his piano music in that it sounds as
though it were written for full orchestra. Witness the title and a
tendency to give certain subjects or phrases the character of single
orchestral instruments or groups of instruments. For instance, the
change between "strings" and "tutti" is obvious at the opening of the
slow introduction, and there is a contrast between the first "string
subject" and the second "wind subject," with its long sustained
notes, in the rondo proper. M-D.

Slàva Vorlovà (1894–1973) Czechoslovakia
Saràdy "Charades" Op.32 1953 (CHF) 69pp. I. Lento: Introduction leads
directly to Allegretto giocoso; imitative; cheerful; accompanimental
figures in Piano II with melody in Piano I. II. Hvězdička: Lento,
repeated notes in Piano I, chordal in Piano II; leads to Andante
sostenuto, melodic; leads to Andante senza sostenuto, rhapsodic.
III. Tři domy: Lento, melodic octaves; Allegro, repeated notes in
alternating hands punctuated with chords. IV. Uhàja: melodic ideas
interspersed with cadenzalike material; leads to Andante, chordal,
trills, *pp* ending. V. Vosy: Lento introduction moves to Allegro
molto; dancelike. Colorful if a little dated. M-D.

W

Alex Raoul Wachtmeister (1865–1947) Sweden

Prelude and Fugue (J. Church 1919; LC; BrM) 18pp. Expansive, in Romantic style. M-D.

Diderik Wagenaar (1946–   ) The Netherlands

Praxis 1973 (Donemus) 116pp. Symphonie for two pianos, oboe ad lib. Performance directions in Dutch and English; geometrical notation described. Harmonics, tremolo chords alternating between hands, dynamic extremes, sectional. Avant-garde. Would appeal only to the most adventurous and determined pianists. D.

Joseph Wagner (1900–1974) USA

Festival Processions 1936 (PIC).

Sonata with Differences 1952 rev.1963 (MS at Pepperdine University, Malibu, CA). Three movements, neo-Classic. Nicolas Slonimsky, who suggested the title, described this music as a work that "might well be used as a manual for the study of counterpoint." M-D.

Wladyslaw Walentynowicz(1902–   ) Poland

Inspirations (AA 1973) 10 min. Three pieces.

Ernest Walker (1870–1949) Great Britain

West Africa Fantasy Op.53 (OUP).

Waltz Suite Op.60 1934 (OUP) 25pp.

Both sets of pieces are written in a traditional idiom with some attractive moments. M-D.

George Walker (1922–   ) USA

Sonata for Two Pianos 1964 (Gen 1162 1981) 35pp. Adagio non troppo: chromatic chordal four-bar theme leads to ten contrasting short variations; the espressivo chordal theme returns to conclude the movement. Presto: octotonic, legato in Piano II contrasted with staccato in Piano I, quieter dynamics. Adagio: sustained, varied meters, dramatic gestures. Allegro tranquillo: legato e dolce opening leads to a ben articolato section featuring runs in one instrument punctuated by rhythmic octaves in the other; these contrasting materials form the basis of the movement. Both Romantic and neo-Classic influences. Logical structuring and warm and evocative expressiveness permeate the entire piece. M-D.

Fried Walter (1907–   ) Germany
Concert Waltzes (Zimmermann).

Philip Warner (1901–   ) USA
Pop Goes the Weasel 1959 (PIC). Clever arrangement, highly effective, the perfect encore. M-D.

Guy Warrack (1900–   ) Great Britain
Prelude, Polka, Fugato and Furiant 1938 (Bo&H) 5½ min.

Werner Wehrli (1892–1944) Switzerland
Variations and Fugue on a Jolly Song Op.18 (Hug).

Karl Weigl (1881–1949) USA, born Austria
Night Fantasies Op.13 (AMC).
City that Was. Dances from Old Vienna (AMC).
Norwegian Dance (ACA).

Jaromir Weinberger (1896–1967) USA, born Bohemia
Polka and Fugue from the opera *Shwanda* (AMP 1940; UCLA) 24pp. Masterfully transcribed by the composer. A Vivo con brio Polka prefaces the lengthy Allegro Fugue. M-D.

Leo Weiner (1885–1960) Hungary
Variations on a Hungarian Folksong Op.32 (EMB 5260 1969) 23pp. Rhythmic theme and seven variations. Attractive writing in traditional Romantic style with Hungarian flavor. Contrast of dynamics, moods, and harmonic color. M-D.

Hugo Weisgall (1912–   ) USA
Fugue and Romance Op.2/1 1939 (TP; AMC) 12pp. This early work by a strong opera composer is from the ballet *One Thing Is Certain*. Effective subject and countersubjects, flowing lines, dramatic chordal and scalar ending. The Romance is anticlimactic. M-D.

Julius Weismann (1879–1950) Germany
Nine Variations on a Theme in A Op.64 (Steingräber).
Partita Op.107 (Steingräber).
Sonatine "Ille terrarum" Op.122 (Steingräber). Romantic style, neo-Classic. M-D.

Leopold Welleba (–   ) Austria
Concert Waltzes Op.1 (Dob 3412; IU) 19pp. A glorified, fluffy Viennese

concoction with all the late nineteenth-century window dressing. M-D.

Jean-Jacques Werner (1935–   ) France
Sonata (Societé d'Editions Musicales Internationales 1979) 17pp. For piano duet or two pianos.

C. E. F. Weyse (1774–1842) Denmark
Etude Op.51/4 (WH).
Etude Op.60/1 (WH).

Charles Whittenberg (1927–   ) USA
Structures for Two Pianos (ACA) 14 min.

Charles Marie Widor (1844–1937) France
Contes d'Avril ("April Tales") Suite concertante (Heugel). Part I: Ouverture. Sérénade illyrienne. Adagio. Presto. Part II: Guitare. Appassionato. Romance. March nuptiale.

Jean Wiéner (1896–   ) France
Cadences (Sal). Jazz. Java. Tango Argentin. Final (Paso doble).

Joseph Wieniawski (1837–1912) Poland
Brother of the famous violinist Henri.
Fantaisie Op.42 (Schott 1886; LC) 37pp. Expansive nineteenth-century idiom, shows strong Franck influence. M-D.

Margaret Wigham (–   ) USA
Concerto for Two Pianos (R.D. Row 1959) 24pp. Three well-balanced movements with a jazzy closing, traditional style. Int.

Wolfgang Wijdeveld (1910–   ) The Netherlands
Kermesse Op.17 1935 (Donemus) 7 min. Polytonal, chordal tremolos, clusters, long scalar figuration, chromatic. M-D.

Friedrich Wilckens (1899–   ) Austria
Robes Pierre & Co., Kriminal-Balletsketsch (UE).

Raymond Wilding-White (1922–   ) USA, born Great Britain
Sonata (MS available from composer, c/o School of Music, De Paul University, 804 West Belden, Chicago, IL 60614) 427 bars. Many tempo changes, dramatic antiphonal opening, some glissandi, neo-Classic in orientation, well spaced over entire keyboard, basically tonal, trill effectively utilized. M-D.

Becket Williams (1890–1956) Great Britain
Impromptu and Double Fugue (Curwen).

Esther Williamson (1915–1973) USA
Sonata for Two Pianos (Mercury 1949) 28pp. [Untitled]: quarter note =

126–132, expressive flowing lines grow in intensity, contrary-motion chords, dramatic closing. Andante: quartal harmony, lyric, leads directly to Allegro vivace: trills, octotonic, section marked "very rhythmic," grand ritard at the *fff* ending. Neo-Classic. M-D to D.

Malcolm Williamson (1931–   ) Great Britain, born Australia
Williamson's multifaceted creative personality encompasses a personal brand of modal serialism and a riotous stylistic variety, sharing ground with Messiaen, which can embrace simple Romantic lyricism and the grittiest rhythmic and harmonic complexity.
Sonata for Two Pianos 1967 (Weinberger) 12 min. One exuberant and rhapsodic movement, Stravinsky influence, pithy ideas, strongly rhetoric, programmatic suggestions, contains some exquisite moments. "The bare bones of the form are uncomplicated and consist of a thrice-repeated alternation of warring rhythms and a vernal release from tension. However, the micro-structure of the dense opening section and its developed reappearances are extremely complex, presenting little cells governed by a rhythmic sub-structure which cancel each other into immobility. The composer has spoken of rebirth and of the sudden explosion of the Northern Spring, and this section is an apt representation of obscure regenerative forces at work during some winter of the spirit. In the second section there comes the serenity of creative energy canalised (rippling scales and an inexorable rhythmic growth in the first piano's chords), its unpredictably sudden emergence so true to psychology and nature" (Anthony Payne, from record jacket Argo ZRG 704). M-D.
Concerto (Weinberger). For two pianos, eight hands, flute, oboe, clarinet, bassoon, and horn.

Nikola von Wilm (1834–1911) Germany, born Russia
Valse-Impromptu Op.2 (R&E).
Two Character Pieces Op.60/1 (R&E 1887; BrM) 9pp. Introduction; Gavotte. Fluent salon style. M-D.
Preludium and Sarabande Op.62 (Leuckart).
Variations Op.64 (Leuckart).
Waltzes Op.72 (Leuckart 1914; Wheaton College Library, Norton, MA 02766) 15pp. Intrada; Tempo di Valse. A concert set in post-Romantic style, much chromatic usage. M-D.
Easy Variations on "So viel Stern' am Himmel stehn" Op.94 (Rieter-Biedermann).
Vier Volkslieder Op.213 (Rieter 1905; LC) Published separately.

Donald M. Wilson (1937–   ) USA
Wilson is chairman of the composition department in the School of Music, Bowling Green State University.

Stabile I 1965 (AMC) 84 min., alternative duration, 21 min. The two pianists begin playing simultaneously. Piano I plays its 84 measures fifteen times, each time as indicated: using triangle beaters, pizzicato, ordinario, glockenspiel mallets, vibraphone mallets. Piano II plays its 45 measures 28 times, each time as indicated: using triangle beaters, pizzicato, etc. Mode of attack should always be extremely soft, but as bell-like as possible, as indicated in the score. Before starting the performance, both players depress their damper pedals and weight them down with some object until just before the final chord of the piece. Unusual and fascinating sonorities. Avant-garde. M-D.

Dorothy Wilson (1904–   ) USA
Dance Diversion I (AMC) 7pp. For two pianos, eight hands. Tonal, rhythmic, flowing lines, big climax. Int. to M-D.
Dance Diversion II (AMC) 8pp. For two pianos, eight hands. Ensemble writing fits the players nicely. Int. to M-D.
The Grapevine (Tone Clusters) (AMC) 1p. For two pianos, four or seven or eight hands. Outer lines have melody and bass while inner parts provide the cluster accompaniment. Int.

Philip Winsor (1938–   ) USA
Melted Ears 1975 (CF) 12pp. Based on material from Beethoven, Brahms, Chopin, and Rachmaninoff, plus Winsor's own considerable contribution. The performers are told to improvise heroically (using theatrics mildly), always in a grand manner; to modulate freely, but logically; and to keep in the style. They are to draw from both previous material and their own repertoires. They should not attempt to coordinate their keys or their harmonies. Traditional and graphic notation, clusters (expanded trill clusters), harmonics, some lines may be played in any order. Hilariously effective. Avant-garde. D.
Cindy 633: Loya Called Is Waiting for the Plummer (a drone for one or more pianos, preferably amplified) 1979 (MS available from composer: c/o School of Music, DePaul University, 804 West Belden Avenue, Chicago, IL 60614). Avant-garde. M-D.

Jan Wisse (1921–   ) The Netherlands
Cristalli 1959 (Donemus; Impero Verlag 9017) 8pp. Three short untitled movements with only tempo indications. Serial, pointillistic, some ad libitum sections. Complex but gentle and deliberate in character. M-D. to D.

David van de Woestijne (1915–   ) Belgium
Sonate 1955 (CeBeDeM) 15 min.

Frank Wohlfahrt (1894–1972) Germany
Marsch für zwei Klaviere aus "Die Passion des Prometheus" (Bo&Bo

1958; LC) 9pp. Neo-Classic, freely tonal, many major sevenths, full chords juxtaposed with octotonic writing. M-D.

Leopold Carl Wolf (–   ) Germany
Phantasiestück Op.24 (Br&H).

Christian Wolff (1934–   ) USA, born France
Duo for Pianists I and II 1957–58 (CFP 1962). Parts for each piano but no full score. Extensive performance directions. The work has no beginning or ending, these being determined only by the situation under which the performance takes place. All materials are indeterminate, the only indications being the areas of limitation provided by the composer (the use of pianos, no silences between performer responses). Less concerned with the definitive roles of rhythm and form than with the essence of sound for its own sake. Restricted number of pitches, generous use of silence, performers allowed various choices. Avant-garde. M-D to D.

Ermanno Wolf-Ferrari (1876–1948) Italy
I Gioelli della madonna (The Jewels of the Madonna) Intermezzo No.2 (Weinberger 1957; BrM) 12pp.

Stefan Wolpe (1902–1972) USA, born Germany
Seven Pieces for Three Pianos 1951 (PIC). These pieces are manifestations of seven organic modes arranged in order of increasing complexity and differentiation of space and time, sonority and texture, shape and gesture. The three pianos are protagonists who become progressively more independent as they overlap and interweave with the complex statements. M-D to D.
Lazy Andy Ant (Seesaw). For two pianos and voice.

Kevin J. Wood (1947–   ) USA
Hexentanz 1976 (MS available from composer: One Bennington Place, Freehold, NJ 07728) 7 min. One movement. M-D.

Ralph W. Wood (1902–   ) Great Britain
Nocturne and Dance 1941 (J. Williams 1951; BrM) 19pp., 10 min.

Arnold Van Wyk (1916–   ) South Africa
Three Improvisations on Dutch Folk Songs (Bo&H 1944) 8 min. To the Market. Prayer for the Homeland. The Silver Fleet.

Ivan Wyschnegradsky (1893–1979) Russia
In 1917 Wyschnegradsky devised a system of quarter-tones with a motto, inspired by Heraclitus, "Everything flows." In 1924 he formulated the concept of "pansonority," which in his nomenclature meant a discrete continuum of quarter-tones.
Ainsi parlait Zarathoustra Op.17 1929–30. Symphony for four pianos

(L'OL 1938) 84pp., 24 min. Pianos I and III are tuned normally, pianos II and IV a quarter-tone higher. Tempo giusto; Scherzando, Lento; Allegro con fuoco. Traditional forms, much chromatic usage, changing meters, many tremolo figures, clusterlike sonorities, glissandi, three against two, free rubato sections contrasted with motoric dance rhythms, massive buildup of sonorities at conclusion.D.

24 Preludes im Vierteltonsystem für zwei Klaviere Op.22 1934 rev.1950s (Belaieff 1977). Vol.I: Preludes 1–12; Vol. II: Preludes 13–24. These pieces use the 24 "tonalities" of a 13-tone "diatonicized" quarter-tone scale. The two pianos are tuned a quarter-tone apart. Austere, dramatic works in which thick chords frequently alternate with disjunct medium-tempo single-note lines. Rich textures, varied moods. D.

See: John Diercks, *NOTES* 35/2 (December 1978):431–32 for a review of this work.

Jurg Wyttenbach (1935–   ) Switzerland

Nachspiel in drei Teilen 1966 (Arv Viva AV87) 15pp., 8 min. Three-part, post-Webern style, pointillistic, clusters, glissandi, trills. Part I begins in lower register and works to extremes of keyboards. Part II is *ff;* Part III *ppp.* Avant-garde. D.

Theóphile Ysaÿe (1865–1918) Belgium
Variations Op.10 e (Schott Frères 1917) 37pp.

Z

Harold Zabrack (1929–   ) USA

Sonata for Two Pianos 1975 (MS available from composer: c/o Westminster Choir College, Princeton, NJ 08540) 64pp. Allegro maestoso: SA, bold thematic treatment, brilliant octaves, dramatic, brilliant chromatic runs, relaxed mid-section, appassionato crescendo conclusion. Andante espressione: cantabile theme, freely tonal, intense buildup to end, sudden *pp* ending. Introduction, Allegro con brio: pointillistic, incisive and rhythmic, broad gestures, pizzicato effects, quasi–French horn sonorities, expansive chords, quasi-cadenza, glissandi, Allegro vivace coda. Beautifully laid out for both instruments, apocalyptic in spirit, arresting. Requires seasoned ensemble pianists. D.

Scherzo (Hommage à Prokofieff) (Bo&H) Originally for solo piano, arranged for two pianos by the composer. Rhythmic motives alternate between instruments, an exciting display piece. M-D.

Vasily Zagorsky (1926–   ) USSR

Rhapsody 1968 (USSR) 55pp., parts. For two pianos, violin, and four percussionists. Percussion includes: timpani, small drum, legni, bells, triangle, tom tom, campane, patti, cassa, tam tam, crotali, gong. One large colorful movement, in the style of Khachaturian. M-D.

Henri Zagwijn (1878–1954) The Netherlands

Petite Suite (in stile antico) 1944 (Donemus) 15 min. Preludio; Fughetta; Minuetto; Giga. Based on the notes ADD-BAGGE. Traditional pianistic treatment, a few MC sonorities. M-D.

Suite Sinfonica 1943 (Donemus) 30 min. Entrata; Fuga; Scherzo; Serenata; Rondo alla gigue. A large tonal work with healthy doses of chromaticism; contains some effective moments. M-D to D.

Daniele Zanettovich (1950–   ) Italy

Invenzioni su un tritono (EC).

Aleksandr A. Zhuk (–   ) USSR

Concertina Op. 32 (USSR 1976; LC) 23pp. Lento introduction leads to Allegro giocoso. In Kabalevsky style. Int.

Hermann Zilcher (1881–1948) Germany
Symphonie Op.50 1924 (Br&H). This is an original work for two pianos, not an orchestral work. The title is suggestive of the symphonic conception of the piece. Schumann and Brahms influence. M-D.

Bernd A. Zimmermann (1918–1970) Germany
Zimmermann combined influences from many different fields in his compositions and used the collage technique.
Perspektiven 1955 (Schott 4910) (Music for an Imaginary Ballet) 27pp. Involved rhythms, clusters play an important role for the first time in serial music, glissandi, pointillistic, trills. Two pianos are needed to imbue the thematic material with broad gestures and sonorities. A sprightly dialogue dance of bright motifs between the instruments, Schoenberg-Stravinsky influence. An accessible, colorful piece of serialism. D.
Monologe 1960–64 (Schott 5427) (Hommage à Claude Debussy) 17 min. Reduction by the composer of his work of the same title for two pianos and orchestra. Despite its title, this work is a dialogue, not only between the pianists but also between fragments of music, old and new. Seven serial sections, integrates collage techniques and fragments from *Jeux* of Debussy, the Bach chorale prelude "Wachet auf, ruft uns die Stimme," Mozart, Gregorian chant. Fragmentation, extreme eclecticism. M-D to D.

W. Zizold (–   )
Konzertstück Op.13 (Lienau). Introduction and Scherzo.

Tomislav Zografski (1934–   ) Yugoslavia
Sonatina C (Izdanje Udruzenja Kompozitora Makedonije 1964; LC) 11pp. Allegro; Andantino; Allegro molto. Large span required. MC. M-D.

Ramon Zupko (1932–   ) USA
Nocturnes 1977 (CFP 66866) 18 min. Six movements tied together by various rhythmic, harmonic, and melodic elements; sometimes lyrical, sometimes more intense. Careful dialogue between instruments, which come together to play unison phrases at key points. The two pianists lay out a firm polychordal structure of three major triads. Calm Impressionistic chords are invaded by alien figures that complicate the texture and build to a big inside-the-piano crash. The composer makes the most of the spots where his materials clash. M-D.

Peter Zwetkoss (1925–   ) Bulgaria
Dialog (Edition Modern 1101) 9 min.

Annotated Bibliography

This section, an extension of the entries following individual composers and single compositions, concentrates on English-language books, periodicals, and a few dissertations. These sources are most helpful when used in conjunction with the musical scores.

Altmann, Wilhelm. *Verzeichnis von Werken für Klavier vier und sechs-händig sowie für zwei und mehr Klaviere.* Leipzig: Verlag von Friedrich Hofmeister, 1943, 133pp. Arranged in two large sections: A. Original Works; B. Arrangements and Transcriptions.

Appleton, Vera, and Field, Michael. "Is There a Two-Piano Dilemma Today?" *Musical Courier* 136 (August 1947):9. Deals with two-piano literature and program problems.

Bartlett, Ethel, and Robertson, Rae. "Two-Piano Playing is Chamber Music." MA 64 (March 25, 1946):39.

Blesch, Eulalie W. "The Study, Analysis and Performance of Selected Original Two-Piano Music of Contemporary American Composers." Diss. Columbia University, 1976, 154pp. The analytical portions of the study focus on the following compositions: Copland, *Danzon Cubano;* Corigliano, *Kaleidoscope;* Dello Joio, *Aria and Toccata;* Persichetti, *Sonata,* Op.13; and Hovhaness, *Vijag,* Op.37.

Brodsky, Vera. "The Art of Two-Piano Playing." Part VII of Albert Wier, *The Piano,* pp. 338–374. New York: Longmans, Green & Co., 1940. An excellent essay dealing with 1. The Essentials of the Art; 2. A Survey of Original and Transcribed Music for Two Pianos; 3. A List of Classical and Modern Works for Two Pianos.

Brozen, Michael. "Two Pianos—Twenty-Five Years." MA 82 (November 1962):54. Concerns the 25th anniversary of Vronsky and Babin's concerts in the USA.

Cedrone, Frank. "Profile of a Piano Team." PQ 103 (Fall 1978):43–46. Concerns the two-piano team of Markowski and Cedrone.

Chang, Frederick M., and Faurot, Albert. *Team Piano Repertoire.* Metuchen, NJ: Scarecrow Press, Inc., 1976, 184pp. Part 2 deals with two players at two pianos; part 3, three or four players at two pianos; part 4, three players at three pianos and four players at four pianos; part 5, arrangements and transcriptions.

Cheadle, William and Louise. "Piano Ensemble Performance: From Memory or From the Score?" *Clavier* 17 (December 1978):34–35.

Comfort, A. "Solving Problems at Two-Pianos." *Etude* 71 (May 1953):11f. An interview with Arthur Whittemore and Jack Lowe.

Contiguglia, Richard and John. "Twin Keyboards." *Music & Musicians* 20 (August 1972):9.

Duncan, Claude. "Teaching Duo-Pianism." *Clavier* 6/2 (February 1967):20f.

Field, Michael. "Piano Music for Four Hands: A Forgotten Treasure-House." MA 67 (October 1949):27.

Friskin, James, and Freundlich, Irwin. *Music for the Piano.* New York: Rinehart, 1954; Dover, 1973. Contains a useful section on two-piano literature, pp. 340–53.

Harvey, Jonathan. *The Music of Stockhausen.* London: Faber & Faber, 1975.

Henderson, A.M. "Duets for Two Pianos." *Proceedings of the Musical Association* 52 (November 1925):1–11.

Jackson, Robert. "Gold and Fizdale." MA 83 (August 1963):16. An interview with this two-piano team.

Kirshbaum, Bernard. "The Art in Duo-Piano Performance." AMT 30/4 (February–March 1981):27, 59.

Klein, D. Arkus, et al. "Pianists by the Pair." ARG 30/9 (May 30, 1970):814f.

Lhevinne, Josef and Rosina. "Four Hands that Play as Two." *Etude* 51/12 (December 1933):809–10. An important essay on two-piano playing.

Lhevinne, Rosina. "The Spirit of Ensemble." *Pan Pipes* of Sigma Alpha Iota 41/3 (February 1949):162–81. An essay on historical, aesthetic, and practical points of two-piano playing.

Luboshutz, Pierre, and Nemenoff, Genia. "The Art of Piano Ensemble." Etude 69 (January 1941):5, 58. Discusses aesthetics and technique of two-piano playing.

Lyons, James. "Teamwork." MA 75 (January 1, 1955):10–11. Two heads have proved better than one in the case of Whittemore and Lowe.

McCarthy, S. Margaret W. "Two-piano Music around Beethoven's Time: Its Significance for the College Teacher." *College Music Symposium* 17/2 (Fall 1977):131–43. Focuses on music for two pianos written between 1770 and 1830. Includes a prehistory of the medium, starting with the contribution of Giles Farnaby, and explores the reasons for its growing appeal around the time of Beethoven. Contains a detailed discussion of selected two-piano pieces by Johann G. Müthel, Clementi, Mozart, Dussek, Eberl, Moscheles, and Chopin and a checklist of two-piano works by 56 composers from the period.

McRoberts, Gary Keith. "An Annotated Catalogue of Original Two-Piano Literature 1950–1970." Thesis, California State University, Long Beach, 1973, 33pp.

Maier, Guy. "Two-Piano Ensemble." In "The Teachers' Round Table," *Etude* 46 (Februray 1938):87.

————. "Second Piano Parts." In "The Teachers' Round Table," *Etude* 59 (November 1941):744.

Merkling, Frank. "Silvery Partnership," MA 75 (March 1955):10, 15. Celebrates the 25th anniversary of Bartlett and Robertson.

Miller, Hugh M. "The Earliest Keyboard Duets." MQ 40 (October 1943): 438–57. Deals with Farnaby's piece for two virginals and with the two earliest compositions for two performers at one keyboard.

Moldenhauer, Hans. *Duo-Pianism*. Chicago: Chicago Musical College Press, 1950, 400pp. The outstanding book on the subject but now somewhat dated.

Moscheles, Ignatz. *Recent Music and Musicians*. New York: Henry Holt & Co., 1875. Da Capo Press, 1970. References to two-piano performances of Moscheles with Cramer and Mendelssohn. The composer's works in this medium.

"Music for Two Pianos." MT 94 (March 4, 1953):123–24.

Orem, Preston Ware. "About Pieces for Two Pianos." *Etude* 56 (September 1938):565–66. Historical comments and repertoire, stresses use of antiphonal effects produced on two pianos.

Pattison, Lee. "Ensemble Piano Playing." *Pacific Coast Musical Review* (n.d.):72.

Penn, Dorothy P. "An Interview with Vitya Vronsky Babin." *Clavier* 17/2(February 1978):12–16.

Prosniz, Adolf. *Handbuch der Klavier-Literatur 1450–1830*. Vienna: Doblinger, 1908. Good source for references to early works for two pianos.

Schramm, Harold. "Piano Ensemble Music." PQ63 (1968):5.

Scionti, Silvio. "The Fascination of Two-Piano Playing." *Etude* 57 (September 1939):567, 602. Historical discussion, opinions on and repertoire for two pianos.

Thomson, Virgil. *The Art of Judging Music*. New York: Alfred A. Knopf, 1948.

Turrill, Pauline Venable. "The Two-Piano Idiom: An Analysis and Evaluation." Thesis, University of California, Los Angeles, 1951, 189pp.

"Two Pianos, Four Hands." *Musical Opinion* 76 (November 1952):97.

Yarbrough, Joan, and Cowan, Robert. "Two Pianos—An American Idiom." *Clavier* 14/4 (April 1975):18–23.

————. "Another Look at Duo-Pianism." MJ 26/2 (February 1968):30f.

————. "Two Pianos on Tour." MJ 28/6 (June 1970):26f.

Indexes of Special Ensembles

Works for Two Pianos, Four Performers

See under:
Arnold
Bank
Dahl
Glazunov

Grainger
Gurlitt
de Haas
Hoffman, H.
Holmes

Kenins
Loevendie
Mendelssohn
Nakada
Powell

Saint-Saëns
Schmidt, Y. R.
Schultz
Williamson, M.
Wilson, D.

Works for Two or More Pianos and Other Instruments

See under:
Andriessen, L.
Babbitt
Bartók
Berio
Boehmer
Boesmans
Bolcom
Bolling
Bon
Bresgen
Brockman
Brown, E.
Constant, M.
Conyngham
Cope

Cox, M.
Dao
Dessau
Feldman
Gilbert
Grainger
Guyonnet
Gyring
Halffter, C.
Hampton
Harrison
Johansen
Jørgensen
Kagel
Kasemets

Kerr
Kolb
Koppel
Lanza
Leibowitz
Lockwood, L.
Luedeke
Macero
Malipiero, R.
Markevitch
Mendes
Montague
Ott (with audience
    participation)
Ranki

Reynolds
Riedstra
Ries
Rogers
Rowland
Schuster
Smith, S.
Souster
Stibilj
Stout
van der Valden
Wagenaar
Williamson, M.
Wolpe
Zagorsky

Works for Pianos and Tape

See under:
Bäck
Bruzdowicz
Hampton

Hays
Hiller, L.
Kolb
Lanza

Mills-Cockrell
Montague
Moss

de Pablo
Perera
Reynolds

Works for Three Pianos

See under:
Beurle
Brown, E.
Cotel
Feldman
Frid

Fritsch
Gibson
Godowsky
Hiller, L.
Lanza

Liberda
Louvier
Luening
Mendes
Montague

Mullins
Nunes
Osieck
Takemitsu
Wolpe

Works for Four or More Pianos

See under:
du Bois
Brown, E.
Cage
Chapple

Czerny
Feldman
Goodenough
de Haas
Hampton

Kupkovic
Mendes
Milhaud
Nunes

Schwartz, E.
Stockhausen
Takemitsu
Wyschnegradsky

Miscellaneous Works

Music for More than One Piano
An Annotated Guide
By Maurice Hinson

Music for more than one keyboard instrument dates back at least to the piece "For Two Virginals" by Giles Farnaby (ca. 1560 – ca. 1620), found in the *Fitzwilliam Virginal Book*. The line of development continued through the Baroque, Classical, and Romantic eras; and the two-piano medium is still strong today, with many twentieth-century composers, in their desire for new timbres, writing for previously untried groupings.

In an alphabetic listing by composer, *Music for More than One Piano* describes works for two or more keyboard instruments, composed mainly since 1700. Maurice Hinson covers all the standard composers and introduces contemporary composers of merit. He also includes what he considers outstanding transcriptions of works originally written for the piano and other media.

The range of combinations can be seen from the indexes, which contain such categories as works for two, three, four, or more pianos; for two or more pianos with other instruments, voice, or tape; for piano and harpsichord; for two player pianos; and for two pianos tuned a quarter-tone apart. There are compositions to be performed on two pianos by one, two, three, and four players, as well as one work for two players, two left hands.

Hinson answers the key questions: What is there? What is it like? Where can I get it? For each entry he provides the date of composition or publication, the publisher(s), the editions available, the number of pages, the performance time, and the level of difficulty.